To Cindy
Always sh...
Never hide!
Mary Perrine

Hidden

by
Mary Perrine

Hidden
Copyright © 2020 by Mary Perrine

Cover by LLPix Design
Editing and Formatting by BZHercules.com

To my husband, Mitch,
who supported my dream before the first keystroke
of this story.
And to my children, Brandon and Taylor.
I love you all beyond measure.

ACKNOWLEDGEMENTS

A huge thank you to everyone at *10,000 Lakes Publishing* for helping me bring my first novel to fruition. A special thanks to Sean Bloomfield and Colton Witte for taking a chance on an unknown writer. I will be forever grateful. I look forward to this exciting journey and hope it is a long and successful one.

Thank you also to Bridget Keen Christianson, DeeAnn Eickhoff, Bobbie Knutson, Barb McMahon, Cheryl Meld, Ruth Wotring Novak, and Linda O'Neil for reading and rereading my novel—selflessly sharing your time, thoughts, and ideas to make the book so much better. A big thank you to Beth Lynne at bzhercules.com. She has a unique gift of understanding the written word and making sure the storyline is airtight. She also responds to my emails both day and night.

An incredible amount of love goes to my children, Brandon and Taylor, for telling me I can do anything I set out to do; they helped me see that writing wasn't a pipedream. And finally, a special thank you to my husband, Mitch, who has served as my all-time back rubber, encourager, idea bouncer, and chocolate supplier. I could not write without his love and support. He has always been my first reader and my best critic.

I love and appreciate all of you so very much.

PROLOGUE

THIRTY-TWO YEARS EARLIER

The sun beat down on her tiny ten-year-old body as she lay in wait on that Sunday afternoon. She could feel her skin tightening as it baked red; she scrunched her forehead to feel how badly it was burned. It hurt more than it had the past weekend or the one before that. She reached beyond her nest and pulled out two handfuls of the fresh grass, laying the cool blades across her forehead, then tugging her hat down over them, all the while calculating how many more hours before the sun would drop beyond the trees and it would be safe enough to sneak back into the house.

Looking back, she could never be certain why she let her guard down on that particular day—whether it was the extra warmth of the sun shining down on her or the coolness of the earth against her back. Nothing inside of her felt any different from the other hundred or so Sundays she had spent hiding out there, praying God would take him away before it was too late.

The giant oaks that lined the right side of the hill cast shadows that worked their way across the incline as the day eased toward sunset. The bees hopped from one flower to another, pollinating the colorful splashes of wildflowers that grew all around her hiding place. A fuzzy brown and black caterpillar made his descent down a tall, green reed, and she marveled at how normal life on the hillside seemed.

She felt her chest expand as she drew in a breath so deep, she thought her lungs would explode. It was the first real breath she had taken since *this* fight had begun. She repeated the prayer, as she drew in a deep breath and slowly blew it out, directing the rush of air toward a feathery dandelion. The white seeds scattered across the tall grass and floated down to the

1

earth until they too were hidden amidst the overgrown weeds. Repeatedly, she whispered her wish before blowing at the weeds, sending the seeds afloat. Soon, every dandelion stem surrounding her stood tall and bare. Her deep breaths had left her lightheaded, and she yawned as she momentarily closed her eyes.

Pressing her head deeper into the crook of her arm, she yawned again. The leaves rustled as they danced in the warm afternoon breeze, occasionally stopping long enough for her to hear the silence of the hillside.

She pressed her back into the ground and curled her shoulders forward, moving only as much as she dared, not enough to be noticed. She stretched her sunburned arm downward before rolling onto her side, where she squirmed until her tiny body once again slipped into the divot. Again, she camouflaged herself with the tall grass before settling in until dark.

The churning in her stomach had begun to ease as she hummed a calming lullaby. For as long as she could remember, this had been her life; from Friday night until Monday morning—when she heard her father's car door slam, whisking him away for another week in the city, nearly two hours south. This was how she survived. Survival meant hiding on the hillside until dark when she would sneak back into the house and into the depths of her closet, her body tucked beneath a wide, low side-shelf, her blanket wrapped tightly around her as she waited out the long night.

From the hillside, she watched the fluffy white clouds slowly drift overhead. A parade of oddly shaped animals passed above her as her daydreams took her far away.

She stretched again, trying to ward off the sleep that had slowly begun to ease its way in. Some of her grass covering slipped away, but she didn't notice. A tiny brown ant crawled across her hand and down the tip of her finger. As she watched it zigzag back and forth, her eyelids fluttered and then closed, leaving her unprotected—an open target.

***

The first blow hit her in the side, partially connecting with her lowest rib. A rush of air escaped so violently, it threw

2

her backward. She rolled farther away and curled herself into a ball, tightly wrapping her arms around her head. She knew the next blow would be worse. Her father's second kick was a direct hit to her lower back. The pain shot up her spine, but she refused to scream. She knew how much satisfaction it would give him if she appeared in the least bit weak.

Watching him through a small opening between her elbows, she saw his jaw tighten as he pulled his leg back again, aiming for nothing, kicking for maximum pain. But as he let loose, she rolled away from him. The missed connection threw him off balance and he fell onto his back, his head bouncing as it connected with the hillside.

She jumped to her feet and took off running up the hill but stopped when she realized he wasn't chasing her. Cautiously, she turned and took one silent step toward her father and waited. Slowly, she inched her way back down the hillside, skidding on a small patch of gravel. An irresistible need to know if he was breathing pulled her closer.

Bending over his still body, she watched his chest for the slightest movement. When she saw nothing, she bent sideways, tipping her ear toward his face, ready to recoil in escape, but all she heard was the chirping of the birds and the rustling of the leaves. She held her breath. A tiny river of blood oozed from the corners of his mouth and nose. The whiskey smell was strong, and she leaned away from him before drawing in a breath.

As she stood up, an overwhelming thought hit her full force. Her eyes darted back and forth between the house and her father. If he was out here, where was her mother? What had he done to her? The fighting never stopped until he passed out. Unless... She again turned to scale the steep hill. Once again, she slipped on the gravel, her foot pressing against her father's shoulder. She pushed herself upright and began the slow climb toward the top, but she had taken only one step when she felt his hand latch onto her ankle. He jerked her leg out from under her and she fell—landing on her elbows, hard. Grasping at the base of the tall weeds, holding on to keep from sliding down the hill, she tried to right herself. She felt his hand grab the back of her shirt, and she spun around, jerking herself free. Her father

3

was on his knees, unsteadily swiping at her with his long, muscular arms. Dropping her head down, she dove into him, sending him backward down the hill, tumbling out of control. She skidded on the loose gravel and tall grasp but saved herself by grabbing the root of a tree that had worked its way out of the soil. She watched as he rolled over and over—his arms flailing in all directions as he attempted to stop himself.

With her hands covering her ears to block out his screams, she again hummed the familiar lullaby as she rocked back and forth, watching until her father came to a sudden stop at the bottom of the hill. Was this another of his tricks? She didn't care this time; she wasn't going to wait around to find out. She'd had enough of his abuse. The anger welled up inside of her, and she could feel the heat slide up her cheeks. As she turned toward the house, she stepped on the edge of a large rock. Bending over, she dug around it, digging at the ground with her already filthy fingernails until she unearthed it. It was bigger than she had expected. Struggling, she hoisted it above her right shoulder and pitched it in her father's direction. The rock landed far from him but continued rolling and bouncing down the hillside, stopping just inches from his head. Something inside her snapped, and she screamed at him—all the words she had wanted to say for as long as she could remember—all those forbidden words he had repeatedly screamed at her and her mother.

Then, she stopped. In the silence of that afternoon, she spewed one last phrase she hoped would be too late for him to hear. Her words were slow and deliberate, and she trembled as she shouted down the hillside. "I hope you're dead! Then you'll finally leave us alone!" Spinning on one foot, she climbed up the steep bank and raced toward the house—toward the only real safety she had ever known—her mother.

CHAPTER 1

THIRTY-TWO YEARS LATER

Claire inched forward in the Starbuck's drive-thru, stopping only inches from the dented rear bumper of a silver minivan filled with unruly preschoolers. *Coffee*—she needed coffee; didn't just *want* it; she *needed* it. She didn't want a latte or a cappuccino or any of the other drinks she usually picked up on her daily outings. Today, she wanted it black—hot and strong. What she really wished for was a caffeine drip, for it to be pumped directly into her bloodstream. After all, she'd already put in an eight-hour day.

She'd been up since 3:08 a.m. when Jade had interrupted another of the nightmares that invaded her sleep nearly every time she closed her eyes lately. Her heart had been racing, pounding in her chest. Claire wasn't sure then, and didn't know even now, if it had been the nightmare or her daughter's panicked voice that had caused the intense reaction.

"Mom? Mom, wake up!" Jade's whisper slipped into her sleep, blending perfectly into the gut-wrenching dream. The little girl in her nightmare tugged on the woman's arm, begging her to open her eyes. Tears trickled down the child's face as the salty liquid ran between her lips and into her mouth. Suddenly, someone was pulling the little girl away from her mother, and the child screamed, "Mom! Please, wake up!"

Claire gasped as her eyes flew open. Her daughter stood over the bed just inches from her face, both hands pulling on her arm. "What? What is it? What's wrong, Jade? Are you okay?"

"Mom, don't be mad!" Jade's tear-filled eyes sparkled in the moonlight that flooded through the window above the bed. "I need your help! I have a history assignment I forgot to finish! I can't have another late assignment. I just can't!" Jade's whisper grew louder as she pleaded for Claire's help. She tugged on the sheets that still entangled her mother.

Claire fell back onto her sweat-soaked pillow. She closed her eyes as a sigh of relief escaped from her trembling lips; she threw an arm across her forehead and drew in several calming breaths. But even as the adrenaline rush slipped away, Claire's anxiety did not.

"Jade," she warned.

"Don't even say it. It's my fault. I know I blew it, but can you help me, please?" Jade's whining irritated Claire, but she said nothing.

Reaching for her daughter's hand, she held it above the mass of sheets as she untangled her legs. Once freed from the final knot of damp, silky turquoise sheets, she tossed them over the top of her husband, who again lay coverless—curled into a ball with his arms tucked around him. She laughed as she listened to Michael's soft snoring. He had slept through another of her nightmares and the unveiling of yet another *Jade crisis*. She brushed her lips gently against his cheek and marveled at the tranquility on his face. If only she could find a small piece of that. No matter how tiny it might be, it had to be a million times better than the stress of what she kept hidden deep inside.

"Come on, Mom! Hurry up!" Jade impatiently pulled on her mother's arm again. Claire shifted her position closer to the edge of the bed. "Don't you get it? We can't have a late assignment again!"

Claire lightly snorted. "No, I guess *we* can't, can *we*?" She touched her daughter's shoulder as she climbed out of bed. "Even if it is...what? 3:08 in the morning." A small moan escaped when she realized the actual time. She stretched her arms toward the ceiling as a yawn snuck out.

Wrapping her outstretched arms around her daughter, Claire held on for much longer than she knew Jade could possibly stand. The warmth of her daughter's skin melted into her own, and she didn't want to let go. She knew the days of hugging Jade were numbered. Adolescence was a mean creature.

Jade's arms wiggled up into the small space between the two of them and she pushed Claire away. "Mo-om," she whined through gritted teeth. "Come on! You're wasting time."

"I'm coming," Claire conceded. "Go get everything set up and I'll be down in a minute."

"Don't be long! We need to get this done." Even under the cover of darkness, Jade's frustration was obvious as she stormed out of the room.

Super Mom! Claire looked at Michael, thinking he was awake, but the words she thought she heard had come from within. *Claire, you can't fix everything for the kids. You know that, right? One day they won't need you—or even want you to fix their problems. What are you going to do then?* It had become his mantra. He said it several times a week, and she knew he was right. What *would* she do then?

Shuddering, she hugged herself, rubbing her hands along her arms, trying to alleviate the goosebumps that had sprung up. With the nightmare still close enough to touch, still riding that fine line between reality and fiction, Claire drew in a deep breath and held it for a moment. Her heart had finally slowed, but it still beat in a random, unsettled pattern. *Reality,* she remembered her mother saying, *is what you can touch, what you can feel against your skin. It is what you can hold in your hands.* Tonight, she had felt every bit of that nightmare. It scared her to death that, with each one, the line between reality and fiction was beginning to fade. She shivered again and wrapped her arms more tightly around herself to stop the shaking—her fingertips absently moved up and down the length of the wide scar that ran from her shoulder to her elbow. *Reality or nightmare?*

Quietly pulling the bedroom door shut behind her, Claire froze as the door latch clicked. Again, she held her breath as her stomach exploded. The nightmare stirred again. Through pursed lips, she let her breath quietly escape. Then, ever so slowly, she let go of the door handle and slipped into the shadows of the hallway to check on her son.

Henry lay sideways across his twin bed; his feet solidly pressed against the dark wall, his head and one arm hung off the side of the mattress. Claire untangled his arms and legs from his twisted Spiderman sheets and gently scooped him into her arms. Henry's limp body was dead weight as she struggled to lay her cheek against his. She breathed in his all-boy scent—the smell of sleep and a faint aroma of shampoo. He squirmed in her arms before settling himself against her chest. Claire clumsily rocked him back and forth, softly humming a familiar lullaby of long ago.

Finally, settling him back into his bed, pulling up and tucking his covers around him, she bent down to kiss his cheek. She glanced at the clock on Henry's nightstand. *3:14 a.m.* She knew Jade would be looking for her at any moment, but she didn't want to move. Her son still needed her—not for what he could get from her—just to be his mom.

Claire gently laid her hand on Henry's forehead. She brushed his hair away from his face and bent over him. "I love you, buddy, more than you'll ever know," she whispered.

"Mom, come on!" The angry call came from the bottom of the stairs, nearly echoing in the empty hallway.

Mimicking her daughter's latest teenage angst, Claire rolled her eyes and whispered, "You know what, Henry? Even when you become a teenager," the corners of Claire's mouth turned up slightly, "I'll still love you." Then, in the dark, as she kissed her son's forehead, Claire felt the final grip of her nightmare fade away.

Running up the stairs, two at a time, Jade grabbed her mother's hand just as Claire reached the top of the landing. "Geez, Mom, what took you so long? I've been waiting forever!" Her words were sharp, foreshadowing the vicious teenage years yet to come.

Jade again tugged on Claire's arm. "Come on, Mom. You've wasted enough time just getting down here." Silently, Claire cupped her daughter's cheek before continuing toward the kitchen. Her eyes snapped shut as she flipped on the shockingly bright island lights. One eyelid slowly opened, and the other followed.

"Mom, what are you doing? We've gotta get this done." Jade followed on her mom's heels, nearly colliding with her when Claire stopped. "This is important. You're acting like it's not."

And there it was—the guilt that Jade had recently begun hurling at her mother—the guilt Claire was growing used to. It wasn't the words; it was the attitude and the sharpness that stabbed at Claire. It made every muscle from the top of her head to the bottom of her feet tense, every nerve tingle. Had Claire used that tone with her own mother? She could not recall ever being disrespectful as a child, at least not to her *mother*. But things had been different then. There had been secrets she had been protecting, secrets that could have escaped if she hadn't been careful. Back then, it had been better to be safe than sorry. Claire was certain she had been nothing like Jade. Silence protected secrets; Jade had no secrets to protect.

Claire counted to ten to keep from saying something she would regret later in the day. Pasting on a teeth-gritting smile, she turned toward Jade. "Honey, I'm going to make a quick pot of coffee. I'm not even awake yet." She fumbled with the handle on the freezer door before pulling it open and extracting the coffee beans. She pushed the door shut and leaned against it for no more than a split second. Her daughter tracked every movement. A heavy sigh filled the kitchen, but Claire chose to ignore it. A second one followed, longer and louder than the first. "I get it, Jade, but my eyes aren't even open yet. Just give me a minute."

"Mom! You don't have time for coffee! We've gotta get this done!" The anger in Jade's voice grated over Claire like fingernails on a chalkboard. Again, she counted, biting her cheeks to keep angry words from slipping out. Slowly, she conceded it was going to be Jade's way whether Claire liked it or not. This was one battle she was not willing to fight.

"Okay, Jade, you win. I'm coming." Claire picked up the coffee beans and opened the bag. The aroma of the frozen beans didn't help, not like a cup of black coffee would have, but it was the best she could do. With a frown, she closed the bag and slipped it back into the freezer. Then, wrapping an arm around her daughter, she led her to the den.

Super Mom!

***

At 6:15 a.m., as Claire began dumping supplies back into plastic bins, an audible yawn slipped out. She shook her head and rubbed her eyes, trying to wipe away her exhaustion. Jade planted her head on the desk, close to the computer

9

keyboard. Her eyelids fluttered before they closed. In another minute or two, Claire was certain there would be a puddle of drool there as well.

Shaking her daughter's shoulder, Claire laughed. "Oh, no you don't! You need to head upstairs and get ready for school. I'll finish cleaning up down here."

Jade turned her head slightly to the right, burying her chin deep into the crook of her arm, almost smothering her whine. "Please, Mom, can't I stay home today? Just this once? Or maybe you could take me in later—after second period— just before history." Jade yawned and let her head fall back onto her arm. "I'm soooo tired."

Claire didn't miss a beat. "You know, sweetie, had you done this last night or even last week, or whenever it was assigned, you wouldn't have had to get up before the crack of dawn." Then, glancing up at the clock, Claire felt her heart soften; still she was quick to dismiss any thought of letting Jade off the hook. "Sorry, hon, this was your decision. I know you don't want to, but you have to go to school today—on time."

Suddenly, the desk chair shot backward, slamming against the work-table, and Jade popped up and stomped out of the room. Claire heard her clomp up the first three stairs before the noise stopped and the house became silent again. She shook her head as she bent over to pick up the pencils and the cup that had flown to the floor during her daughter's heated exit. As she stood up, she bumped into Jade. Her daughter awkwardly wrapped her arms around her. "Sorry, Mom. Thanks for the help." And with that, she was gone—quieter and with less drama than her first exit.

How many years did adolescence last anyway?

Moving silently around the room, slipping supplies back into drawers and onto shelves, Claire's mind drifted back to her own childhood. She had promised herself, from a young age, that her family would never suffer from *her* past. "Whatever it takes." She shivered as she whispered the words aloud. She would do what her own mother had not done, what she could not do because of her father. She would do whatever it took to keep them happy and safe.

CHAPTER 2

Claire balanced on the edge of her mother's twin bed, her feet planted firmly on the floor, supporting most of her weight. The soft hum of the fluorescent lights and the usual drone of activity from the hallway at the Autumn Woods Nursing Home seeped into the room.

"Margaret, you have to use your walker or you're going to fall," one of the nurses scolded a patient in the hallway.

"Oh, for crying-out-loud! I'm 97 years old. Stop telling me what to do, you old biddy."

"I'm *not* kidding, Margaret." There was a pause followed by, "Wait! Did *you* just call *me* an old biddy?"

Claire chuckled, thankful for the interruption in the awkward conversation she was having with her mother.

Another nurse reprimanded a man who was rocking back and forth in his wheelchair, banging his head into the wall just outside her mother's room. "Mr. Harvey, you're going to hurt yourself. Here, let me help you back to your room."

"Stop! Stop touching me!" he screamed. "Help! Police! This woman is trying to rob me! Help me! Somebody, help me!"

Claire jumped as the sudden ringing of her cell phone cut through the commotion in the hallway. Tess's arm instinctively reached forward, grabbing the TV remote control from the nightstand that had become a dumping ground for a dozen or so Andes Mints foils, a pile of wadded-up tissues, and anything else she had touched in the last twenty-four hours.

Tess pulled the remote close to her face. "Hello," she sang. "Hello! Hello!" she impatiently barked into the remote, her volume increasing each time she spoke. Her hands shook as she pressed the remote closer to her face. "Listen here, buster, don't think I don't know you're still there. You'd better listen to me. You're just taunting an old woman and I won't stand for it. Now stop it!"

When she jabbed at the power button of the remote control, the voices and music of another commercial that played quietly on the television at the end of the room faded into silence. Tess dropped the black and silver device onto her lap as she clicked her tongue. Angrily, she waved her arms through the air. "That was rude, I tell you! Just plain rude! I don't understand how anyone can call you and then just hang up." She leaned back in her chair and crossed her arms. "Back in my day, we had manners...

"Mary Claire, what's wrong with you? Wipe that stupid grin off of your face or I'll wipe it off for you. I taught you better than that. It's just so rude." Tess leaned forward and pointed her finger directly into Claire's face. "I'll tell you one thing, Missy; I'd better *never* catch you doing that—or those children of yours either. Manners! That's what's wrong with these children today; they have no manners. Why just..."

In the mirror over her mother's dresser, Claire caught her reflection again, but it wasn't 42-year-old Claire she saw—it was her ten-year-old self.

It was a sunny, late April morning more than thirty years earlier—the day of her father's funeral. She and her mother stood next to the simple gray steel casket. The lid was closed; it had never been opened, but she knew he was inside. She had seen his lifeless body as he lay on the garage floor on that fateful day. She knew there was no way he could still be alive, but an unsettling feeling washed over her, and she felt as if she was being watched. She spun her head to the left and then to the right but saw no signs of him or anyone else looking in her direction. She released the breath she had been holding; holding her breath was just another way she had learned to hide.

Claire took a single step forward and reverently touched the cold metal top of the casket with a single fingertip. She wanted to peek inside. She could not recall ever being this close to her father without having to become invisible—but she was done with that now. Anger grew inside of her and she fought the urge to kick the box, to pound on the lid, to scream at him for all the suffering he had put them through. But just knowing he was gone was enough—for now.

The scent of orchids floated through the church, so strong they made her eyes burn and her nose itch. In small groups, people approached them to pay their respects, shaking her mother's hand, uncomfortably wrapping their arms around Claire. The church had been filled with people, her father's business associates, many of whom had been on the receiving end of her father's temper, and all the locals—who did not have a clue. They believed the O'Brien family had been something they were not.

Claire fidgeted with the handkerchief her mother had tucked into the pocket of her dress. But the white hanky was useless. She felt no sadness over the loss of her father, and even though she tried to make a show for others, she could not make even one tear fall.

As she watched the groups of people who had come to say their final goodbyes, there was something that struck her as strange; none of them were crying either. Not one person shed a tear, including her own mother. Were they as happy as she was that he was gone? As she stood in her homemade navy-blue sailor dress, white gloves, and navy and white brimmed hat, a smile spread across her face—not a little grin or even a smirk, but a full-fledged ear-to-ear smile. For the first time ever, she realized her father would not walk through the door on Friday night, wouldn't bring with him the fear he tracked in every weekend. She would never have to inch her way down that hillside again or hide in the depths of her closet buried beneath blankets and quilts, under that low shelf. She was free—finally free!

Her mother had seen her smile, noticed how it continued to widen right there in front of her father's casket, and she squeezed her hand—not a gentle, loving squeeze, but an angry one. It was enough for Claire to erase it from her face. But even so, she continued to smile on the inside.

The smile slid from Claire's face as she scooted back onto the bed, leaning away from her mother's rant. No longer listening to the words, Claire studied Tess. The perfectly coiffed, jet-black dyed hair of her younger days was now laid gray and flat, parted and combed to one side. Her face had aged almost overnight. The fine wrinkles and imperfections she had kept hidden beneath the same light-colored Cover Girl make-up she had always worn were deeper now, more obvious around her eyes and mouth. The bright red lipstick Claire had repeatedly hidden and replaced with a lighter, more subtle shade had returned, and extended far beyond Tess's natural lip line, spreading into the deep crevices around her mouth.

Claire reached for a Kleenex. "Mom, let me help you with your lipstick. You have a little…"

"Dammit, Mary Claire!" Tess turned her head and fought Claire's help as a child would fight her own mother. "Leave me alone. I'm not four years old. Stop treating me like I am." She slapped a hand over her mouth and glared at her daughter. With a muffled voice, she called, "Ha! Can't touch me!" Tess giggled like the small child she had become.

Claire sadly leaned back onto the bed. She knew her mother was in there somewhere. She had seen glimpses of the person Tess had once been. But with every passing day, those moments were less frequent. The disease was winning. Alzheimer's—one. Tess—zero. It was driving a wedge between them—this one permanent, unlike the temporary one that was growing between her and Jade.

Claire's face began to burn; she could feel the heat as it inched its way up her cheeks all the way to the tips of her ears. She despised this disease that was chipping away at her mother's memory, breaking off bits of it daily, slowly erasing the person Claire recognized.

She felt her shoulders sag forward, heavy with the sadness she felt. Refusing to give in to the tears that had begun to build, she turned away from her mother. Family photos lined the dresser, and they brought a sense of comfort to Claire, memories of Tess in another time, another place—when life was real for both of them, easier to understand.

"Why's it so damn quiet in here?" Tess's words were almost always harsh now—often pointed and cruel. "You'd think a bunch of old coots lived here." Her eyes darted about, searching the sparsely furnished room, finally landing on the TV that hung from the ceiling. "Unbelievable! That stupid thing shut off again. I've had nothing but trouble with that thing since I moved into this dump." Her head turned sideways, and she gave Claire a nasty glance. "It goes off all the time. Every time that damn phone rings, *it shuts off*! I keep telling them it's broken, but they won't believe me. They talk to me like I'm stupid. I can hear it in their voices."

"Mom, I know…"

"Don't even try to tell me you know." Tess cut her off. "You don't have a clue what it's like to be old and all alone. Yes, Mary Claire, you heard me—alone. People laugh at you behind your back. All day long, I sit here watching people come and go…knowing that when they leave, I might never see them again. You *don't* know, Mary Claire. You don't have any idea at all. So, don't try to tell me you do."

"Mom, that isn't what…"

"I want out of here, Mary Claire. You dumped me here…" Her voice suddenly grew quieter; her hands shook as she stared down at the tissue she had shredded into countless pieces.

Tess's actions gradually slowed. Her words were lost in the midst of a long pause. Her head fell back against the back of the chair, and a gentle puff of air escaped from her lips as her shoulders slumped forward. The shredded tissue drifted from her hands and fell to the floor, piece by piece. As quickly as her tirade started, it was over.

Tess was gone, had mentally faded away. She had left the now and was trapped somewhere else: in a different dimension, in the past or maybe even the future, but she was no longer with Claire in that moment. As with all her episodes—as Dr. Sedgewick called them—Tess would never remember this outburst, and for that, Claire was thankful.

By the time Claire had listened to her mother's *It's rude to hang up on anyone, The TV is broken so what are you going to do about it?* and *You dumped me here* outburst, she knew she had missed the call that had started her mother's entire blow-up. As Tess sat silently staring in the direction of the window, seemingly unaware the curtain between her section of the room

15

and her roommate's was drawn and blocking her view, Claire reached for her cell phone and listened to the message.

Claire's muscles tensed as she heard the school nurse identify herself. "Hey, Claire. This is Nurse Angie from the elementary school. I'm afraid Henry had a small accident this morning in PE." Claire jumped up and grabbed her oversized purse as she dropped a quick kiss on her mother's forehead. Then, flinging her bag onto her shoulder, she raced from the room without looking back, her mind focused solely on her son as she headed toward her car.

Angie's message continued. "Henry's fine, but I think you should probably take him to the doctor and have his ankle checked out. He does have some swelling, but I don't think it's broken. Can you call me back when you get this message? 555-0416. If I don't hear from you soon, I'll try to call your husband. Oh…and try not to worry. Henry's one of the tough guys."

Try not to worry? Impossible! Claire thought as she raced her Lexus out of the parking lot. It was her job to worry.

CHAPTER 3

"Michael, stop! Henry needs to tie his shoes before he breaks his neck!" Claire was bringing up the rear as the four hiked the rocky path toward the river. She was still a bit gun shy after Henry twisted his ankle at school days before.

Her husband turned and wove his way past his children, parking himself in front of his wife. He placed one hand on each of her shoulders and held her at arm's length. "Claire, stop worrying. Kids fall; it's what they do. If Henry gets hurt, it'll teach him to keep his shoes tied." Claire opened her mouth, but Michael pressed a finger to her lips to keep her from interrupting.

Her husband threw his arms into the air. He stared into the sky as he sarcastically cast out another of his *life lesson tales*. "Ladies and gentlemen," he patted Henry on the head before sending his arm skyward again, "throughout all of history, mothers have tried to save their sons from the demise of the ill-fitting shoe. Let's take a look back." His voice suddenly became nasally and high-pitched as he mimicked an old woman. "Tutankhamen, stop and hook your sandals, son. You're going to trip and kill yourself. How do you ever expect to grow up to become king?" Michael and the kids laughed as Claire gave him a dirty look.

Claire silently bent over and tied Henry's gray and orange hiking boot and double-knotted it, then she tugged on the other. She spun on her heels, grabbed her son's hand, and took the lead along the path—a trail that allowed only rare peeks at the sun.

Michael and Jade quickly fell into step behind them. They hadn't walked more than ten steps before Claire's words drifted backward. "You know, Mr. Smarty Pants, how do you know Tut didn't trip on the sandal straps his mother told him to hook? I mean, he died when he was just a teenager."

"Hey, Jade!" Michael grinned as he elbowed his daughter while scanning his surroundings. "Did you hear something?"

Jade covered her mouth to keep a giggle from escaping.

As they broke the hill, the river came into view, blue and clear. The sun reflected off the water, sending shards of light in every direction. Wildflowers of yellow, purple, and red lined the banks of the river. Where flowers didn't brighten the banks with their grandeur of color, a multitude of greenery did. Every shade of spring green could be found somewhere along the bank. Fuzzy moss grew atop several large rocks that lay near the water's edge close to the base of a cluster of trees where they stopped.

"This is it!" Claire announced. She threw her arms out to her sides and spun around in a circle, breathing in the midday air. "It's beautiful here." She grabbed the blanket draped over Michael's arm and spread it out on the grassy bank.

Sundays were family day; they had been since before they were married. First it had just the two of them, but even when the kids came along and life got busy, they still made every effort to spend the day together.

"Where's the picnic basket? I'm starving." Michael scanned the area as Claire smoothed down the last corner.

She spun around; her face twisted in confusion. "What? I set it down when I tied Henry's shoe. You were behind me! Didn't you pick it up?"

Michael's head pivoted toward the forest. The entrance to the path was nearly concealed by the thick spring foliage. "I didn't pick it up. I had the blanket. You were supposed to carry the picnic basket. I didn't even see it." His shoulders sagged and he let out a huge sigh. "It's got to be nearly twenty minutes back to the place we stopped. Twenty minutes there, twenty minutes back—we may as well *all* go back. We'll starve to death by then." With his face still turned away from his wife, Michael bit the inside of his cheeks to keep from laughing out loud; he could not face his wife, not without giving himself away.

Claire pushed her way past Michael, plowing into him with her shoulder as she passed. She headed toward the trail, calling back as she took off first at a jog then a dead run. "Fine, I left it; I'll go get it. Keep an eye on the kids, and make sure Henry doesn't get close to the river until I get back." Michael watched her ponytail bob up and down, the sun creating golden highlights in her naturally blonde hair.

Jade lifted her dad's arm and wrapped it over her shoulder as she slipped in close to him. "Oh, Dad, she's gonna kill you. But it's gonna be so worth it." She giggled as she rubbed her hands together.

Henry tugged on Michael's worn t-shirt. "Dad, why's Mom gonna kill you?" But Michael ignored him, keeping his eyes on his wife. "Dad?" Henry whined louder.

Michael caught glimpses of Claire's pink t-shirt as it flashed between the branches and the leaves of the trees. "Five, four, three…"

And there it was—seconds sooner than he had expected. Anyone within a two-mile range could have heard it. "Michael Thomas Stanton!"

Jade's eyebrows shot upward, and her cheeks puffed out. "Oh, Dad!" She laughed. "She used your *middle* name. You *are* in trouble. I don't even wanna be here when she gets back. Wait! Yes, I do. But oooooohhh! She's gonna kill you!" Jade pulled her arms to her chest as she shivered with excitement.

"Daaaaad! Why's Mom gonna kill you?" Henry became more insistent as he bounced his hip against his father's leg over and over until Michael finally rubbed the top of his son's head.

"Ahh, Henry, women just don't have a good sense of humor like men do." He and Jade laughed as they watched Claire storm out of the woods with the tan wicker picnic basket. The basket bounced against her leg as she took long strides toward them.

"Real funny!" Claire called as she continued along the path. "But I have something even funnier for you. You know that bag of Cheetos we had to pick up on the way out here—the ones you swore you'd die if you didn't have? Well, if you really want them, the birds *might* share what's left—that is, of course, if you get there fast enough." Claire pulled the empty orange Cheetos bag beneath the front of her shirt. As she passed the two jokesters, she shoved the bag into Michael's stomach and continued toward the river.

"Uhhhh!" Michael groaned as she shoulders fell.

Jade tugged the bag out of her father's hands. "Are there *any* crumbs left?" As she searched the inside of the bag, she let out a small groan—loud enough to put a smile on her mother's face. Then Claire licked her index finger and placed an invisible tally in the air.

A look of defeat slid across Michael's face. Then, mimicking his best Yogi Bear voice, he declared, "I think we might have made a *boo-boo* with that pic-a-nic basket!"

Jade shoved the empty Cheetos bag into her father's stomach just as her mother had done. "Jeez, Dad, do you think?"

Henry raced after Claire. "Mom, what's so funny? What happened? Nobody's telling me nothin'—and why are you gonna kill Dad?"

Claire wrapped an arm around her son's shoulder. "Henry, men just don't have a good sense of humor like women do."

Henry shrugged his shoulders as the corners of his mouth turned up in question. "That's not what *Dad* said."

***

Claire loved watching her family; there was nothing she enjoyed more. As she lay on her stomach on the old green army blanket, her chin rested in the palms of her hands, her elbows taking the brunt of the weight. A long-lens Sony camera lay on the blanket next to her. Having almost no pictures of her own childhood, her camera was never far away.

Nothing could erase the joy she felt at that moment. A frog-catching contest had gotten underway. The winner would earn the right to choose where they would spend the next Sunday. Hooting and hollering filled the air as the three ran up and down the riverbank, searching for the biggest frog. As each one was captured, the newest prisoner was compared to the current winner housed under a large plastic bucket. Claire served as judge.

Claire snapped pictures of the contest as the sun traveled across the sky, pushing the afternoon with it. The brilliant blue sky was dotted with puffy cotton-ball clouds. Only the movement of her family disturbed the frozen image.

Even with a little creative *scorekeeping* on Michael's part, the number of frogs Jade and Michael each caught far outnumbered those Henry staked claim to. Growing increasingly serious about winning the contest, her son made his way up the bank to where Claire lay snapping candid shots.

Henry plopped down next to her. Dropping his chin onto her shoulder, he threw one arm across her back and patted her bare arm with his damp, frog-germ hands. Claire cringed but didn't move. "Hey, Bud! It looked like you were catching some pretty big frogs out there," she said.

"Was not," he argued, his voice filled with defeat. "Mom, you gotta help me. I need some superpowers or something." Henry lay on his stomach and pressed his face against hers. "Do you have any magic like you used to have when I was little?"

Claire laughed at his seriousness as she rolled over and pulled him into a huge bear hug. *Supermom! Magic powers!* She was expected to do it all.

"You know, Henry. I might have packed some superpowers just for you."

"Really?" he whispered. He pressed his face closer to hers. "Don't tell anyone else, 'kay?"

Claire drew an X across her chest and raised two fingers into the air. "Cross my heart and hope to die! Stick a needle in my eye," she whispered.

"Oooooooo!" Henry cooed as he rubbed his hands together. Claire started digging through the oversized backpack. It held an arsenal of extra *just in case* items: Band-Aids, sunscreen, calamine lotion, Neosporin. Claire pushed past the bag of smaller tubes and bottles and pulled a red, white, and blue beach towel from the bottom of the bag. Holding it above her head in triumph, she declared, "Superpowers, Henry. If you want superpowers, you've got superpowers. Just tell me this— what do Superman, Batman, and Wonder Woman all have in common?"

Without missing a beat, Henry declared, "A *mom* who knows how to get superpowers!"

Claire laughed loud enough to attract the attention of Jade and Michael. "Yeah, Henry, that's right. And this mom…she knows how to get superpowers too." Claire loosely tied the cape around her son's neck. "Now raise your right hand." Claire waited for her son to follow her direction. "Other right, buddy!" Henry quickly switched hands.

"I know!" he said as his cheeks turned a rosy pink. "I was just checkin' to see if you'd notice." The two of them pressed their heads together and giggled.

"Okay, ready?" Claire asked. Henry excitedly nodded his head. "By the *powers* vested in me, in accordance with the Superhero Moms of the World," she continued, "I dub you Super Kid. Go forth and prosper…or catch frogs…or whatever you want to do."

"Cool, Mom! Thanks!" And with that, Henry squished her cheeks between his froggy hands. "You're better than Superman's mom even, I bet."

"Yeah, and don't you forget it!" Claire called as he flew off toward his mission.

Claire pressed her face into the blanket and rubbed it back and forth to remove the frog slime from her cheeks. When she lifted her head, the flapping of her son's cape made her the happiest mom in the world.

Superhero, Claire thought with a laugh. But her joy was short-lived as a memory from her past pulled her down. She, too, had been only five years old.

***

FIVE YEARS OLD

She had found a pale blue towel, torn and shredded. Pulling it from the bottom shelf of the linen closet, she was certain no one would mind if she used it. It looked worse than any of the rags her father kept in his garage. She tied the towel around her neck and raced through the house—flying. She wasn't a five-year-old anymore—she was a superhero, the kind who rescued people from burning buildings and evil villains— the kind who never had to be invisible because everyone *needed* them. Everyone *loved* them.

Superheroes *flew* everywhere, and she knew that. She flew up the stairs, taking them as fast as her little legs could carry her. She flew down the stairs, running one hand down the side of the wall to keep from tripping, always leaving the other out in front of her, superhero style. She flew in and out of her bedroom, through the kitchen, around the center island, and through nearly every inch of the house before she flew into the living room. But the sight of her father reading the Sunday paper stopped her in her tracks; her superpowers froze. She had been certain he was gone for the day.

She didn't breathe; she didn't move. She squeezed her eyes shut and wished for a real superhero to swoop down and save her. But no one came—not even her mom. It wasn't until she heard the snap of the footrest of the leather recliner that she spun around and raced toward the doorway, trying to escape before her father could catch her.

She felt the yank on her cape as it cut across her throat. Her tiny body stopped midstream before tumbling backward and out of control. She tugged the towel away from her throat, desperately trying to untie the stubborn knot. The back of her head cracked against the floor, creating sharp flashes of bright light around the edges of her eyes. She lay on her back, facing the ceiling with her arms out to her sides. Her eyes blinked rapidly, trying to bring the room into focus, but it was impossible. Her superpowers had betrayed her. They were useless against the one person she needed protection from—her father: the man who stood over her now, the man who hated her more than anyone else in the world.

Still too dazed to move, she watched through a cloud of blurriness as her father's eyes widened and his jaw tightened. The vein running along his temple bulged blue with anger. His cheeks burned red, and the color crept upward toward his forehead.

His arms shook as he lifted his foot, slamming it down across the tips of her tiny fingers, crushing them and holding them in place. A high-pitched sound filled the room, but she did not recognize it. She just wanted it to stop. It hurt her ears.

"Shut up! Shut up, you little brat! Look what you've done to that towel. You've completely ruined it! Now *both* of you are just pieces of trash!"

Her father turned and stormed out of the room, shoving her to the side with his foot, as if she were nothing.

She waited until she heard the screen door slam, then

she untied her makeshift cape. Her fingers throbbed as she folded the torn towel into smaller and smaller rectangles, carefully matching the corners each time. Then she pushed it all the way to the bottom of the kitchen trash can, covering it with the other garbage.

CHAPTER 4

"Well, I think we're pretty much done here," Claire said as she set the folder containing the PTA meeting notes on the conference table in front of her. She slipped off her purple tortoiseshell glasses and set them on the table in front of her. "Is there any other business we need to discuss?"

"I've got something," Ellen blurted out. "What's the deal with the PTA board retreat next week? We haven't heard anything. Is that still in the works or is that something else that's fallen by the wayside with the changeover in administration?" Her voice dripped with sarcasm as her eyes shifted from Claire to the new principal and back again.

Claire's eyes flashed a fierce warning.

"What?' Ellen's palms turned upward in front of her, mimicking the actions of every middle school student in the building. "I'm just asking. I need to know if I need to make plans with the devil to keep my kids next week." She turned toward Ben, also a single parent, and rested her chin on the back of one hand, batting her long eyelashes. "Because I could definitely use a little adult time."

Everyone laughed—except for one person.

Will Ryan, Willow Brook Middle School's principal, repeatedly drew a dark black line on the yellow notepad in his leather portfolio. The pen cut a slit several pages deep before he finally clicked the end and tucked it into the slot on the inside of the cover. His lower jaw shifted from one side to the other before he flipped the book shut.

"Yes." He closed his eyes then twisted his neck to the left before opening them again. "The board *work* session will be next week—Thursday and Friday, the fourteenth and fifteenth. The days will be long." He looked directly at Ellen before he spoke again. "And there will be *little* time for socializing."

Ellen snapped her fingers as she smiled at Ben. "Looks like I won't be going then."

Will ignored the levity of the comment and continued with his impersonal speech. "We'll meet at the Oakdale Retreat Center...same as last year. Your *old* administration said it was fine, so I figured we'd use it again. I've got information on rooms."

His words had been carefully chosen—pointed and few—and Claire cringed at his tone. When he finished, he looked only at her. His head tipped back as his chin jutted in her direction. "Let me know who's planning to attend by tomorrow. I'll have my secretary make the arrangements." Will quickly stood up, sending his rolling chair gliding backward. He turned and walked from the room as all eight board members watched him cross the office and slam his office door shut.

Sam shook his head in disbelief. He leaned backward in his chair and stretched his arm toward the door, giving it a quick push with his index finger. He waited for it to close. "What in the hell is with him anyway? He shows about as much emotion as a road-killed possum." He slapped one hand down onto the wood-grain Formica. "The man sat there the entire time, not saying one word until Ellen asked about the retreat. Isn't the administration supposed to...lead? Administrate? Something? *Anything at all?*" His volume continued to climb, as did his frustration.

Char shook her head. "About the only thing he's cut out to administer is Advil," she said dryly. "That man gives me a throbbing headache!" She pressed her fingers to her temples. "And he's so cold! He's got about as much warmth as a block of ice." Then, as an afterthought, she added, "In the *wintertime.*"

Laughter filled the room, making Claire glad Sam had had the foresight to close the door.

"I'm telling you, he's hiding something. I don't know what it is, but I swear something's going to come out sooner or later. And I just hope it's not going to make us regret hiring him any more than we already do," Chris added.

Claire listened to the others question their belief in Will

as a leader. She did nothing to stop the conversation because she one hundred percent agreed with their statements. As far as she was concerned, Will was a self-centered, unemotional man who cared only about himself.

"I agree. I think we made a poor decision in hiring him last spring. What were we thinking? Was the competition so pathetic, it made Will look good?" Jen asked.

"I don't know how he got hired; I wasn't on the committee. But I do agree—he's hiding *something*." Sam's face turned into a full-blown grin. "Let's just hope it's not a body."

"Sam!" Jen rebuked as she gently slapped his arm. "That's a terrible thought!"

"Well?" Sam's shoulders rose in question.

"You know, you bring up a good point, though." Jack's brow knit itself together as he bit his lip.

"What? About the *body*?" Sam teased.

"No, but there *is* something he's hiding. I guess the real question is, *How're we going to find out what it is?*"

The room grew quiet as ideas churned in each person's mind.

"Wait! I've got…" Ben paused as he took out his wallet and rifled through it. The others silently watched as he pulled pictures, cards, and scraps of paper from the worn brown leather shell. From the last slot, he pulled a small white card and waved it in the air. "Here it is! I have a cousin who's a PI. He might be able to…"

"Okay…okay," Claire finally felt the need to step in. "I don't think we need to go *that* far. We have no proof that Will has done anything illegal or criminal. After all, he had to pass the background screening before the district could hire him, so he couldn't have anything worse than a few minor traffic violations on his record." She paused as she let a grin slide across her face. "Besides, as far as I know, being an *ass* isn't illegal in Colorado." Giggles rose from all sides of the table.

"Ooooh, Claire! Such language!" Ellen teased as she slapped her knee. "And to think I let my little Brandon play with your Henry! Not much of a role model, are you?"

Claire gave her a sideways grin before turning toward Ben, all the while biting the inside of her cheeks to stop herself from a full-blown laugh attack. "Hold on to your cousin's card, though. You never know when we might need it. I hear the superintendent's thinking about retiring in a year or so."

The room once again erupted with out-of-control laughter.

Ben hastily tucked his collection back into his wallet. "Yeah, well, laugh if you want, but my cousin owes me. And I honestly don't think it's such a bad idea." His face suddenly morphed into a huge smirk. "I'd love to be the one to dig up dirt on that loser."

"Alright! Enough said on that subject." Claire swiftly moved the conversation back to the upcoming retreat.

***

As she flipped off the lights in the now-empty conference room, Claire paused before stepping into the main office. A nagging feeling poked at her stomach. A simple overnight trip should not be a big deal, but something about it bothered her more this year than ever before. She didn't know what it was. She completely trusted Michael with the kids, so why did her stomach feel like she had just gotten off the biggest rollercoaster in the world?

***

The clock on Claire's dashboard glowed *11:47 a.m.* as she drove her car into the garage. She pressed the opener and waited for the moaning of the door to finally stop before she pressed the four-digit code that opened the door between the garage and the house. She quietly slipped into the mudroom, disarming and then rearming the security system. The sequence of beeps announced her return.

After leaving the PTA board meeting, she ran some errands and then met up with the neighborhood women for a girls' night out. Claire smiled as she recalled the spirited events of the evening.

The uptight tuxedoed manager had visited their table as they neared the end of their appetizers. "Ladies," he murmured softly. When they did not stop talking, he cleared his throat and tried again, "Ladies, I'm happy to see you're having a good time. However, we do have other customers who would like to enjoy their dinners as well. Do you think you could keep it down just a bit?"

That was only the first of his many appearances. He reprimanded them again, about twenty minutes later, this time without the friendly smile that had accompanied his first visit. And finally, a half-hour later, he reappeared—his voice almost a hiss that time. "If you cannot keep your voices down, I will have to ask you to leave. Do I make myself clear?"

So, they left—but not before Celeste planted an exceptionally loud kiss on his cheek before she sashayed through the restaurant and out the double-doors. The poor manager looked as if he was in shock as the rest of them passed by—each one tucking a $20 tip into his hand as they followed Celeste out of the restaurant. They had not left silently either. Giggles, hoots, and hollers had traveled with them as they headed out of the door.

Claire, the last one to leave, had watched the stocky, uptight manager as he fanned the money out. A lopsided grin broke loose as he called out, "Come again, ladies. Anytime!"

Leaving the restaurant had not put an end to the party. The festivities had simply moved to the parking lot, where the laughter continued for another forty-five minutes or so.

As Claire followed the parade of cars home and into her neighborhood, each car peeling off the road and into one driveway or another along the route, she realized how badly she had needed the laughter. It had cleared her head and left her at peace for the first time in days.

CHAPTER 5

Checking both the lock on the door and the security alarm a second time, Claire wandered into the kitchen—her favorite room of the house—with its oversized stainless-steel appliances, walk-in pantry, and twelve-foot island. The room looked as if it had been remodeled by one of the hosts of HGTV.

Michael had left one small pendant light on over the center island. A row of identical lights ran the entire length of the quartz countertop. This particular light had become the family nightlight; the one that was only shut off once *everyone* was home, safe and accounted for.

The countertop was nearly barren save for a large bouquet of multicolored roses Michael had sent the day before and a Deruta pottery bowl of fresh fruit. At a second glance, Claire noticed two bright pink sticky notes directly beneath the light. One was written in Jade's girly handwriting with its flowing curls and heart-dotted I's: *Mom, I need markers for science class*. The other was in Henry's large kindergarten print: *Mom, I love you! Henry*. There was a P.S. on the bottom of Henry's note from Michael that read *Me too!* Claire read the note a second time and then a third, her smile continually widening.

In the shadows of the night, Claire felt her way up the curved staircase and into Henry's room. Henry lay half on and half off his bed—an apparent every night occurrence. Claire slid him back into place, aligning him to the life-size Spiderman who stared up at her from his sheets. She pulled off the match to the sock she had found downstairs. Then she planted a gentle kiss on his sweaty forehead. As she left, she turned back for a final look at her son. The white glow of the moonlight reflected off his mirror and wrapped him in a bright light that made him appear almost angelic. A grin slid across Claire's face; she knew Henry better than that.

Across the hall, Claire opened the door of her daughter's room. There she found exactly what she had expected—a lump in the middle of the bed. Jade was nearly invisible to the outside world. If nothing else, her children were predictable. As she gently pulled the covers back to expose her daughter's head, a flashlight rolled onto the floor, scattering a random pattern of light across the white carpet and pale purple walls. A thick mystery book lay cradled in Jade's arms. Claire extracted it from her grip and set it on her glass nightstand.

"Mom, don't! I'm reading that," Jade sleepily chastised her mother, making a half-hearted attempt at grabbing the book before rolling toward the wall.

"Sweetie, it's almost midnight and you have school tomorrow. You need to go to sleep."

Silence. No words came from Jade, just the shallow breaths of peaceful sleep.

She clicked off the flashlight and tucked it back into a pile of stuffed animals—the secret spot where Jade hid everything of importance.

Closing Jade's door, Claire slipped through the hallway and into her own bathroom. Under the cover of darkness was where she had always felt comfort. While most people hated the murkiness of the night, Claire treasured it. No one could read her emotions; no one could see how much she hurt. She could hide from everyone and everything.

But on that night, Claire spent an unusually long time in the darkness of the bathroom—alone—hiding from even herself.

Finally, losing her battle with exhaustion, Claire ducked into the bedroom and slipped between the lavender-scented silky sheets on her bed. Michael slid toward her, pulling her into his arms and locking them around her waist. He ran a single finger up and down the side-seam of her nightgown. The contrast of the cool sheets and the warmth of his body sent a shiver down her spine.

With his eyes still closed, he sniffed the air around him. "Hmmm, you smell just like my wife. She's out late tonight, so we have time for a quickie." Michael chuckled at his own joke, then snuggled his face into the softness of Claire's neck. "I didn't hear you come home, Hon. When'd you get in?"

Claire laughed out loud. She turned her head and buried her face into the thickness of her pillow to stifle the sounds that escaped. "I swear, Michael, you wouldn't hear a freight train if it plowed right through the house, would you?"

"What'd you say?" Michael joked again.

Claire playfully slapped her husband's shoulder. "Some protector you are. I might as well get a dog. He'd protect me, keep me company, *and* love me unconditionally. Honestly, that's about all you're good for."

Michael leaned up on one elbow and brushed his lips across hers. "Ahhhh, but there are some things that I can do that a..." Claire giggled and let him work his magic.

Slowly, passionately, they made love for the first time in nearly a week—not by choice, but by the craziness of their schedules. As their pulses slowed, as they beat as one, Claire fell into a deep, peaceful sleep. She knew she was safe, protected, and loved.

***

As morning approached, Claire felt the nightmare begin to weave its way into her sleep, its long tentacles pulling her deeper into the uncontrollable black hole. It began to overthrow the peacefulness that Michael had wrapped her in just hours before. As with all the others, once it started, there was no stopping it. She felt herself falling into the abyss of the nightmare as it spiraled out of control. Subconsciously, she wrapped the sheets tightly around her arms and clutched the bars of the headboard, but even with all of her thrashing and preparation, the dream didn't halt; she felt herself being sucked up into the depths of the hell she had known since childhood.

...something was following her. She could not see what it was, but she could sense its presence. It remained hidden in the shadows of the night as she hurried along the unpaved road. She could feel its eyes watching her, boring into her, sending fiery sensations through every inch of her body. Her spine stiffened, and her head began to tingle as the hairs on the back of her neck stood up. Her heart thudded and she could feel the

pace of her steps move in time to its beat. As her feet picked up speed, a cloud of dust swirled around her legs, climbing upward toward her face, nearly choking her. The blue forget-me-not flowers, clutched tightly in her sweaty palm as she pumped her arms faster and faster, were taking a beating as they whipped back and forth. She was afraid to turn, afraid to see what was behind her, and yet she wanted to know what or who her predator was. She could feel it gaining on her, closing the gap between them faster than she could close the one between herself and her house.

The lights ahead of her cast out a warm, yellow glow, leading her home. She tried to run faster, but her short legs could not move any faster than they already were. She tried to scream, but even as she forced her clenched jaw open, the only noise that escaped sounded like the whine of an injured animal.

The white wooden railing that ran up the stairs was within her grasp. Her hand reached for it as she skipped the first step, her little legs taking them two at a time. Eight steps—six—four—two... Suddenly, without warning, the rubber toe of one shoe caught the front edge of the step and she felt herself fly forward, her entire body slamming into the screen door. In the chaos of the moment, she tried to right herself, pushing backward far enough to give her the space she needed to yank the door open, but as she did, she felt the bony fingers of a hand latch on to the back of her neck. She felt the heat where the hand touched her skin. Once again, she tried to scream, but the sound was swallowed by fear.

A second hand tightly clutched onto her small shoulder, but despite that, she did not give up. She fumbled with the steel door handle, a handle that stuck more often than not. She repeatedly jerked it, throwing her weight backward with each pull, jiggling it as hard as she could. She refused to let go, refused to succumb to whatever was pulling her from behind.

A face slowly began to take shape from behind the shadow of the dense metal screen in the door. Her eyes focused only on that shadow—on the face she was certain had come to save her. As it slowly moved from the shadows and into the light, she froze. Her father's face was pressed so close to the screen, she could feel his hot breath as it seeped through the tight mesh grid. His cold blue eyes grew larger, and she could feel his hatred more than the hands that held her in place.

One corner of his mouth lifted upward into a wicked sneer as her eyes pleaded for his help. Her mouth moved in uncontrollable silent screams. But slowly, deliberately, he reached backward, slamming the heavy, wooden door shut with a bang.

Time stood still as the click of the lock echoed.

Then, with one blue forget-me-not still pressed into her sweaty palm, she fell backward into the arms of her nightmare.

Claire's body jerked into a sitting position. One hand had been tightly squeezed shut. Fingernail indents lined the palm of her hand, and she massaged it with her other thumb. Her heart thudded. Her breaths were jagged and anything but silent as they ripped through the stillness of the night. Claire tried to convince herself she was safe, that it had only been another of her nightmares, but even that knowledge did not help this time.

Unwinding the silky sheets from around her body, she tugged them up to her neck as protection against the unknown. She pulled her knees to her chest and hugged them tightly as she rested her chin against her kneecaps, lying on her side in a tight ball. She sucked in deep breaths through her nose and slowly released them through her mouth, praying for control. Even though she wasn't cold, she shivered uncontrollably. This time, the nightmare had been too real. This time, it seemed to have crossed from fiction into reality. It had radiated with the same intensity she had experienced as a child. No matter how hard she tried, she could no longer find the line between the reality of her childhood and the deceit of the nightmare. Somewhere, it had faded.

Her eyes scanned the bedroom, moving through the dark, taking in the shadows of the night: the bedside lamp with the oversized shade, the large leather chairs—strewn with the clothes Michael had discarded on his way to bed—the family photographs she could not make out but had committed to memory... She had to remind herself—this was her reality.

With her chin still resting on her knees, she focused on each item as she counted her breaths. *One in—one out. Two in—*

two out... She waited for the nightmare to fade, but even as the minutes ticked away, even as she counted each breath, even as she felt her heartbeat return to a normal rhythm, even then, she knew the nightmares would never let her go.

Absently, she slipped her hand behind her head and massaged the ache at the base of her neck. Her head throbbed in time to her racing heartbeat.

As she turned onto her back and slid her legs toward the bottom of the bed, she carefully smoothed the sheets around her. A gut-wrenching sob shuddered through her, throwing the bed into a spasm. Claire quickly slapped her hands over her mouth and tensed her entire body to keep it from shaking. She lay frozen as she grabbed onto the next sob, trapping it in the back of her throat, not letting it escape through her clenched jaw. In his sleep, Michael rolled away from her and pulled the covers over his shoulder. She watched him, hoping she hadn't woken him. He had dealt with enough of her craziness—more than enough to last him a lifetime.

Lying there, listening to his slow, steady breathing, she tried to match her breaths to his. Finally, when she was certain Michael did not know she had lost it once again, she let her tears fall—dealing with her past—alone.

CHAPTER 6

For two days, rain poured down on the town of Willow Brook. Small rivers flowed through Claire and Michael's yard, creating tributaries off the wider branches. More than once, Claire stared out into the gray mist and wondered if it would ever stop.

She shivered as she trailed Karen through the door and into the darkness of the covered porch. With one hand, she buttoned the middle button of her black cardigan as she slipped past the yellow glow of the windows. The rims of the wine glasses she held in her other hand clinked together as she hooked an arm through her best friend's elbow. In perfect synchronization, they plopped onto the whitewashed wooden swing. It rocked back and forth as Claire slipped off her flip-flops and tucked her feet beneath her. She covered them both with the blanket that hung on the back of the swing.

She held out both glasses as her friend filled them with white wine. Karen set the bottle in the planter at the end of the swing, lodging it into the corner to keep it from tipping. The two sat for a long time in comfortable silence, rocking back and forth as they stared into the heavy rain.

"I could sit here all night long," Karen murmured as she reached for the wine bottle and refilled their glasses.

"Yep, just the three of us—you, me and Chardonnay." Claire laughed at her own joke as she tapped the edge of Karen's glass with her own.

The screen door slid open, and Jade poked her head out. "Mom, Dad and Matt want to know if you want them to join you or if you guys want to be left alone."

"Alone!" the women called out in unison, giggling like a couple of schoolgirls.

Jade turned and called back into the house, "Sorry, Dad!

They said they don't want to hang out with a couple of losers like you two," she teased.

"Jade!" her mother laughed.

Her daughter shrugged, slid the screen door shut, and wandered down the porch to where the women were seated. She plopped into a white wicker rocker that sat near the swing. She slipped her bare feet onto the edge of the ottoman and rocked herself back and forth, matching her movement to the rhythm of the women's swing. Jade stared off into the distance and let out a sigh. When her sigh wasn't answered, she let out a louder, more pointed one.

"Alright," Karen said, turning her attention to the girl. "I'll bite. What's buggin' you?"

"Nothin'," she pouted. Jade suddenly stopped rocking and turned toward her neighbor—after all, this was her chance to be heard. "Well…" But her shoulders immediately dropped in defeat. "Never mind. You'll just side with my mom anyway. Grown-ups *always* stick together." Claire ignored the scowl Jade cast in her direction.

Karen's sideways grin was lost in the shadow of the night. "Not always. There's a lot of stuff your mom and I don't agree on," she said as she patted Claire's knee.

Jade crossed her arms. "Oh, yeah. Name one," she challenged.

"Well," Karen thought for a moment, "alright, here's one. She thinks Matthew McConaughey's hot, but I'm much more partial to Oscar the Grouch. That green fur just does something to me." The two women giggled as Jade rolled her eyes. "Just try me." Karen offered a listening ear.

"Ha-ha!" Jade mocked. She sized Karen up, debating about sharing her dilemma. "Okay. So…" She took a deep breath and blurted it out in one long sentence. "One of my friends is spending the summer at her family's beach house out east and she asked me to go with, but of course, like always, Mom said NO." She sucked in a quick breath before adding her final dig. "She's so unfair. She won't even *think* about it."

Karen leaned her elbow on the arm of the swing and hid her grin behind her hand. "Oh, Jade, honey, you're *only* twelve years old. You'll have lots…"

Slamming her fists down on the arms of the rocker, Jade squealed, "See! I knew it. You just immediately take her side and won't even think about my side." Jade took out her frustration on the rocker as it bounced back and forth.

Karen tilted her head toward Jade. "Maybe you're right. Tell me."

Caught off-guard by Karen's offer to actually listen, Jade froze in mid-rock. "Well..." She looked at her foot as she slid her big toe along the edge of the ottoman. "Well..." she said again, frustration woven into the word. "I-I just really *want* to go," she whined. Then, at her lack of a better explanation, she growled, threw her arms into the air, and stormed off across the porch and back into the house.

The women chuckled. "At what point does logic sink in?" Claire asked. "I think my daughter may have been absent the day common sense was passed out."

Karen glanced into the window to watch Jade's retreat through the kitchen, but what she saw made her forget about Jade entirely. She elbowed Claire, pointed to the window, and whispered, "Look!" Michael's arms were out to the sides, his head tipped back, a half-full bottle of wine balanced precariously on his chin as his entire body wobbled to keep it from falling. Matt kept an eye on his watch, obviously timing the challenge. Karen shook her head. "And so, there you have it; neither one of them has any common sense either. Who in their right mind would chance wasting wine? Look at those two little boys in..." A loud crash drowned out her last word.

Michael stood in a puddle of red Bordeaux and broken glass, his eyes wider than usual. "Dammit! I could have beaten you if Jade hadn't slammed the door." That statement immediately started a lighthearted argument between the two men about when the door slammed versus when the bottle fell.

"Well, at least I know who Jade gets *her* genes from. And as for you, my friend, you should be glad you and Matt *don't* have kids." Claire smiled.

"Clai-re." Michael's voice was as smooth and sweet as pumpkin pie as he turned her name into two syllables, his head pressed against the screen of the door.

"Sorry, Michael. I'll tell you what I tell the kids: you

made the mess—you clean it up!"

As he disappeared into the kitchen, she threw her arm around Karen. "Oh, darlin', we *deserve* more wine. Keep pouring."

Claire had never had a best friend until she met Karen. She had only had surface friendships—friendships that had rules. As a child, she would have given anything to have had a friend, but she had too many secrets to keep, too many things to hide.

***

SIX YEARS OLD

She heard the cars slowly pass by her house; one car door after another slammed shut delivering children to her neighbor's birthday party. Laughter rang out as they raced around in anticipation of the big event.

She had been watching since the early morning. When she realized what was happening, she made her way into the woods behind the Clark's house. She hid there, just out of view, watching as her closest neighbors decorated for Ella Mae's sixth birthday party. Pink streamers hung from the lowest branches of the trees, where they danced in the gentle breeze. Helium balloons of pink and white floated together, anchored to the four legs of a large picnic table—the table that would later hold a special birthday cake. Six small card tables had been set up, covered in a tablecloth of either pink or white, creating a checkerboard pattern. Party hats and favors had been set at each place. Excitement floated through the air. She wished with all her heart she could be part of it, but like always, she had not been invited.

Her back and legs ached from hiding, crouching in the thicket. She took a step backward and flopped down onto a rotting stump. She leaned her chin in the palms of her hands as her elbows rested on her knees. Closing her eyes, she let the liveliness of the children surround her as she imagined being the guest of honor, imagined that *she* was the one wearing the silver plastic birthday tiara—*not* Ella Mae.

A rumble in the distance signaled an approaching storm, and she watched Ella's mom glance toward the sky in her direction. She dove behind the branches of an evergreen tree and hoped that her bright yellow t-shirt had not given her away.

The rumble continued to grow, and rain began to fall. Ella's dad grabbed the cake, and her mom hustled the children into the house, leaving the backyard with all its rewards forgotten. A few paper hats tossed around in the wind that preceded the storm. Ella's birthday tiara flew off the table and was covered by one of the plastic tablecloths that had taken flight. Ella Mae had taken it off to put on the blindfold to play a game.

She wanted that crown, wanted it more than anything else in the entire world. Then, in a split-second decision, she raced into the yard, dove under the tablecloth, snatched the tiara, and bolted back into the woods.

Her t-shirt and jeans were soaked by the time she reached the stump, but she didn't care. She walked through the woods until she found a small opening, canopied by a thick cluster of trees, intermixed with several evergreens. Carefully, she used her foot to clear the forest floor of the rust-colored pine needles and dried leaves. She sat down on the damp ground, where she slowly and majestically placed the crown on her head. Instantly, her shoulders rose and her back straightened. She lifted her chin and glanced into the distance as if looking at her royal subjects.

"I am the queen. Today is my birthday, and I would like you to throw me a party." She quickly added the word *please* to the end of her request, as it was out of character for her to *demand* anything.

Suddenly, a blood-curdling scream brought her imaginary party to a screeching halt. Pressing the tiara to the top of her head, she worked her way back through the woods until she could once again see Ella Mae's backyard.

"Daddy, you have to find it!" Ella stomped her feet. "It was right there!" She threw her arm outward, pointing toward the large table. "I left it there before it started to rain!" She stomped her feet harder and carried on like a toddler, screeching and grunting. From where she stood, she could see Ella's fists curl into tiny white balls as she wailed, demanding her father find her birthday crown. Her father searched fruitlessly, all the while making excuses about it being carried away in the storm.

"FIND IT!" Ella Mae screamed. "Find it NOW...or...or...or I'm telling Mommy!" Ella angrily folded her arms across her chest as she threatened her father.

Quietly, she pulled the tiara from the top of her head and read the word *birthday* out loud. Her thoughts were conflicted, and they pulled equally in two directions. It was Ella's birthday crown after all, and she didn't hate Ella, but on the other hand, she had never had a birthday crown—or a party, or a cake, or a present, or even real friends of her own. She deserved to have at least the birthday crown. That was all she wanted.

Taking one last look at the crown, she slipped it back on her head. Ignoring Ella Mae's tantrum, she strolled back to her canopy in the woods, where she knew she would spend the rest of the afternoon—at least until dusk when she would move to the safety of the hillside.

***

No, Claire had never had friends—not a best friend, not a real friend—not until Karen moved next door. For the first time in her life, she felt she had someone she could tell anything to. Well, *almost* anything.

CHAPTER 7

Claire yawned as she slipped through the door of her hotel room. The PTA board session had exhausted her emotionally, but she was too anxious to feel the physical exhaustion. Hitting redial on her cell, she paced the room as she counted all six rings before the answering machine picked up yet again. She bit her lip as she hung up before the beep forced her into leaving another message. *Where could they be?* No answer at home and Michael's cell went directly to voicemail.

She checked her watch for what felt like the hundredth time in the past hour: 9:30 p.m. She focused on the detailed list she had left for Michael. None of it went past 9:00.

Claire had left nothing to chance. All Michael had to do was follow the plan, but her husband was her exact opposite— laidback and carefree. It was why she had given him such specific directions.

She dropped onto the end of the bed and stared into the oversized mirror. An electric current started to buzz inside of her—she was certain something was wrong; she could feel it.

Holding the phone tightly in her palm, she stood up and paced the floor of her hotel room. A visible path had begun to show in the deeply napped carpet, fibers flattening as she repeatedly walked the course. Her legs felt rubbery; they wobbled with each step, almost buckling beneath her. She could hear her pulse pounding in her ears as she walked. Her fingers began to tingle; she could feel herself growing dizzy. Her breathing became more and more labored, and the spicy egg rolls she had eaten for dinner sloshed in her stomach, slowly working their way upward.

Stop worrying! she chided herself. *Michael won't let anything happen to the kids.* Claire knew that, but even so, after her own childhood, she didn't trust anyone—at least not completely—not even her husband.

Even as a small child, Claire trusted no one, except her

mother, and as time passed, even that changed. That complete lack of trust in anyone was what allowed her to become invisible. She learned to hide in a room full of people. It had not taken much; she just stopped existing and began surviving. It was something Claire knew better than anyone else—especially when her father was around.

***

FIVE YEARS OLD

Kindergarten was meant to be fun—at least that was what the few adults she had met had told her. From the older kids on the bus, she had heard it was the beginning of thirteen years of misery.

She did not mind the teachers or the other kids, but she hated being away from her mother. She hated being dragged away by that orange monster every morning as her mother waved goodbye to her, an extra-large smile plastered across her face. She longed to be snuggled tightly against her mom's chest, wrapped warmly in her arms as her mother sipped her coffee over the top of her blonde head. She loved the smell of the steaming drink and her mom's floral perfume as they swirled together and floated through the air.

Mondays through Thursdays, she had begged to stay home, to spend time glued to her mother's side as she baked, mended clothing, and cleaned the house that never really seemed to get dirty. On those mornings, her mom would crawl into bed with her, pull her tightly against the curve of her body, and tell her how much she loved her sweet little girl. It was Monday through Thursday that she lived for more than any other time.

She loved having her mom's hands work their magic on the snarls that had crept into her baby-fine hair overnight, gently untangling each one. Her mother tied bright-colored bows to the bottom of each perfectly plaited braid. Standing in front of the full-length mirror, she knew for certain she was the most beautiful girl in the world—because her mother had told her so.

With her Cinderella lunchbox in her hand and a cloth handkerchief spritzed with her mother's perfume tucked deep inside her pocket, she would sadly leave the house.

And on those four mornings, she would slowly drift

toward the bus stop, turning to take frequent peeks back toward the house.

From the front porch, her mother would wave to her, and she would wave back until her arms ached. Even long after the bus had picked her up and the house was no longer in view, she would continue to wiggle her fingers in the tiniest wave, afraid to stop—afraid that doing so would break the feeling of safety she felt during the week.

But on Fridays, everything was different.

On Fridays, she had a feeling a five-year-old could not put into words. It was a mixture of sadness, anger, and fear all rolled into one tight ball, and that feeling would lodge itself in the middle of her stomach, where it would continue to grow as the clock ticked off the seconds that brought Friday evening closer. She could not explain it, and she never shared that feeling with anyone, not even her mom. But every Friday morning, from the moment she opened her eyes, the knot grew. Slowly crawling out of bed, as the unnamed emotion tumbled deep inside her stomach, she felt the happy footsteps that had carried her through every other morning of the week turn into slow, silent movements. She could feel her heels slowly lift off the ground until she walked only on her tiptoes, holding her nightgown tightly around her legs so it would not make the swooshing sound she loved during the rest of the week. She was slowly becoming invisible.

She knew those slow and silent movements were how she could remain under her father's radar when he returned on Friday evenings. If she had been able to name the change she felt, she would have called it *survival*. She had perfected surviving around him. And it worked—most of the time.

***

With her head still pressed to her knees, Claire felt her hotel room begin to shrink again; the walls moved inward, suffocating her. Jumping up, she raced to the window, flipping on lights as she ran. Tossing the curtains to the side, she jerked the window open, slamming the glass pane to the left. She shoved her head out of the screenless opening and drew in a deep breath. The cool night breeze brushed against her flaming cheeks.

She leaned on the window frame, breathing deeply, drawing in breath after breath from the wide-open darkness until the spinning began to slow. She pulled her head back through the window but left the glass and the curtain open, allowing the lighted room to seep outside.

The clock glowed an angry red: *9:58.*

Her heart skipped a beat, and she felt herself slipping away again. She dropped to her knees and leaned against the bed. She grabbed two fistfuls of the thick down comforter and buried her face deep within. Droplets of sweat rolled from her forehead and down her nose.

Claire knew this wasn't normal. Michael had everything under control. She loved him with all her heart, but at this moment, she did not trust him—and that feeling only made her anxiety worse.

10:08. Where are they?

Suddenly, the shrill ring of her cell phone cut through the room. Her heart skipped a beat—and then another. She let it ring three times, sending another burning shot of adrenaline into her stomach. Bad news could wait. And if everything was okay, she did not want to appear overly anxious—even to Michael.

Her hands shook as she finally pressed the button.

She found her voice, but it was unsteady; it pinched tightly in her throat. "H-hello."

"Claire? Are you okay?" The sound of Michael's voice echoed through her head as if he were calling to her through a canyon.

"I'm fine. I'd just fallen asleep." She cringed at the ease with which the lie escaped.

"I'm sorry, hon. We can talk in the morning."

"NO!" The word came out a little too loudly. "I'm awake *now*." She forced a laugh.

She could feel her shoulders droop as the anxiety and tension slowly fell away. The adrenaline rush she felt earlier had left her exhausted, and it took all her concentration just to focus on his words.

"I tried to call you earlier tonight," Claire said. She would never admit her panic, would not allow even Michael to get close enough to glimpse into the craziness she battled on a daily basis.

"Yeah, sorry about that. The battery on my phone died. I forgot to charge it last night." Michael yawned and Claire heard a soft moan as he stretched. "We just got home a few minutes ago. Grayson called an emergency meeting late this afternoon." She could hear his voice fade in and out as he loosened the knot of his tie, moving away from the phone and then back. "Turns out he's making me the lead attorney on Senator Prescott's case." He drew a deep breath. "This is huge, Claire. If I can prove self-defense, I'll make partner."

"That's incredible! I am so happy for you."

"I spent the evening with Grayson and the legal team he's compiled." Michael grew silent. "Claire, you do understand what this means for the family, right? If I take this case, it'll be the year from hell. The thing is, when I am around, I won't really be there. We're already scheduled to go south next week. Are you going to be okay with this? Are you going to be able to handle that I am in and out of our life—with little control—for the next year or so?"

"Honey, you've worked for this your entire career. Don't worry about me; I can hold down the fort. I'm just so incredibly proud of you."

"You're just the ego boost I needed tonight," Michael teased.

"I know, right?" Claire laughed. Unable to wait one second longer, she blurted, "So…how are the kids?"

"The kids are fine. Karen picked Henry up after school, and Jade went with Sydney's dad to soccer. Karen picked her up at the field. She had some meeting or another tonight, but Matt took them to McDonald's; then he kept the kids until I could get home. Henry was already asleep on the couch and Jade was in the kitchen working on her homework."

Claire cringed; she hated fast food, but Matt made sure the kids got fed, so she let it go. "I don't know what we'd do without Matt and Karen. They've been there for us more than once."

"Your daughter was in quite a mood tonight," Michael said. "She was waiting for me in the kitchen and practically pushed me out the door as soon as I had Henry in my arms. When we got home, she went straight to her room. When I went up to kiss her goodnight, she would hardly talk to me."

"Why is it she's my daughter when she gets in these moods?" Claire laughed. "I'm guessing she was probably tired. You didn't pick them up until almost ten, you know."

"I just think she hates it when you're gone. She seemed pretty upset with me for working tonight, so I just let it go. Are you sure you're up to becoming a single parent while I work on this case?" Michael laughed as he added, "And have my name added to the sign that will read *Grayson, Delaney, and Stanton.*"

"Oh, I can handle the kids. It's you I might not be able to handle." Claire shook her head. "So, as for your daughter, well, she's becoming a teenager. I've seen signs of *that* recently."

"Yeah, well, I'm not sure I like it." His voice cracked with emotion.

"I wish I was home."

"Honey, you'll be home tomorrow night. Enjoy your time away. Try to pretend you're an adult and you have a real life for once." Michael chuckled.

"I just hate being away from you and the kids."

"I know," he said, yawning.

"Will you give Jade and Henry a kiss for me?"

"You got it, hon. Night, Claire. I love you."

"I love you more."

"Yeah, that's what you think."

A bittersweet smile crossed her face. Her family was home, and they were safe. Other than being there herself, what more could she ask for?

Claire dropped her phone onto the plush comforter. As she threw back the covers and wandered to the bathroom, along nearly the same path she had worn into the carpet not long before, a joyful sigh slipped from her lips—but a small knot had already begun to grow in the pit of her stomach.

CHAPTER 8

The hotel lobby was nearly empty when Claire set her suitcase down in front of a vending machine. She shoved two dollars into the slot and pressed a button. The Diet Coke banged its way through the machine and came to a sudden stop. Claire popped the top and closed her eyes as she guzzled nearly a third of the can. Then she slid into an overstuffed retro-looking chair and finished the rest of the can while she waited for the others to arrive.

The lobby had been decorated in a 1970s motif. Orange, lime green, and bright blue furniture was carefully arranged on top of the wild geometric patterned carpet. The end tables were plastic and round—simplistic and reminiscent of that era. Chicago's "Saturday in the Park" played in the background; Robert Lamm's and Peter Cetera's voices were as smooth as silk.

Claire checked her watch; she was driven by time. When it was fashionable to be late, she was unfashionable. She was always early. From early on, she had taught herself to feel time so she could synchronize her disappearances with her father's appearances.

The elevator doors opened and the ruckus from inside overflowed into the lobby, drowning out a Kansas song. Claire laughed as she pointed to her watch, indicating the group's tardiness.

Like a mother hen, she collected their room keys and moved toward the counter. She set her bag next to her feet, sliding it between herself and the desk. She dropped her purse on the bright Formica but kept the shoulder strap hooked over one arm. With all of her belongings within her control, she paid the bill for the board members' hotel rooms.

Will Ryan stood next to her—his back erect and rigid, his face, long and lean, completely devoid of emotion. In nearly every interaction Claire had ever had with him, he had never laughed, had never even smiled. As far as she knew, he had never shown compassion, empathy, or curiosity to or about anyone else. His heart and his head appeared to be cut from stone.

Will had come to the school with excellent references from his previous district, but it was as if those recommendations had been written about someone else. The words the interview team had read on paper and the words Claire would use to describe Will were complete opposites: *caring/thoughtless—nurturing/neglectful—people person/selfish—*and the list went on and on. How had they not noticed this in his interview? How had the committee missed something so blatantly obvious?

Claire had served on the hiring committee, and from the first word Will spoke, *she* had had doubts. Others believed he showed the promise of a great leader, but she saw something different. She had always been an excellent judge of character—of reading people before others could. Will's answers were smooth and professional, polished, and practiced; some might even describe them as textbook. However, it had been the words left *unspoken*, the pauses that fell between his answers that had rubbed Claire like sandpaper—so much so, that she was the lone *no* vote in hiring him. The committee could not understand her apprehension. Claire had wondered if she had somehow missed the unveiling of the human side of Will, because she had not seen it.

Claire secretly watched him as he stood next to her, paying his own bill from his administrative account. She saw no glimmer of the man described in his impeccable credentials. All she saw was an empty shell. After almost a year, Willow Brook's public opinion of him was split; the school was running fine with him in charge—financially and academically—but there were those who, like Claire, saw through his façade.

The exposure Claire had to the student perspective was limited to Jade and her friends. *He's okay. We just don't deal with him. He's just another adult at school.* What happened to the principal being a leader, a role model? From what she could tell, Will Ryan was neither.

Claire studied him as she waited for her receipt to print.

Appearance-wise, he was a good-looking man: tall, dark, and handsome. Those were generally the first three items a woman checked off in her quest for the perfect man. However, deep down, most people wanted someone who had passion, someone to share the joys and the sorrows of life. As far as she could tell, Will could do neither of those. He did not seem capable of enjoying life, and that far outweighed the fairytale of *tall, dark, and handsome.*

The desk clerk startled her with his return. "I'm sorry, Ma'am. We seem to be having difficulty with the printer. It'll be just another minute or so." Claire nodded.

She absently clicked the pen open and closed before looking back at Will. He drummed his fingers on the countertop and stared toward the door. No wedding band, Claire noticed. She knew he was single, but standing this close, she noticed a slight narrowing of his ring finger, a faint tan line too. *Had* he been married? Recently divorced? Maybe that was what brought him to Willow Brook—an opportunity to escape, or maybe it was a change of scenery. It might also explain why he could have dated any number of single women from the area but chose not to. No one had ever gotten more than a simple hello from Will—and it had not been from lack of trying. Simply put, he was unreachable, and even though she had no other evidence than his obvious lack of emotion, Claire was sure Will had a past he was trying to outrun.

The older of the two clerks handed Will his paperwork, which he carefully folded in three and tucked inside the breast pocket of his suit jacket. He reached for the black leather briefcase he had set on the floor between them. As he stood up, his face was within a foot of Claire's. His dark brown eyes locked with hers, and there he remained—halfway up, making no effort to stand nor bend back down.

"Excuse me, Ma'am." Claire jumped again as the clerk touched her hand. She could feel her cheeks burn red as Will finally straightened and walked away. "Your receipt is ready."

Fiddling with the zipper on her sweater to avoid eye contact with the clerk, Claire took the paperwork, folded it in half, and shoved it into her purse. Keeping her face tilted toward the floor, she slowly turned back to the group, hoping the scarlet color of her cheeks had faded. *What had just happened? Why had he stared at her like that? Why hadn't she looked away?* Claire lifted the handle of her bag and began wheeling it toward the door to join the others.

As they made their way through the hotel door, a man with a long, narrow case bumped into Claire. Something stirred inside her and she was nine years old again.

***

NINE YEARS OLD

November was the killing month—the month she hated more than any other. It was deer hunting season, and death rang out with every shot that echoed deep within the nearly leaf-barren forest that surrounded her house.

She was not allowed to leave the house during hunting season, but on those rare occasions when she did go out, it was only with a blaze-orange hat and jacket. Covered from head to toe, she nearly drowned in her father's hunting clothes. She hated those clothes—not the color or the size—but for what they represented. They smelled of sweat and her father's musky cologne, of mothballs and death. Hiding in the back of her closet on those weekends and waiting out her father's anger and rage was preferable to wearing something he had worn, something that had ever touched his skin.

She also hated November for what it did to her mother. It was November that trapped her mother in the kitchen. On weekends, her father brought streams of men home from his office in the city to deer hunt. On those weekends, her mother was expected to provide for the men's every need: cook meals, pack lunches, pour drinks. She never rested. Her whole existence was purely to serve the men who had temporarily taken her home away from her, making *her* feel like the intruder.

From the time the men arrived, their mission was clear: track down and kill as many deer as possible. They sat around making intricate plans on Friday nights as they guzzled beer into the wee hours of the morning. Then, rising before dawn, even before the roosters down the road could signal the morning light, they would wolf down the breakfast her mother had gotten up especially early to make. Washing the food down with several mugs of coffee, they would leave the house, headed deep into the dense forest, moving silently—with a deadly purpose.

Standing at the window, she would watch them go, watch as the thicket of trees and brush swallowed them, the neon orange disappearing in the dimly lit sky. But even when the color disappeared into the woods, she would continue to hold her breath, waiting to be sure they were really gone.

There was no safety, not while the men were there, not while they hunted in the woods just yards from her house. But once she knew they were gone, even for a few hours, she felt she could finally breathe. She was finally alone with her mom.

Later in the day, the men would often return with deer that had been gutted, dragged by a rope that had been tied around their limp necks; the fur covered in hardened tufts of red, dried blood. Enormous brown eyes stared sightlessly at her, begging her for help. As if she could ever be powerful enough to take on her father and his so-called friends. The old oak tree near the hillside, near *her* hillside, became the final resting place for what remotely resembled the gentle animal she remembered darting in and out of the brush along the edge of the woods.

A thick bristled hemp rope was tossed over a sturdy branch, and the men worked together to hoist the dead animals off the ground, celebrating their conquest with cigars and beer. There the deer would hang for days before finally being hauled off to be butchered. The animals returned as packages of waxy white paper. The words written in permanent black marker described what the deer had become: steaks, sausage, ground venison. Those packages were stored in the freezer for whatever her father deemed the perfect occasion—parties or gatherings— when stories of the hunt could be told repeatedly, each man one-upping the other with tales of the greatest deer hunt ever; the details changed every time the stories were told, their lies increasing in size.

Often, there were three or four deer hanging from the thick oaks scattered around the yard. Even at nine years old, she knew it was trophy hunting. It was a way to show their neighbors that her father and his friends were amazing hunters. But to her, it was all just a gruesome act of evil against a defenseless creature, a spiral of destruction that—in her mind—would eventually destroy them all. The stench of death permeated even the walls of the house and reminded her that no one was safe near her father—no one.

If the hunt had been successful, the men usually headed back to the city on Saturday night, taking their bragging rights with them. However, a man named Roy had begun overstaying his welcome. She didn't like Roy. His smell, his actions, even his hazel eyes emitted a danger that convinced her to keep her distance. But she also knew if her father was kept busy with his hunting buddies, he would not have time to bother with her. She knew he would still hold his power over her mother, making her wait on them hand and foot, but to her father, *she* would remain invisible on those killing weekends. Being invisible was the only way to survive.

Roy slept in her bedroom, even though there were extra rooms upstairs. Too drunk to climb the stairs, he kicked her out the first weekend he came to hunt. Her room was small and sparsely furnished. The pink, blue, and green gingham curtains and bedspread were a stark contrast to the white walls and pale pink desk. The room did not fit a man like Roy. It fit a little girl; it fit *her*.

While he lay in her twin bed, contaminating it with his very being, she waited the night away, waited as it slid slowly into morning, knowing he would be gone in less than twelve hours.

The open beds upstairs were off-limits to her. Her father had made that perfectly clear. *Your mother doesn't need to be cleaning up after a little brat like you. You ain't worth her time.* So, while the men were there, her bed was the couch, but she was forbidden to lie down on it until everyone else had gone to bed. In the morning, the living room needed to be spotless before the men rose. There could be no evidence she had slept there, had ever been in the living room at all during the night. More than once, her going to bed and her getting up time were separated by less than a couple of hours. It was more than should have been expected of a nine-year-old. Her mother had told her father that once—and only once. That one time had been enough to make sure she never forgot to wake before all the others on hunting weekends. That one time had left her mother nursing a split lip and a black eye. If she was to protect her mother, she needed to be on guard at all times—follow every rule.

One Saturday night, after her mother had spent the entire evening waiting on the men as they drank themselves into oblivion and they finally stumbled to bed, her mother passed by the couch, kicking it gently, unnoticeably with her foot, too afraid to bring unwanted attention to her child, who lay hidden behind the couch. The girl had not needed her mother to signal to her; her subconscious warned her. It told her when it was safe to come out.

She had developed an innate talent for instinctively telling time. She didn't need to keep one eye on the clock at night; she felt the time. Her body had its own internal timepiece; it was one more piece of survival. At the first sound or movement inside the house, she was able to wake herself, moving quickly and quietly—escaping back behind the couch.

On that Saturday night, it was nearly 2:00 a.m. when she heard her father throw a log on the fire, drunkenly stabbing at the wood with the blackened fireplace poker, sending orange sparks fluttering down onto the slate floor that surrounded the fireplace. He whistled, off-key, as he slammed the metal and glass doors shut. She counted the creaks of each stair as he clumsily moved from one to the next, bumping into the walls on either side of the stairway, stopping himself more than once from tumbling backward. An invisible child would know where to step, would know every board that creaked—a drunken father would not.

She counted the fifteen creaks and listened for the echoing slam of his bedroom door before she crept out from behind the couch where she had been lying, hidden inside the bunched-up flannel sleeping bag, waiting for the room to be all hers.

She smoothed the worn green bag out over the top of the nearly perfect couch cushions. Her entire body longed to lie down, to let sleep consume her. Her legs ached from being crammed into the tight quarters for so many hours, and she could hardly wait to stretch them out, to let her muscles relax, if only for a handful of hours.

As she crawled into the bag, she could feel the warmth of the fire as it roared from the fuel of the new log. Slowly, silently moving the zipper, tooth by tooth, down the side of the sleeping bag, trying to avoid even the slightest noise, she threw the top of it over the back of the couch. The heaviness of the bag created too much heat to lie beneath near the recently stoked fire. As her muscles began to relax, exhaustion filled every inch of her mind and body, pushing out anything but silence. She fell asleep as she watched the orange sparks snap and skitter across the logs.

Suddenly, Roy was there. She felt his presence before she saw him. At first, she thought it might be a vision, something her mind had conjured up. She peeked, lifting her eyelids just enough to see the outline of his body, a dark shadow sitting in the rocking chair less than eight feet away. His gaze was fixed on her. He did not know she was awake. She didn't want him to.

Through the tiny slits of her eyes, open just enough to see shadow and light, she carefully watched him—the tipping of his head, the movements of his hands as he first smoked his cigarette and then snuffed it out in the glass ashtray he held. The dying flames reflected orange off of his glasses, and even though she couldn't see his eyes, she knew he was staring at her. She felt her insides start to crawl; it felt as if bugs had taken up residency under her skin. Her mind screamed for him to leave, but he remained in the chair, his face never turning away from her. His breathing grew loud and deep, almost as if he had been running.

She lay in perfect stillness. Her nightgown felt too thin; she wished she had chosen her heavy flannel pajamas instead. She would next time. Her body shivered and she rolled over, facing the back of the couch, feigning sleep. She shivered, not from the cold but from fear. As if being guided by her dreams, she pulled the sleeping bag up over her tiny body, burying even her head beneath the weight of it. Instinctively, she pulled her legs toward her chest and rolled her body into a tight, familiar ball, her arms locked around her knees. There she remained frozen, lifeless. Yet her senses were on high alert. She finally heard him leave, clumsily wandering down the hallway and into the downstairs bathroom. She trapped a breath in her lungs and held it until it burned; she was afraid to let it escape for fear he would return. There was not a moment of sleep that night. The clock on the wall ticked like a time bomb, foreshadowing her eventual destruction. And for the first time, she longed for morning to come, for the light to erase the fear of this night.

But even as the darkness slowly turned to daylight, as sunlight crept up the wall on the other side of the room, she was not sure which was worse: this man who had watched her in the night or the return of her father's anger once Roy left after breakfast.

She knew her father; she could figure out *his* next move because he was usually predictable. She knew how to hide in the shadows and remain invisible around him. She did not know Roy; she had no defense against the unknown.

CHAPTER 9

At 6:49 p.m., Jen's Chevy Tahoe, in obvious need of new shocks, bounced down Claire's street. The houses in the neighborhood were huge. When she and Michael built their house, they wanted it to be classically elegant, yet homey. They had chosen the Rivercrest development because of the river that wound its way behind the house. *You'll be sorry, Claire,* her mother had said. *That house is too damn big! You'll be cleaning day and night.* Claire didn't see it that way; she saw the beauty: the location, the gardens, the view of the river. She also felt something in this home she had felt nowhere else—safety. No matter where she turned, which room she walked into, a feeling of warmth almost always overwhelmed her. For the first time ever, the place she lived was not a house; it was a *home*.

Even after her father's death, she and her mother lived in one apartment after another. She had never had a place to call her own.

Thick white columns supported the long roof as it angled down over an exceptionally wide porch. Yellow and red petunias hung from baskets attached to each of the eight pillars that lined the front of the house. Small, four-sided gazebos graced both ends of the wrap-around porch; an old-fashioned wooden swing hung inside of each. Flowers of yellow, red, and white bloomed in several smaller beds and in enormous red and brown ceramic pots. Oversized double doors welcomed visitors into the enormous foyer.

With her overnight bag clasped tightly in one hand and her purse slung over the opposite shoulder, Claire climbed the brick stairs, counting each of the six steps as she did so. The massive trees, mostly maples and elms, cast shadows across the front of the house and porch, blocking it from much of the early evening sun. Setting her bag near the door, Claire slipped past the front window, which was covered by a double layer of sheers that were kept pulled as the day spilled into evening. She settled onto one of the swings and listened to the voices that escaped through the open windows, a silent observer into her own family.

A car turned onto her street off in the distance. She could hear it travel along the road, moving closer, passing in front of the picket and wrought-iron fences that separated each yard. It wasn't until the car turned into her driveway that she smiled at the humor of its appearance. Again, she slipped unnoticed past the window and met the driver at his car.

Seconds later, Claire stood on the front porch and pressed the doorbell. As the door opened, she held the pizza box toward her husband. "You cooked, I see!"

"I believe I told you I would." Michael grinned as he leaned over the pizza box and planted a kiss on his wife's lips. Then he whispered in her ear, "And how much do I owe you for this delivery, ma'am?"

Claire's smirk fell away. "Hmmmm...I'll get back to you."

After grabbing his wife's bag off the porch, Michael dropped it in the entryway. With the pizza still in one hand, he hugged his wife, nearly lifting all one hundred and ten pounds of her off the floor.

A sudden explosion of excitement filled the room. "Mom! Mom, I knew you'd come home. I told Jade you would." Henry flew into Claire's arms, hitting her at a dead run before she was ready. Michael grabbed the back of his son's shirt to keep him from crashing onto the ceramic floor, nearly dropping the pizza in the commotion.

Bending down to her son's level, Claire said, "Of course I came back, Henry. I always come back." She stood, lifting him with her. He wrapped his legs around her waist and his arms around her neck.

Henry awkwardly turned toward his sister, who remained in the background. "See, Jade! You were wrong! I told you she'd come back." He tightened his arms around Claire's neck and pressed his forehead and nose to hers. Then he whispered, "She's so mean. She told me you weren't coming home...ever."

"Well, I did come home, Henry. I told you I would, and I always keep my word." Claire tipped her head to one side, just enough to see around her son. Jade stood in the doorway of the den; her face tilted downward. With a bit of effort, Claire shifted her son onto her left hip, balancing him in one arm. She held her free arm out as an invitation to her daughter. "Do I get a hug from you too, honey?"

Jade inched forward, keeping her eyes downcast until she was close enough for Claire to pull into a hug. "Hey, baby. I missed you, but I'm home now," she said as she planted a kiss on the top of Jade's head.

Her daughter leaned her forehead into her mother's shoulder and whispered, "You shouldn't have gone." Then she wiggled out of her mom's grip and raced upstairs to her room. Claire flinched at the sound of the slamming door.

Michael shrugged; his lips pressed tightly together. "I know. I don't get it. She's been upset since yesterday morning, right after you left."

Henry squeezed Claire's cheeks between his chubby hands, turning her face to meet his. "*I* get it, Mom. *I* know why she's bein' so mean."

"Why, Henry? What is it?"

He shook his head. "I think she's going through the *change-a-life.*" He whispered his last words as if they were dirty.

Neither of his parents could keep from laughing. "Ohhh, Henry, I don't think that's it, but if you do find out what it is, you'll let us know, won't you?"

"But, Mom, that really *is* it," he insisted. "Benjy said his grandma went through the *change-a-life* and she was crabby all the time." Squirming sideways so he could see his father, he asked, "Dad, did Mom ever go through the *change-a-life?*" Henry continued to whisper the phrase, still unsure of its appropriateness.

"Don't get me involved in this one, Henry. This is a woman thing. I think you're on your own here." Michael peeled Henry from his mother's grip. "But just the same, son, I think it's time we had a talk about women."

Henry scrunched up his face and sighed. "Okay, but can we eat *first*? Girls make me not wanna eat."

"Sure, Henry." Michael chuckled as he winked at Claire. "Being around *girls* sort of makes me not want to eat either—but not quite for the same reason."

Confusion clouded Henry's eyes for a split second, but he reached out and patted his dad on the back of his head. "It's okay, Dad. Nobody gets girls!" Then Henry threw one arm around his mother and pulled her into a three-way hug. He laid his cheek on Michael's shoulder and patted Claire's cheek. "Don't worry, Mom! It's okay. You ain't a *girl* no more anyhow."

Michael pulled Henry away from Claire and laughed. "Alright, bud, I think we should have that talk *before* dinner."

"Da-ad!" Henry whined.

Claire smiled. "Henry, go wash up before you and Dad have your talk. And while you two do that, I think I'll go let Jade know it's time for dinner." Claire said, then she turned toward the stairway.

"Yeah, well, good luck with that," Michael declared. Then, pressing his hands over Henry's ears, he whispered, "Maybe she'll be done with *the change* by the time you get there."

"Oh, let's hope so," Claire called back over her shoulder.

"I heard that!" Henry yelled. "I heard that...and I don't think I was s'pposed to!"

***

"I'm not hungry!" Jade insisted. Her lip quivered as she added, "I'm tired...and maybe mad. I missed plans with my friends last night because Dad had to work late." Jade pulled the covers over her head.

Claire studied the lump of bedding her daughter had become. "Do you want to talk about..."

"NO! Just leave, okay?"

Claire sat on the edge of the bed and rubbed her daughter's back, "Okay, but if you do..." Her words drifted off. The last thing she wanted to do was to push her daughter away. "Well, anyway, we'll save you some pizza in case you get hungry later."

She leaned down to kiss the lump she thought was her daughter's head but, as she did, Jade threw back the covers and grabbed Claire tightly around the neck and refused to let go. "Honey, what is it? What's wrong?"

Silence hung heavily. "Don't ever leave me again. Dad just doesn't get it."

Claire unhooked Jade's arms from around her neck. She leaned back and studied her daughter's face. "Did something else happen?"

"No, Dad's just a *guy*. He doesn't get it. He'll never understand."

"Understand what?"

Jade watched her mom's face before she answered. "Me—*my* life."

"Oh, honey," Claire cooed. "Everyone thinks their life is hard and that no one else…"

"Just leave me alone, Mom." Jade rolled onto her side, away from Claire, ending the conversation. "You don't get it either!"

"Honey, you know I'm always here for you."

"Mom, just go eat! Your pizza's getting cold." Jade pulled the covers over her head. "I just want to go to sleep."

Claire watched her daughter for a few seconds longer. Henry was right; maybe it was *the change—the change* into teenage-dom. But even in her head, as she thought the words: *the change*, just like Henry, she whispered them, because those two little words scared her to death.

***

As Claire climbed into bed, Michael closed his laptop, set it on his nightstand, and flipped off the light. He slid across to her side of the bed and drew her into his arms, pulling her toward him as if she was a rag doll. She snuggled her head into the space between his shoulder and neck, laying one arm across his chest. His body felt warm and strong against hers, and she clung to him as Jade had hung on to her.

It was nearly midnight when Claire finally rolled away from Michael—pulled into the depths of another nightmare.

***

She could feel the heat before she smelled the smoke. No alarm could be heard, except the one in her head screaming for her to run. The fire was dancing on the ceiling of the basement just below her room. She could feel the heat against her bare feet. She ran to the door and grabbed the handle, but the knob was too hot to touch; her fingertips burned as she jerked them away. She kissed the tips of them, just as her mom would have done, but she felt no comfort.

Her only escape was the window. She climbed onto her bed and slid the glass pane to the side, staring down at the ground—a distance nearly five times her height. It had never seemed that far before. Repeatedly, she slammed her tiny fists against the screen until she finally dislodged it from the grooves that held it in place. She watched it tumble toward the ground, bouncing as it hit.

She glanced back into the room, but the black smoke was already beginning to sneak under her door. Her lungs tightened, and she coughed and choked as the smoke crept toward her. She turned back to the opening and leaned her head out as far as she dared, breathing in the night air that had not yet been scarred by smoke. She moved closer to the edge of her bed, hoisting herself onto the wooden window frame. Except for the crackling of the fire, as it ate away at the floor and walls outside of her room, the night remained quiet. No sirens or voices could be heard.

The room was suddenly filled with light as the reddish-orange flames crept under the door, sneaking into the darkness. She pressed her mouth and nose into the crook of her elbow and breathed into her pink flannel pajama top. She watched the flames dance across the floor and toward her bed, trying to decide how long she could wait before she had to jump, praying for help to come. "Mom!" she screamed into the fire. Where was her mother? "Mom!" she wailed again.

Deciding it was time, she took one final look back into her room. Wisps of smoke smothered the few toys she owned; the orange and red flames lapped at the bottom of her bookshelf and she could see her books being eaten by the orange monster. Baxter, her teddy bear, was tucked under one arm, and she clung to him.

She choked, gasping for air as the fire moved closer to the bed. Turning back to the outside, she tried to keep her balance as she crouched on the windowsill. She rubbed her burning eyes and she squeezed them tightly shut. She buried her face in her bear, filtering her breaths through his fur.

Then, from out of nowhere, she heard a voice telling her to grab on. The voice was hidden somewhere behind a thick cloud of smoke, hidden on the deck about five feet to the right of her bedroom window. She caught only a shadowy glimpse of a man through the smoke that was billowing out of the doors and onto the deck. Kissing Baxter, she tucked him into the waistband of her pajama bottoms, then dropped over the side, clinging to the windowsill as she dangled from its edge. Adjusting her grip, she stretched one arm in the direction of the voice, toward the outstretched hand until it grabbed onto her wrist. Counting to three in her head, she pushed off the side of the house. Her tiny body swung sideways toward the deck, the deck's railing slamming into her shoulder as she swung into it again and again.

She swayed back and forth like a pendulum, dangling below the bottom edge of the deck, still too many feet above the ground. Pain ripped through her arm as if it were being torn from her body and she watched the blood seep through her pajama top. The ground moved below her as she twisted with each violent cough that worked to expel the black smoke from her lungs.

Finally, she felt the tug on her arm as her body was being lifted back to the safety of the deck. But at the top of the deck, her eyes met his. He held her tiny body out and away from the railing—at arm's length. She tightened her grip as she felt his loosen. She dug her fingernails into his hands, pleading for his help. "Father, please! Please, don't let me fall," she whimpered. His eyes looked like glass, and even through the smoke, she saw how much he hated her. He tightened his grip for one moment, pulling her almost close enough for her to wrap an arm around his neck, but she did not dare let go of his hand—she knew she couldn't trust him. Grimly, she prepared herself for the fall. She watched in horror as her father's lips curled into a wicked smile and he peeled her fingers back—and let go.

***

Claire screamed. She could feel herself falling. Instinctively, she pulled her hands toward her face. A pair of arms reached out and grabbed her, tightening their grip around her waist, saving her from the freefall of her nightmare. Sobs exploded from her as she tried to grab onto reality. No words needed to be spoken; the nightmares had become nearly as common as breathing for Claire, and for Michael too.

As she lay drenched in sweat from her night terror, safely tucked in her husband's arms, Claire knew she needed more than help—she needed answers.

CHAPTER 10

"Mary Claire, I haven't seen you in weeks," Tess scolded. No one had called Claire by that name since she was ten years old, no one except her mother.

Claire bent down to kiss her mother's cheek, sheltering Tess from the grin that appeared. "Hi, Mom. I know I haven't been here for a couple of days, but I was just here on Saturday. Remember, I brought Jade and Henry for a visit?"

"Don't lie to me. I know when you are lying."

Tess reached up and jerked the calendar down from the wall, sending the red plastic tack flying across the room. Claire dropped to her knees to search for it before someone in bare feet found it. With the calendar turned toward her daughter, Tess repeatedly tapped on the first day of the month—a red line circled the number one.

"See, Mary Claire. I marked down the last time you came. I *always* mark down your visits, and the last time you were here was on the first of the month." Tess thrust the calendar in her daughter's direction.

Awkwardly grabbing the calendar, Claire turned two pages, "Mom, look. You have the wrong month. That was in January. It's March."

Leaning back in her chair, Tess's shoulders slumped forward just a bit. "I don't even know what month it is, Mary Claire," she said quietly. Claire kneeled on the gray and white terrazzo floor, settling herself directly in front of her mom. Tess bent forward, moving closer to her daughter. "Look closely," she insisted. "Does it look to you like my head's screwed on straight today, because damned if it doesn't feel a little crooked!" Tess laughed at her own joke. "I'll tell you one thing, missy, growing old ain't for sissies." Then she fell backwards against her chair.

"Oh, Mom, you're not old."

"Don't give me that shit. I've been old since the day I

65

was born; old enough to know better and old enough to make better choices than I have in this lifetime. And I sure as hell should be old enough to know that I was looking at the wrong damn month too." The corners of Tess's mouth sagged downward; the wrinkles that surrounded them looked deeper than Claire remembered them being, even on Saturday.

Still kneeling on the floor in front of her mother's chair, Claire picked up Tess's hands and gently rubbed them with her thumbs. "It's okay, Mom. We all get confused from time to time."

Jerking her hands out of her daughter's, Tess huffed. "Yeah, well, in my world, I seem to be having more confused days than good days lately." She angrily crossed her arms in front of her chest.

Claire felt her heart break for her mother. What Tess said was true—there were more bad days than good ones recently, and that number was slowly increasing. But what hurt Claire the most was knowing her mother knew it was happening, and she hadn't lived the life she deserved. Easing herself up and onto the side of the bed, Claire's mind wandered to the days before her mother had been diagnosed with Alzheimer's—to the days when her father was still alive.

Outward appearances had portrayed them as the perfect family: her father—tall and muscular—quite handsome in his expensive suits—always driving fancy vehicles. No one else in the entire town could afford the things her father could. Her mother: a beautiful woman, shoulders always pressed backward, her head held erect, refined to perfection. When in public, she had always been dressed in the finest clothing and had been adorned with the most expensive jewelry money could buy. And, of course, there was Mary Claire—the perfect daughter: cute and polite, with *the sweetest smile this side of Denver*—according to the old church ladies.

Everyone wanted to be like them, but no one wanted to *be* them. Her entire family kept their distance; they stood apart from the crowd. Other than a word spoken in passing, the townspeople typically stayed away as well. Her family had kept the *real* O'Briens hidden: the controlling, abusive father; the fearful, submissive wife and mother; and the nearly invisible daughter.

She and her mother executed every movement of their life like a perfectly choreographed dance. If they faltered—gave any public indication their family wasn't as perfect as her father had portrayed—they would pay the price through the wrath of Edward. Claire had been on the receiving end of a willow switch more than once—the first time at just four years old. Those whippings were all it took to remind her how an O'Brien lived—in public and in private.

Every week, one hour before church, as Claire knelt in the confessional, a thin, black screen separating her from Father Harwood, she made up sins to confess.

"Bless me, Father, for I have sinned. It has been one week since my last confession." She could feel the sweat beading on her forehead as she desperately tried to lie her way through the five-minute declaration of guilt.

Claire never struggled with The Holy Father's commandments—it was her father's directives that left her reeling. Even one small infraction meant a trip to the garage and a beating with a fresh willow switch he took great pleasure in cutting and stripping while she watched.

No, Claire rarely broke her father's rules—even if it meant lying to a priest.

All she had wanted was to be a child—to run and play, to drag dirt and mud into the house and jump on her bed, to leave messes where messes did not belong and to invite friends over—but she did not do any of those things. She could not because, if Claire misbehaved, her mother was also held responsible.

On one rare occasion, Claire had entered her father's office and had accidentally broken a vase that had belonged to her father's mother—a grandmother she was told had died long before she was born. Even though her mom hugged her and told her accidents happened, she knew her mother worried all week about her father's reaction.

On Friday, she took Mary Claire aside and told her she would tell her father that *she* had broken the vase—that she had left a window open while cleaning and the wind caught the curtain and knocked it over.

But Claire knew what was coming. They both did. No story would save them—truth or lie. Yet Tess made Claire practice the lie so many times, she started believing it herself.

When her father returned that Friday night, it took him only minutes to notice the missing vase. The house, spotless with its barebones furnishings, made a missing item easy to detect. A creature of habit, Edward entered the house, went directly to his den, and bellowed for a beer. He ignored her and her mother just as he had every Friday night for as long as Claire could remember.

When his voice boomed through the house, Claire felt it like a bass drum thudding in her chest; each word yelled with a staccato beat through gritted teeth. "Where in the hell is Mother's vase? Tess!" His body shook with uncontrollable anger as he leaned into her mother when she appeared in the doorway, a beer in one hand. His face contorted in rage as Claire hid behind her mom's skirt.

Tess's voice cracked as she told the lie. "I was cleaning in here, and I opened..."

"Shut up! Just shut up, you bitch! You're lying!" He turned away from her and then spun back on his heels, pressing his fingers around her neck, squeezing tightly enough for her mother to struggle. "You wouldn't know the truth if it slapped you across the face!" Then, as if trying to prove his point, he backhanded Tess across the face so hard, it knocked her, Claire, and the beer into a heap on the floor, his large ruby ring slicing through her mother's lip.

Nearly growling, her father turned toward her. "Mary Claire! Where's Grandma's vase?" He grabbed her by the arm, nearly tearing it from its socket as he jerked her to her feet, pulling her from the tangled pile she and her mother lay in. Her legs twisted beneath her mother's weight as he jerked her free. "Stand up!" Red, angry splotches had grown on his neck and face. The anger had squeezed his chest and his voice grew hoarse and strained. Clasping each of her upper arms in his enormous hands, Claire winced as his grip tightened around them; her fingers started to tingle, then suddenly went numb. He bent down at the waist, standing with his nose nearly pressed against hers.

He clenched his teeth. "Tell me the truth and tell me NOW!" he screamed.

She squirmed, trying to make eye contact with her mother, but her father held her in place, keeping her from turning around. She closed her eyes and pictured her mother lying on the floor, fighting the tears that threatened to fall. She knew Tess would not give in to her father's anger; she wouldn't give him the satisfaction of winning, and Claire wouldn't either. So, just as they had practiced, she told him the story of the wind breaking the vase. The other story, the one where *she* had broken the vase, was no longer real; she had to stand by her mother's words and protect her from her father.

When she finished, her father shoved her aside, tossing her back into the heap that was her mother—his discard pile.

"Clean this up!" he screamed. "You both smell like a brewery!" Then he disappeared. Claire latched on to her mother; she did not want to let go. She gently pressed her tiny fingers against the gaping hole on Tess's lip and silently vowed to teach her mother to become invisible too.

Within seconds, they heard the whine of the garage door followed by squealing tires as the car raced down the driveway, spraying rocks and sand against the house. Tess hugged Claire as tightly as Claire held her mother; they rocked back and forth as the seconds turned into minutes.

In less than an hour, they heard the car squeal back up the driveway, skidding to a stop on the gravel. Claire raced to her room, falling as she flung the door to her closet open. She quickly shut the door, rolled herself in a blanket, and scooted beneath the low shelf. From her hiding place, she could hear her mother in the kitchen. Pots and pans banged together as she cooked dinner as if nothing had happened.

The screen door slammed as her father stormed into the house. From her dark hiding place, Claire heard the drill as he screwed hasps on every window, fastening padlocks to each one—including the one in her bedroom. The windows would never again open.

Claire and her father went to church that Sunday, her mother clearly absent from their *perfect* family. Everyone who asked was told her mother was sick. He squeezed her hand, too hard, as a message for her to remain silent as he accepted the congregation's get well wishes for her mother. Silence was the only thing that would save her, so she smiled and let the women pat the top of her Sunday hat and pinch her cheeks, just like they did every other week.

***

Claire shook the memory away and focused on trying to get information from Tess. "Mom, do you…"

Tess smiled. "Sarah's coming to play the piano for us today. I just love when she comes. She plays the old songs I remember from my childhood. Today's Bingo day too. You should stay for Bingo, Mary Claire. We always have good prizes." Tess's words were animated, almost childlike.

Claire smiled at her mother. "That's good. I'm glad you like it here. It sounds like they have lots of fun things for you to do."

She could feel her mother slowly slipping away. The cycle was all too familiar; Claire knew her time was limited. Just like every other visit, before long, Tess would be gone— sometimes silent, sometimes incoherent. Often, the stages she went through overlapped or traded places. Some days they passed more quickly than others. Today, Claire could not take a chance. There were questions she needed answers to and she had to ask them while her mother was still lucid enough to give her the information she needed.

Peeking behind the curtain that separated her mother's side of the room from that of her roommate's, Claire asked, "Where's Lois? Is she off with her family today?"

"Huh…that old biddy? Who knows! She's so nosey. She's probably out rounding up some gossip…or more likely spreading it." Claire flinched. In the past, Tess had never spoken a bad word about anyone except her father, but the older she got, the more Alzheimer's ate away at the loving side of her mother. Tess's lack of compassion and her increasing volume often left Claire searching for the mother she once knew. She had suddenly become more like the other residents at Autumn Woods and less like Tess.

"Mom!" Claire scolded. "You shouldn't say those things. She might hear you."

Tess looked indignant. "Are you kidding me? That woman's so out to lunch, she wouldn't know if this entire place exploded around her." She shook her head, never taking her eyes off her daughter. "Unbelievable, Natalie! You, telling me what to do. When did you become my mother?"

Claire took her mom's hand. "Mom, it's me, Claire."

"What?" Tess asked. "Of course it's you. Do you think I'm that old and dumb that I don't know my own daughter?"

"No, Mom. It's just that you called me Natalie."

"I did not," Tess argued. "You need to listen."

Claire swallowed hard. She didn't want to fight. She hadn't come for that. She had too many questions.

"I'm sorry, Mom. It's just that…well, I've been wondering about something. Do you remember when we lived out in the country—when Father was still alive? There are so many things I *think* I remember, but I don't know if they're true or not. Right now, all I have are fuzzy pictures." Her mother's eyes widened; fear shone on her face.

"Do you ever remember him locking me out of the house?" Claire stood, pacing the room as she waited for her mother's response.

When she turned back, she saw anger building on Tess's face. Her mother leaned forward, digging her fingernails into the arms of the recliner. "Really, Mary Claire! You always did have an imagination that was bigger than you. Why does it matter anyway? Your father did a lot of things he shouldn't have. He wasn't *exactly* the most patient man. Some things are simply better left forgotten."

"No, Mom. This isn't one of those things. I *need* to know what was real and what wasn't."

Dropping her head backwards against the recliner, Tess stared up at the ceiling. "You know, you weren't the easiest child to raise, and your father wasn't the easiest man to live with either. The two of you mixed about as well as oil and vinegar."

Claire tilted her head to the side. "I don't remember it that way. I mean, I remember him not having patience, but I don't remember being a difficult child." Claire knelt next to her mother's chair. "Besides, this memory is different. It's just so real. I remember I was running, trying to get away from something—or someone. Do you remember that? I was screaming—begging someone to help me." Claire stood and leaned against the door frame, feeling the cold of the steel against her back. She closed her eyes and conjured up pictures from her nightmare.

"Okay, so, maybe you *don't* remember that, but was there ever a fire? Did we ever have a fire at our house?" She moved toward the dresser and picked up an old, framed photo of her and her mother. They were standing in front of a restaurant. Claire was about twelve years old. She could tell, because of their smiles, the picture had been taken *after* her father's death. Still holding the photo, she turned toward her mom. "I remember standing on the ledge of a windowsill. I had Baxter, my bear, and Father tried to grab my hand, but instead of helping me, he let me fall."

Tess remained silent as she watched her daughter fight with the questions of the past.

Claire's chin dropped to her chest and she felt an overwhelming sense of grief. She dropped back to her knees and laid her head in her mother's lap. "Please, Mom. Were any of these memories real?"

Tess stroked Claire's hair with one hand, tucking it behind her ear as she had when Claire was small. She absently ran the index finger of her other hand along the scar that ran the length of Claire's upper arm. "Honey, some things are better left alone. The past is the past for a reason. Move forward, Claire."

"I can't, Mom. Don't you see? I can't move forward until I know what really happened back then."

Claire moved to the edge of the bed again. A tightness pulled at her chest.

"Mom, please tell me this. Why did Father hate me so much? Why couldn't he just love me for me?" A sob nearly swallowed her words. "Why didn't he love *you*?"

Claire's head hung down and she rocked back and forth on the edge of the bed as she waited for her mother to answer. Lifting her head, her shoulders dropped as her eyes met her mother's. Physically, Tess sat in the chair with her head tipped back and to one side, but the Alzheimer's had crept back in. For this day, the cycle was complete. Tess's eyes were glazed over—as blank as an empty sheet of paper. But her lips moved almost undetectably—at first.

"Oh, Wanda," Tess whispered; her lips grew more animated with each passing word. "When did you get here? I haven't seen you for the longest time. How was your trip, dear?" Tess stared blankly over Claire's shoulder. Claire knew no one was standing behind her, but still, she turned to look.

The only person behind her was in her mom's mind. Tess's sister had been gone for nearly six years. She had died just before Henry was born. It was shortly after that Claire noticed Tess's failing memory.

Claire watched her mother's face as it made the transition to complete incoherence. She longed to be a part of her mother's world just long enough to find some answers, but she could not—it wasn't to be a part of this trip, and she might never know. She had been locked out, just like in her nightmare.

Claire kissed her mother's cheek. "Have a nice visit with Aunt Wanda, Mom," she whispered. "I love you." Then she slipped out the door while her mother continued to talk to the empty room.

CHAPTER 11

Three grocery bags tentatively balanced between Claire and the door. The paper bags leaned against her left arm as she pressed her thumb down on the lever. A stack of mail and the keys dangled precariously in her other hand. The door slid open just far enough to send the bags tumbling into the entryway, hitting the floor with a thud. Oranges rolled across the floor and mail fluttered down in front of her as two brown bags tore open. "Dammit!" Claire shouted. "Why do I *always* do this? What made me think it would be different this time?" Dropping her purse onto the side table, Claire knelt amidst the mess.

After tucking boxes and cans into the torn bags, she hauled them to the kitchen, making several trips, stashing them into the neatly arranged and labeled pantry, refrigerator, and freezer. Except for a handful of eggs and a carton of half-thawed frozen yogurt that had virtually exploded, Claire was able to salvage the rest of her groceries. She scooped up the eggs and yogurt with paper towels and tossed the entire mess into the garbage can. She scrubbed the floor with hot, sudsy water, moving the brush in small, uniform circles. With a damp towel hanging over her shoulder and one in her hand, she stood back to examine her work, bending over to take a quick swipe at a damp spot the size of a quarter.

After tossing the towels into the washer, Claire plopped down on a kitchen stool. She flipped through the mail, shredding the junk and filing the rest into each of the labeled compartments above her desk: *bills, invitations, letters, etc.* She checked her voicemail—there were no messages. For the first time in weeks, she had nothing to do. With the school year ending in a month, her volunteer jobs had dwindled as well. The cleaning lady had taken away her opportunity to even pretend she had cleaning to do—but still, she swiped at imaginary dust.

The house was quiet—too quiet. Claire pressed the button on the stereo. Rod Stewart's voice filled all three levels of the house, but that particular song haunted her with memories. She pushed the preset button over and over: jazz, classic love songs, and country, but the music bored her. The talk radio celebrities were no better, so she turned it off.

The TV was of even less comfort. Even as background noise, the programs frustrated her. Station after station was filled with shows that attempted to solve guests' shortcomings or explored controversial issues that led to heated arguments. The rest of the stations were filled with soap operas or movies loaded with dysfunction and scandal. Claire's past was crazier than any story a writer or producer could bring to life.

Claire checked the clock. *1:30 p.m.* She listened to the seconds tick away before she raced up the stairs, taking them two at a time. A run was exactly what she needed—a chance to clear her head, to breathe. Henry was at a friend's house until after dinner, and Michael had planned to work late, again; the Prescott case devoured his time with her or the kids. Jade didn't need to be accounted for until after soccer practice.

Claire slipped on a pair of gray running shorts that had grown a half-size too small in the past several weeks of her crazy life. She grabbed a yellow t-shirt from the stack in her closet and stretched it out before pulling it over her head as she raced down the stairs. She snatched her old running shoes from the shelf in the hall closet, rejecting two new pairs that were still boxed. With her laces tightened and double-knotted, she headed out the door. After checking the lock *twice*, she slipped the key into the inside pocket of her shorts, zipping it shut as she ran. She checked her watch one more time before heading down the long driveway. She did not stretch—even though she knew she should. The promise she had made to herself to jog until she warmed up enough to run the way she needed to, was broken by the time she hit the road.

Claire ran past Karen and Matt's house, already picking up speed. As she approached Barbara and Walter's house, she waved. A gray-haired couple sat on opposite sides of a small black wrought-iron table on their front porch, half-hidden in the shade of several large trees. A pitcher of lemonade and two tall glasses sat between them.

"Well, m'goodness, Claire, you shouldn't be out runnin'

in the heat of the day like this. You'll make y'rself sick,"
Barbara called out, a hint of her Texas drawl still evident after
eight years of Colorado living.

"Come on, darlin'. Join us for some lemonade, won't
you?" Walter waved her onto the porch. "Made it myself—
when Barbara wasn't watchin' me." He chuckled as he slipped
one hand over his wife's. "It's got 'nough sugar to keep you
running for the next week and a half."

Claire laughed as she jogged in place at the end of their
driveway.

Barbara tipped her chin down and glared at her husband
over the top of her silver-rimmed glasses. "Walter, that is the
last time I'll ever let you make the lemonade."

"Huh." Walter slapped his knee as he turned toward
Claire; a smirk slid across his face. "If that don't beat all. That
plan worked better than I could'a hoped for."

Barbara pulled her hand from beneath her husband's.
She swiped at the air near his head. "You're an old poop, Walter
Harris, just an old poop."

Claire laughed out loud. "Thanks for the offer, but I
need to be back in time to pick Jade up from soccer practice.
Maybe tomorrow." She waved as she started jogging away.

"Well, alright, dear, but we'll be expectin' you for a visit
tomorrow, then. And don't push y'rself too hard. It's awfully
warm out here."

"I promise," Claire called back over her shoulder. Then
she slowly jogged until she turned the corner—just out of
Barb's view.

The day *was* warm, warmer than Claire had expected
for early May. The leaves on the trees were still brilliant spring
green. The flowers were in full bloom everywhere Claire
looked. She loved spring; it was her favorite time of year. The
season always felt like a new beginning for her, a fresh start.
She drew in a deep breath, filling her lungs with the warm air.

With each step she took, Claire felt herself relax. Her
steps and her breathing were rhythmic and controlled as she
turned toward the park, waving to friends and neighbors she
passed along the way.

Maybe her mother was right. What *did* it matter that her

father had hated her? He had been gone for nearly thirty-two years. Why should she still let him have so much control over her thoughts and emotions? This was *her* life now: move forward, focus on the positives—let go of the negatives.

She picked up the pace as she concentrated on each step—*left-right-left-right-left-right*. Her ponytail bobbed as she ran, brushing the back of her neck as it swung back and forth. Sweat rolled down her back, soaking into her t-shirt, tinting it a darker shade than the rest of her shirt. She felt her spirits lift and she made a decision to run more often. It was better than therapy and definitely cheaper.

Periodically, she drew in a deep breath amidst the shallow ones. Visions of her younger self running came to mind, and she allowed herself to momentarily lose focus.

***

In grade school, she had been the perfect child: bright and good-natured. She had been appreciative of every kindness shown to her. She had wanted to make her mother proud—as long as it didn't mean leaving the safety of the sidelines. On the sidelines, no one really noticed her as she faded into the background; no one befriended her or wanted to know her. She was a loner, and that was the only way she knew how to survive. That was when she discovered running. It was the one thing she could do alone, the one thing that set her apart from others. She could blend into the shadows, completely disappearing. It was also one of the only ways she knew she could escape the horrors of her father.

People who watched her run were amazed. They said she ran like the wind. But she was more like the wind than they even knew—not in the way she ran as much as how she lived her life: gently touching the things she loved, changing directions, shifting away from the things she didn't. She could move silently, fluttering the edges of her life—not enough to be noticed, just enough to convince herself she really existed— even if she was invisible. She could go almost anywhere. And when necessary, she could be noticed without being seen—just like the wind.

***

Claire let the memory fade as she veered left onto the

path that ran through the park. The shade was a welcome change as she ran. Her focus switched from herself to the others. The sidewalk was filled with people enjoying the park. The sounds blended together: laughter, babies squealing, wheels of strollers clicking as they bounced along the uneven path, and ducks begging for food.

"Passing on your left," she called as she veered off the sidewalk to pass an elderly couple strolling through the green. More than once, she swerved to avoid a near collision. She began to feel a bit claustrophobic as she ran deeper into the park, darting between and around people. Her breathing became jagged as it matched the inconsistency of her steps.

A fork in the path at the rear of the park provided relief and she checked her watch. The path to the right took her out of the park and back onto the street; the one to the left cut deeper into the woods toward a secluded section that ran along the stream. Without hesitation, Claire headed left, away from the distractions.

The tall trees draped over the top of the path, creating a canopy. The sun's rays cut through the leaves, sending skinny streams of light onto the path. Because of the foliage, it felt at least ten degrees cooler than running through the park. Claire welcomed the temperature change.

Lifting the bottom of her t-shirt, she mopped the sweat from her face as she continued to run deeper into the woods. The path's twists and turns paralleled the water's natural boundaries, but the stream was nearly invisible because of the spring leaves in an amazing array of greens.

A mother deer and baby fawn stood in a small clearing just ahead. Slowing to a jog, Claire cut wide, off the path and along the treeline on the opposite side of the trail. The mother deer nudged her baby toward the stream.

At the end of the clearing, she again picked up speed, forcing her feet to move faster with each step. *Run like the wind!* she repeated over and over in her head, making it match the rhythmic beat of her feet against the pavement.

Just ahead, in a clearing, was a second choice of paths: left and back out of the park or right and along the stream, pushing her deeper into the woods until a second turn would bring her full circle and back to the park. Claire again checked her watch, already knowing what it would tell her.

Her muscles burned as if they were on fire as she pushed the final two hundred yards before the turn. She continued to pick up speed, feeling euphoria as she forced herself to work harder than she could ever remember. She focused on the movement of her feet, lifting them faster and faster, increasing the drumming sound as they touched down against the tar path.

Claire felt a freedom she had not experienced in a long, long time. She wanted to laugh, to release every ounce of negative energy that had built up over the past forty-two years, but she did not. The little energy she had left went into increasing her speed before the turn.

Her breathing grew more labored as her heart slammed inside her chest. In less than ten seconds, she would have to slow and turn back toward the park. Pressing her chin downward, she watched her feet, counting down the final seconds of her run. *Ten, nine, eight…five, four, three…* On two, she lifted her head, ready to slow before making the turn. But it was too late—he was standing directly in front of her.

Claire veered to the right to keep from hitting him full force. As she did, she careened off the paved surface. Her steps clumsily landed on the uneven ground; the rhythmic beat of seconds before was lost. She stumbled out of control as her foot connected with the side of a large rock, sending her flying forward, face first into the dirt; gravel ground into her stomach, thighs, and arms as she skidded to a stop near the stream.

Everything had moved in slow motion, and yet it had taken only a split second for her to go from running to lying within inches of the water. While it happened, she had experienced a heightened awareness—a sixth sense that moved her from participant to spectator. She had seen it all, as if she had been floating above, watching. But the noise, the screaming, pulled her back onto the ground, lying face down in the gravel.

"Oh, my god! Are you okay? I'm so sorry! I didn't know anyone would be out here." Claire heard his mumbled voice as he moved closer to her. It echoed, growing louder and then softer. His words were lost amidst the heartbeat that pounded in her ears.

"Ma'am? Ma'am, are you okay?"

Her body ached. Every muscle convulsed; her thighs, stomach, and arms burned. She could feel the blood seeping from her cuts and scrapes and trickle down her legs, almost tickling the skin that had remained intact.

"HELP!" Again, his voice echoed. "HELP! We need help!" he screamed.

Slowly, she rolled from her stomach onto her back.

The man put both of his hands out, palms outward in warning. "Don't move! I don't think you should move."

Shut up! she wanted to scream…*shut up!* She squeezed her eyes shut even tighter, pressing the heels of her hands into them, hoping to blur the pain. Sharp flames shot through her entire body as she tried to regroup.

"Ma'am? What can I do? Please, answer me." His words came to her as if he were yelling through a tunnel. She still could not understand them. Her screams were drowning out his words again, but she wasn't sure if they were coming from inside her head or if they were escaping into the air. Slowly, she pulled her hands away from her eyes and slid them down to her mouth. It was closed. She clenched her jaw to keep the screams from breaking free.

"Lady, please, talk to me. Are you okay?" the man begged. His voice shook as he spoke. The echo of his voice began to subside; his words became clearer. She could tell he had moved closer because she could feel his shadow across her face, blocking out the afternoon sun.

Claire's eyes remained closed as she concentrated on a plan to get home. She gently lifted her arms, bending and twisting each one, checking for breaks. She did the same with her legs—feeling each of the movements, not watching them. She felt weak and drained as nausea swam in her stomach.

"You're shaking. Y-you're probably in shock." She felt his shadow shift as he turned away from her. "W-will you be okay if I go get help?"

She finally found her voice. It was a whisper, barely audible to even herself.

"What? I-I didn't hear you," he said, leaning closer.

She tried again. "I'm, I'm fine. I mean…" A deep breath shuddered through her as she inhaled, and she forcefully blew it out between her tight lips. "I-I'll be fine when I get home."

The man moved closer to her. "Don't stand up right away. Just sit up first." She still kept her eyes closed, afraid to look at her mangled limbs and torso, afraid of being sick here on the side of the path—in front of this stranger.

A low moan slipped out as she rolled onto her side. "Good idea," she whispered, frozen in place as she let another wave of nausea pass.

Finally, pushing herself into a sitting position, she opened her eyes, blinking her surroundings into focus. Pressing the side of her hand to her forehead, sheltering her eyes from the overly bright sun, she turned toward the man she had narrowly missed. Her breath caught in her throat, and an animal-like sound filled the air: part howl, part scream. A dry heave worked its way up her throat, gagging her.

The sun's light reflected orange off the man's glasses as he watched her overly exposed body. He stood over her, straddling her legs. His hands stretched out to offer help, but his eyes were focused on her legs and stomach—surveying the damage his sudden appearance had caused.

Memories flooded back, and her screams found momentum. Claire shoved him backward, nearly knocking him to the ground. She kicked at him, trying to create space between the two of them. The man stepped back out of Claire's reach.

"What's wrong with you?" he cried. "I'm just trying to help."

"Stay away from me!" Claire screamed as she tried to stand. "Don't come near me! Stay away!"

Her jaw tightened and she fought her pain through clenched teeth. She pushed herself to her feet; adrenaline continued to burn through her stomach. She took one step and nearly tumbled forward. Her next steps were tentative, but she forced her legs to support her weight. Keeping her eyes focused on the man, she watched his every move with as much concentrated effort as he watched hers.

"I-I'm sorry, ma'am. I didn't mean…"

Claire took another step and nearly fell again. He moved

forward, reaching out to steady her, but pulled back as she lashed out again. "Stay away from me! I told you to stay away!" she screamed as she aimed her body toward the path, shaking from fear and pain.

One step, then another, each putting distance between the two of them. Once again, she felt as if she were a spectator in her own life, watching herself run. She ran sideways, continuing to watch him over her shoulder, making sure he had no plans to follow her. Step by step, she pushed toward home: half limping, half running. Heads turned and eyes followed her as her tentative steps carried her back through the park. People quickly parted, stepping out of her way, allowing her full access to the path. And even though everyone saw her pain, saw the wounds that disfigured her body, they all kept their distance— once more reminding her how invisible she had become.

***

Again, Claire struggled with the lock. Her arms shook so badly, she squeezed the key tightly with both hands as she fought to slip it into the keyhole. Fear had left her unable to execute even menial tasks.

She winced when she stepped into the air-conditioned house, slamming the door shut and angrily twisting the lock. A shiver ripped through her, and she wrapped her arms tightly around her stomach. She fell back against the door, her head and shoulders pressing against the cool wood as she tried to gain control of her breathing. She felt numb inside—too numb to feel anything but physical pain.

Her knees buckled more than once as she ascended the stairs one at a time, momentarily resting on each step. She had to direct her movements—*leg up, step, push.* She struggled to make it into the bathroom, steadying herself against the walls and doorways as she passed. No matter how small, every movement she made tore at her muscles.

She pulled the glass shower door open and used both hands to move the lever all the way to hot before stepping out and waiting for the water to heat up. Grabbing scissors from the top drawer of her vanity, she cut off her shorts and t-shirt, slashing at them as violent sobs racked her entire body.

Turning toward the shower, Claire caught a glimpse of

herself in the full-length mirror. Dirt and blood streaks marked her face, legs, stomach, and arms. Tiny streams of red still oozed around places where the blood had begun to harden, leaving scabs—memories of the day—scars of a lifetime.

Again, she pulled the shower door open, stepping into the water as the full force of it pelted against her: strong and hot. The water slapped against her open sores, and she leaned her head against the wall and turned the lever to a cooler temperature. The pain was excruciating: the physical pain on the outside of her body and the emotional pain on the inside. Claire cried out in agony as the memories of the day collided with those of the past. She pounded her fists against the sides of the marble shower, screaming for them to stop. Eventually, her legs could support her no longer, and her body crumbled in a heap on the shower floor, the water cutting deeply into her, eroding the walls she had built over a lifetime.

And there in the shower—not more than two hours after she had decided to let go of the past—her memories returned, full-bore. She did not try to stop them; she couldn't have even if she had wanted to. She just let them come—washing over her like the water.

CHAPTER 12

TEN YEARS OLD

Killing Season had begun.

Sometime after dark, headlights bounced up and down along the dirt road until they turned into the gravel driveway. Dust swirled in the headlights between each car. A handful of vehicles had been abandoned at odd angles, some left in the grass along the driveway.

Snapping off the light, she stepped up onto her bed and pressed her forehead against the window. The men practically dove out of their cars, bending and stretching after their two-hour journey north. Her father stood in the middle of the men, laughing, handing each one a beer as they joined the circle. Their words were lost through the glass that separated them, but the hooting and hollering found its way into the house.

Roy glanced up at her window and lifted his beer toward it. She jumped backward out of his view, nearly tumbling off the edge of the bed as she fell onto the pillows. She knew he could not see her in the dark of the night, yet she still felt exposed. Minutes passed before she eased back toward the window and watched the men pull their gear from their cars: bags of hunting clothes, guns cased in tan canvas and leather.

Dropping his bag to the ground next to his pick-up, Roy pulled his gun from the back of this truck, uncased it, and aimed it into the distance, pretending to fire it; he jerked his shoulder backward—an imaginary kickback as if he had really pulled the trigger. She could tell the other men were admiring his gun, each fingering the rifle before taking it and mimicking Roy's actions.

She felt her arms and hands begin to move, to take the shape of the same gun the others tried out. She lifted the imaginary weapon to her shoulder, carefully pointing it—at Roy. *Ptttchu!* The make-believe bullet pierced him, and she imagined him crumbling to the ground. Still holding her fantasy gun, she turned it slightly to the left, taking careful aim as she once again pulled the trigger. She envisioned her father grabbing for his chest and collapsing in a heap on the ground, lying near Roy. In her mind, the others ran. The corners of her mouth curled upward as she kicked her legs out and dropped onto the side of the bed, her imagination pulling her deeper into the story she had started at the window.

She was nearly blinded when the overhead light snapped on; she covered her eyes against the sudden brightness. "Mary Claire," her mother hissed. "What are you doing in here? Move! Go, now! The hunters are here. Hurry up!" Her mother raced around the room, smoothing out the wrinkles she had left on the bed.

The front door slammed shut and loud voices echoed through the house. "Go, NOW!" her mother loudly whispered as she pointed toward the door.

She dove toward her mother, trying to plant one last kiss on her before the weekend began, but her mother had already turned away and her lips brushed her shoulder instead. With no time left, she dashed from the room and crept along the side of the hallway and into the living room. She silently slipped past the kitchen door and squeezed herself into the small space behind the couch. There she lay on her back on top of the old, smelly sleeping bag as she waited the night away.

She could hear her mother as she raced back and forth, moving about the kitchen—no wasted steps.

"Beer, Theresa!" her father bellowed. "Now!"

"Yeah, beer, woman!" another man called, mimicking Edward's demand, laughing at his own stupid joke.

The bottles clanked against one another as her mother pulled them from the refrigerator. She heard the tops pop off, one at a time as they dropped onto the countertop. She knew her mother had tucked all six bottles into her arm and carried them to the table. A cheer went up when her mom walked into the dining room.

"I'll buy the next round," she heard one man say. "This one'll go down fast. Hustle in here with another round." And with that, she heard her mother slip back into the kitchen.

She allowed herself to doze on and off, hidden behind

the couch, close enough to the kitchen and the dining room to keep an ear out for both her mother and the unruly hunters.

One by one, she heard chairs slide backward; the men drunkenly stumbled off to bed.

***

By Saturday night, the trees were decorated with trophies. Gutted deer dangled from ropes tied around their necks. Their tongues hung sideways from the corners of their mouths as blood dripped from their lifeless bodies that swayed in the breeze. Camera flashes provided evidence that the hunters had triumphed once again over the defenseless animals.

She hated this time of year—hated everyone who was involved in any part of it. On those Saturday afternoons, she refused to go near any windows.

***

Saturday evening marked the end of the hunt for the men. They ate, packed their gear, and drove away—their conquests tightly tied to the roof of their car or tossed into the back of a pick-up. Once again, a cloud of dust swirled around each vehicle as it pulled onto the dirt road. Sitting in the window seat at the end of the upstairs hallway, hidden behind the edge of a heavy curtain, she wondered, as the cars disappeared down the road, how anyone could feel triumph in taking an animal that stood no chance against a gun. But then she remembered the imaginary gun she held Friday night—and she knew.

A lone black pickup remained in the driveway—Roy's. Her father walked back toward the house with Roy by his side. She dashed past several now empty bedrooms she had never been allowed to set foot in and raced down the staircase. She dove behind the couch just as the door opened. She wondered if anyone else would be able to hear her heavy breathing, but just in case, she pressed her face into the stinky sleeping bag to muffle the sound.

The night wore on. Early darkness filled the sky; a winter storm brewed outside. The wind howled through the trees, warning of things to come. Gentle snow blanketed the ground, swirling in the wind before settling in to spend the winter.

She could hear the approaching storm's sounds from her

hiding place. In the darkness of the living room, she could see the snow as it passed by the window above. Voices drifted from the kitchen, tales of the day. Her mother's voice never mixed with her father's or Roy's.

Dishes clinked together, water ran, the refrigerator opened and closed. Food was prepared and again set out for a second meal of the night. It was all cleaned up without so much as a sound from her mom.

Her internal clock registered the time to be just after midnight. Hypnotized by the snow that swirled above her, she fell into a restless sleep; any sleep was better than nothing. She knew she had to be vigilant through the long night ahead. She needed to be on guard against the darkness of the night—against Roy.

As the time neared one o'clock, she heard the gathering break up. The noises that had grown louder with every beer popped open had finally died down. A drunken stupor had captured their ability to remain awake, let alone hold coherent conversations. Her father stirred the fire with the wrought-iron poker he pulled from a hook on the wall; she saw the room brighten with fuel from the extra logs he tossed on top of the embers.

Long after the house went silent, she remained behind the couch. She debated about staying there, cramped in the space that had grown smaller as she had grown bigger in the past year. But the wall was cold, and the draft that leaked through the cheap windows above her made her muscles ache.

Except for the crackling fire, the house was silent. There was not a sound anywhere when she finally pushed her way out from behind the couch, dragging the ratty sleeping bag with her. Silently moving the couch back into place, she crawled in for the long night's watch.

Her mind wandered, touching on familiar things, keeping herself occupied so sleep would not come. When she found herself drifting off, she made up stories, happy tales about families, imaginary families she belonged to.

The storm brewing inside of her and the one that raged around her forced her to refocus time and again, until finally, like a thief in the night, the wind and the snow and the crackling fire stole her ability to remain vigilant. She drifted off to sleep, entering a chamber of nothingness.

***

She felt his hand—first, as part of her dream—warm and rough as it stroked her cheek and neck. Her eyes jerked open. He was bent over her with one knee resting on the edge of the couch. His hand moved quickly from her neck to her mouth. He pushed down hard, holding his other hand near his own face—his index finger pressed firmly against his lips, indicating for her to remain silent. The flames of the fireplace reflected orange off of his aviator glasses. She squirmed, tried to pry his fingers from her face. Her screams were muffled beneath his hand, so she tried to bite him—but she could not fight his size. She heard him snicker at her attempts.

"You got some spunk, don'tcha, kid? That's what I like about you," he whispered. "The first time I laid eyes on you, I knew you had spunk." He bent forward, his hot breath blowing in her face. "You remind me an awful lot of my own girls. They're sweet and pretty, just like you." He pressed his hand tighter over her mouth. "And they love their daddy so much." He kissed her forehead, then her face and her neck. She tried to fight, but as she did, he pushed her head deeper into the cushion, twisting her neck at an unusual angle.

His free hand reached under her flannel pajama top, touching the flatness of her breasts. She grabbed at his hand, digging her fingernails into the top of it. But he shook her off, grabbed both of her small hands in his large one and pressed the whole lot over her mouth. He slid his hand down her stomach and under the elastic waistband of her pajama bottoms—moving slowly downward. She kicked at him, fighting the weight of the sleeping bag that trapped her legs.

"Well, well, well. Looks like we got ourselves a fighter, now, don't it?" He placed one knee across her legs, holding them in place; his weight nearly snapped them in two. His breathing grew heavy as he touched her. The tone of his voice was deep as he repeatedly told her to shut up, that he would kill her if she continued to fight.

He was too big, too strong for a ten-year-old. He had power over her, just like the power he had over the snow-covered deer that hung outside the window. She closed her eyes and let her body go still. She could not fight him off. She gave up trying. At that moment, she shut off her emotions—stored them deep inside of her—imagined nothing.

Emotionless and disconnected from what was happening, she watched him shake as his body moved uncontrollably. His breathing became more labored—jagged, quick, and shallow. His head jerked backward, then dropped forward until his chin pressed against his chest. He stood there motionless for several seconds; his eyes tightly closed. She remained frozen, afraid to move, afraid to bring anything inside of him back to life.

Slowly, he opened his eyes and grinned when he saw her looking at him. He let go of her arms and pressed his hand tightly across her mouth, this time covering her nose too. She grabbed at his hand, trying to free herself—fighting for a breath.

Then, he leaned down so close to her face, she could smell the stink of his breath. "Listen here, you little shit. D'you see that gun over there in the corner?" He motioned with his chin, jerking her face in the direction of the gun, twisting her neck to the side. "If you tell *anyone*, mention even *one* word about this, I'll kill your mother." He let out a laugh, louder than he had intended. Turning toward the stairs to be sure no one had heard, he added, "I could make it look like an accident." He half grunted, half laughed at his ability to make death seem so casual.

"But the sad thing is, that would leave you with that vile scumbag father you hate so much." His eyes sparkled as the fire's reflection danced on the lens of his glasses.

"Your father was right about both you and your mother—you're both more trouble than you're worth. He should have done away with you a long time ago...years ago when he had the chance."

His nose nearly touched hers. "Do you understand me? One word...and BOOM! She's dead. Got it?" She nodded her head as much as possible under the weight of his hand. Then he pushed his palm so hard against her face that she was certain her neck would break.

Suddenly, he let go, but he lifted his hand only an inch

above her mouth, waited for her to scream, to make any noise at all. And when she did not, he spit in her face. Then he walked to the corner and picked up his gun. He pointed it up the stairs toward her mother's bedroom. He watched her face as she watched him. And then he carried it back down the hallway—a reminder of his promise.

She rolled to her side and lay perfectly still beneath the weight of the old sleeping bag. She silently cried so as not to wake anyone. Rage began to grow inside of her, slowly at first, then with a vengeance. She wiped the tears with her sleeve and scrubbed his spit from her face with the sleeping bag. Her eyes wandered the room, searching the shadows of the night, but her mind was too wired to focus on any one thing.

Her jaw tightened and her fingers clenched the top edge of the sleeping bag. Her entire body shook. She hated Roy, and she loathed her father. She despised the life she had been born into. She was no one—no one who mattered anymore. She had lost control of her own life. Roy had stolen that; he owned her now. The only thing she knew at that moment was that she'd never let anyone control her again.

She picked up the imaginary gun and pointed it in the direction of her bedroom, the room where Roy slept. *Ptttchu!* The sound echoed across the living room. She dropped her arms and grinned.

Tossing the top of her sleeping bag over the back of the couch, she tiptoed across the room and hoisted her father's rifle into her arms. She lifted it to her shoulder, just as she had done with the imaginary gun. It was heavy. Her arms shook from the weight, but her anger gave her strength. Pointing the gun toward the floor, she balanced the barrel against one leg. She fingered the bronze-colored bolt—lifting it and then dropping it back down. Again, she lifted the bolt, this time sliding it forward and pulling it back, locking it in place. The click echoed through the room, and she stood perfectly still. No doors opened—but still, she did not move for almost a full minute—keeping her back pressed against the wall. Finally, she stepped over the creaky floorboards as she inched her way down the hallway, toward her bedroom—the room where Roy slept—the gun loaded, ready and perched against her shoulder.

CHAPTER 13

Claire's steps were tentative; she moved almost in slow motion. Her entire body ached—a deeper pain than she had ever known. Not an inch of it had been left unscathed by the fall—every muscle hurt, every scrape and cut burned as if on fire. Her head throbbed, and she tightened her neck and shoulders as she eased down the stairs.

The coffee pot held a leftover cup from the morning rush. She poured it into a tall white mug and shoved it into the microwave, heating it until she could barely hold the cup in her trembling hands.

Claire took a slow sip of the coffee. It burned as she swallowed, ironically sending an icy shiver down her spine. Pain raged inside and out, and she laid her head on the cold countertop to stop the wave of nausea that grew, threatening to expel the small swallow she had just taken.

What had happened out there on that path? she thought as she worked to unwind the pieces of the day. She had completely become unglued when she saw that man's face—the wire-rimmed aviator glasses, the same orange glow that had haunted her for over thirty years.

That poor man! He had not looked like Roy any more than she looked like her own father—not really. He had the same salt and pepper gray hair, parted on the left and slicked to the right. He was tall and sturdy, muscular and strong, but those characteristics were true of hundreds of men, and yet, this man's ill-fated timing had caused her to lash out with all the pain she had stuffed inside for all those years.

Would she have reacted with such intensity had he not been standing over her when she opened her eyes, his arm stretched toward her? It was déjà-vu, and in that moment, the years had fallen away, and it may as well have been Roy standing there.

Nausea again churned in her stomach; vomit worked its

way into her throat, and she swallowed hard to push it back down. She drew a deep breath in through her nose and slowly let it out. The memories of the day haunted her, and she knew letting go of the past was not going to be as easy as she had hoped.

As the clock chimed five times, Claire watched the pendulum swing back and forth. The clock had been the first wedding gift she and Michael had opened—their first possession as husband and wife. Ever since that day, the clock had ticked off moments of their lives together.

Five o'clock. Claire let out a cry—the time suddenly registered. *Jade! Soccer practice!* She had forgotten to pick her up at school. What kind of a mother forgets her own child? As she pushed her stool away from the counter, she grimaced. Biting her lip, she fought through the pain as she eased her damaged body out of the house and into the car. As she backed out of the driveway faster than she intended, she realized her reaction time was slower than it should be.

Her phone beeped and she dug it out of her purse. She scanned the screen as she drove down her street. Three missed calls—all from Jade, all from school: one at 3:33; another at 4:08—a hang up around 4:47.

Soccer practice had been cut short for one reason or another. Jade had been waiting for Claire for nearly an hour and a half. *Why hadn't she called the house phone?* Maybe she had. Maybe there was a message, or several messages, that hadn't registered during her meltdown.

"Call the Middle School," Claire directed her phone, but the number immediately went to voicemail. She tried a second and a third time—with each call, the secretary's recorded voice announced the office was closed.

Traffic was heavy, but Claire scooted in and around other vehicles, taking side streets as often as possible. She was acutely aware of the intense pain in her arms and legs each time she braked or pressed on the gas—each time she turned the steering wheel more than just a little.

5:24 p.m.—Jade had been waiting for nearly two hours by then. Claire knew her daughter would be angry, frightened even. In any event, Jade would have expected her to show up by 4:20, even if practice had not been cut short.

As she raced into the school's main parking lot. A lone car remained—a black Jeep Cherokee belonging to Will Ryan. She abandoned her car next to his.

Claire jerked on the school's heavy glass door. Half expecting it to be locked, she nearly tumbled backward when the door pulled open against her weight. The commons was empty. The wax on the floor sparkled in the overhead lights.

"Jade!" Claire called out. "Jade!"

A custodian appeared from behind a set of lockers, a rag in one hand and a can of window cleaner in the other "Ma'am, can I help you?"

"I'm looking for my daughter—about this tall, sandy brown hair." She held her hand slightly above her shoulder.

"They all look like that," he chuckled. "Sorry. Hasn't been any kids in the building for at least an hour now." Claire's shoulders dropped and he took pity on her. "You might wanna check with the boss, though," signaling toward the office with his chin. "Boss-man's still in his office. Been in there with his door shut since I got here at 3:30. He might be able to help you out." Then he shrugged and walked away.

Claire pushed through the double doors and into the dimly lit office. The only light came through a small transom window high up on the back wall.

Will's office door was slightly ajar. A narrow wedge of light spilled onto the carpet. But as Claire pushed the door open a few more inches, her lips froze around the words she had planned to say. She watched the scene for several seconds, trying to give meaning to what she saw. Jade's demeanor startled Claire. Her daughter sat rigid, almost frozen in a chair in the back corner of Will's office; her hands tightly gripped the front edge of the cushion. Will's jacket was off, his tie loosened; his sleeves were rolled up to his elbows. Claire had never seen him in anything other than a suit, a crisp white shirt, and tie. But it was not the way he was dressed that bothered her; it was the way he stood over Jade—his power and presence clearly a threat to her daughter.

Claire shoved the door hard. The sudden bang startled Will and he stepped backward, clearly shocked by her appearance. His eyes met hers, and for the first time, she saw emotion, something other than the darkness that had always clouded them. She could not read it. It was there for a split second—and then it was gone.

Jade ran to Claire, ducking behind her. She glued herself to her mother's back, eyes downcast. Claire could hear her daughter's whimpers. She knew the drill. How many times had she stood behind her mother in the exact same way—hiding from her father?

She tried to turn toward her daughter, but Jade clutched the back of her mother's shirt even tighter. Claire whispered over her shoulder, "Honey, are you okay? What's wrong?"

"C-c-can we just go?" Claire barely heard the question through Jade's sobs.

"Yes, honey; of course we can."

Will moved behind his desk where he had begun shuffling papers into neat piles. "I would have been here sooner, Will, but something happened this afternoon and…" Claire's confession did not come easy.

Will's eyes grew dark again as he dismissed her tardiness with a partial sentence that drifted off as quickly as it began. "…had work to do anyway." His manner was rude. Her stomach flopped one way and then the other. Between Will's flippant attitude and Jade's sobbing, Claire knew something was terribly wrong, but she was not sure she was willing to go to the place it was taking her.

Jade pulled on her mom, tugged on her shirt from behind, inching the two of them backward—toward the door. Claire turned to face Jade for the first time. Fear washed over her, and sadness tugged the corners of her mouth downward. She recognized it as her own. She had seen it in the mirror, felt it a million times herself. Tears came to both mother and daughter as Claire wrapped Jade in her arms, making a hasty retreat toward the door. "Honey, what *is* it? What happened?" she whispered.

Will's briefcase snapped open; he shoved papers into it. Without ever looking up, he called out, "Jade." Claire froze. "Remember what I told you." Claire felt the nausea from earlier return. She tightened her arm around her daughter's shoulder and guided her out of the office.

As soon as they were in the car, Claire pressed the lock button; she no longer felt safe anywhere. She allowed herself several deep breaths before putting the key into the ignition and starting the car. The cool air blew against her burning cheeks. "Jade, honey, I'm so sorry I didn't get your messages."

Her daughter angrily slapped her hands against the dashboard before knotting them across her chest. "So what happened, Mom?" Jade's sarcastic attitude made Claire cringe. "You told him something happened. What was it?" Instead of facing her mother, looking at the scars she held from her earlier mishap, Jade turned toward her own window, staring at nothing in particular. "What happened that made you *forget* about me?"

Defeated, Claire's shoulders sagged as she touched the raw, already scabbing over sore on her left cheek. "Nothing, honey. Nothing I shouldn't have been able to control." They sat in silence, listening to the hum of the car. Claire reached toward Jade, tried to tuck her hair behind her ear, but her daughter pulled away. "Honey, I could never forget about you. Never! It's just…"

Jade's eyes blazed with anger; her eyebrows furrowed as she turned back toward her mother, her arms wrapped tightly across her chest. "Yeah, well, you did, Mom. You *did* forget!"

Tears stung Claire's eyes, and she looked toward the ceiling to keep them from falling. "Jade, I'm *so* sorry…*so very* sorry." Her voice grew husky as she fought the tears. "But, honey, I think there's more to it than you're telling me. Did something else happen? What did Mr. Ryan tell you?"

Again, Jade turned away from her mother; she pulled her knees into her chest and rested her forehead against them, closing their discussion.

Claire jumped when Will knocked on her window. Without even acknowledging his sudden appearance, she slammed the car into drive and raced out of the parking lot.

CHAPTER 14

Claire ran her hands along the front of her thighs as she stood naked in front of the full-length mirror. The scars that had felt swollen and rough only days earlier had begun to disappear, leaving behind a pink puckered tenderness. She traced the white scar that ran across the bottom of her abdomen, her thumbs meeting in the middle—a souvenir of bringing life into the world. Slowly, she moved her hand toward her arm, brushing her fingertips along the old scar that ran from her elbow to her shoulder. Finally, she slipped a hand under the hair on the side of her head. Her fingertip touched the jagged scar that lay hidden there, and she repeatedly traced the crooked line.

Her old scars had warped in with the new ones in recent days—both physical and emotional. Daily, Claire struggled to separate them, to reclaim her life, but the accident had fused the two time periods together—and no matter how hard she tried, she could not dissever them. One moment she was fine, the next she was hit with a wave of memories that nearly crippled her, making it almost impossible to breathe.

In her good moments, Claire focused on her family, but neither her husband nor her children needed her the way *she* needed them to.

In the past few weeks, Michael had become married to the Prescott case. She couldn't blame him; she had agreed to it, but even their family Sundays had been ignored in recent weeks. He spent nearly every waking hour at the office, often not returning home until dawn broke on the horizon, and then usually just for a quick shower and a change of clothing before disappearing again. Other nights, he slept at the office or in a hotel a couple of hours south. Days would pass without them seeing one another save for the hour or so of silence when Michael fell into bed, often in the same clothes he had worn to work. He rarely had time to call home. None of that mattered; Claire did not have the energy to hold a conversation with him anyway.

Her son did not need her any more than her husband did. Almost overnight, Henry changed from her baby boy into a little man. She felt like a mother bird watching her fledgling attempt to fly, knowing she could not save him if he fell. Only, unlike the mother bird, she wasn't *pushing* him out of the nest— he was jumping—and she let him go.

Since the accident, the same day Claire had forgotten her daughter, Jade had become even more sullen and silent; she moved along the edges of the family, not crossing paths unless it was necessary. She never spoke unless she was spoken to, and even then, her answer almost always came as a shrug. The few words she did speak were succinct, well-chosen syllables at best. She brooded over joining her mother and brother for meals, making life so miserable that Claire left trays of food outside her daughter's bedroom door, only to pick them up later, nearly untouched. Claire was grateful for the days her kids were in school and she had time alone.

"Jade, it's time to leave for soccer practice," Claire said as she gently knocked on the door to her daughter's room. She waited almost a full minute before calling again. "Jade?" A muffled response hurled through the closed door.

"Honey, you don't have a choice. Your team needs you; they *depend* on you." Claire pressed down on the levered door handle, but it did not budge. Less than an inch and a half of wood separated them, yet they may as well have been standing on opposite sides of the world.

Claire pressed her head against the door frame and listened as her daughter moved about her bedroom. Objects slammed against the walls as Jade angrily tossed them, each thud taking Claire back to her own childhood. When the door finally opened, Jade emerged in her soccer gear—one sock pulled up only halfway, her shoelaces untied. With her soccer bag tossed over her shoulder, she pushed past her mother, almost knocking her down. "Ridin' my bike," she announced in a whisper so quiet it took a moment to register.

Grabbing her daughter by one shoulder, Claire forcibly turned Jade toward her. "Honey, let me..." Tears stung her eyes; she refused to blink, refused to set the flood in motion.

"No, Mom!" Jade jerked free of her mother's grip and ran down five steps before stopping on the landing. "You just don't get it! You haven't been here when I needed you." Her footsteps pounded as she raced out the front door, slamming it behind her. The slam reverberated in the silence that surrounded Claire. The tears that had formed earlier started their descent down her cheeks; the salty liquid rolled into her mouth and dripped off her chin. She moved to the front window as she watched her daughter ride away, widening the gap even further.

An overwhelming ache surged through her, and she wrapped her arms around herself and slid down the wall as she waited for it to pass. She agonized over the loss of her perfect family—over the loss of herself. She had always been fragile—but now she was broken.

She curled her fingers into tight fists and pounded them on the carpeted floor until her arms ached, too heavy to lift. Her neglected fingernails dug into the palms of her hands, slicing through the pad below one thumb. She opened her hand and watched the blood trickle out before balling her fist closed again, digging the nail into the same cut, squeezing harder than she had before. Frustration, anger, bitterness, and hatred churned through every inch of her, picking up speed, spinning inside of her—sending her spiraling downward.

When she hit bottom, she felt her life snap—her entire life unwound like a broken spring; it lay before her—bent and broken. Slowly, her hands opened as they fell to her sides onto the carpeted floor. A sudden rush of air escaped, and she turned her head as if she did not recognize the noise. The tightness in her shoulders fell away and her body went numb as she fell headlong into the depths of despair.

CHAPTER 15

Claire remained on the floor until darkness fell, hidden by a sofa that sat between the stairs and the entrance to the upstairs sunroom. Both Henry and Jade passed by her several times, but neither of them looked for her. She heard the refrigerator door open and close more than once, but the simple sound did not register—it was distant and foreign.

At dark, Jade pushed Henry into his room and closed the door, but she never said a word before going into her own room and locking the door behind her.

It was the click of the lock that brought Claire to the present—not the same Claire she had been a month ago, and not even the same person she had been earlier in the day. Whatever had snapped inside of her had awoken the person she had fought to keep locked away all those years.

Claire struggled to stand, listing side to side until the room stopped spinning. In the darkness of the night, she silently crept down the stairs and into the kitchen. She turned on one overhead pendant light before picking up the laptop and centering it under the stream of brightness.

The laptop sprang to life with the tap of just one button; the familiar sound echoed across the open kitchen. Claire twisted her mouth to one side, staring intently at the screen as it made the transformation from black to a brilliantly colored photo of Henry and Jade. It was that picture that made her put the computer down and walk away. What was she thinking? What was she doing?

At the sink, she rinsed out the dishrag and scrubbed the already clean island again. She worked from one end to the other, scrubbing in small circles around until she made her way back toward the computer. Her kids smiled at her from the screen. The mist from the waterfall in the background had created a rainbow behind them. Her fingertips touched the photo, brushed against Jade's cheek, settled on Henry's lips.

Watching her children's faces, she bit her lip as she slid her finger across the trackpad, sending the cursor toward the web browser. When she tapped it, Jade and Henry disappeared.

Slipping onto the tall stool, Claire balanced her fingers above the keys, letting them hang in midair. But once her ring finger reached up and typed the letter *W* into the search engine, the rest of them followed as if they were strung together— *whitepages.com*. The page popped up. She took a deep breath before slowly filling in the information she knew. *Last name: Moses. First name: Roy. State: CO.* She stared at the screen, drumming the fingers of one hand on the countertop while nervously chewing on a hangnail on her other hand. She told herself she only wanted to know if he was still alive. Did he still live in the city, less than an hour from where she now lived? It couldn't hurt to find out that information, could it? Claire absently rubbed the crease that had formed between her brows. Her mouth twisted again from side to side as her little finger hovered above the *Enter* key before she finally let it fall.

Within less than a second, the information popped onto the screen. *Roy J. Moses, 78, 1787 Hauser Circle, Golden, Colorado.* Claire knocked the stool over as she jumped away from the computer. She shuddered. A chill ran down her spine, and she wrapped her arms around herself as she began to shake uncontrollably. Roy *was* still alive. Tears began to form—tears of fear.

Claire righted the chair before pulling a notepad from the cupboard. She hastily copied down the address, her shaking hand creating such a mess of the numbers and letters that she did not even recognize it as her handwriting. She did not know why she wrote it down; she didn't even want it. Leaving the address lay on the island, Claire walked away but returned seconds later. She couldn't stop herself; she was like a gawker at a car accident. She touched the address, running her fingers lightly over the yellow paper. At first, it was just simple knowledge: a place. But as the moments passed, the knowledge grew into anger, and the anger turned to fury. This piece of paper and the simple words it contained enraged her. She crumpled it into a tight ball, squeezing it until her knuckles grew white. Then she forcibly pitched it into the trash can and stormed from the room.

She had taken no more than five steps past the doorway before she returned, retrieving the wrinkled paper from the top of the garbage can. She smoothed out the note and committed the address to memory—repeating it over and over. Two hours south of the place she had grown up. Just sixty minutes north of where she lived now—*sixty minutes.*

Mapquest showed it at fifty-three point two miles from her driveway to his. Claire lived just fifty-three miles from the person she hated and feared more than anyone else in her entire life—except her father—but he was dead. She pulled up the address on her phone. Then she clicked on the history button, deleting both *whitepages.com* and *mapquest* from the computer's memory.

She snapped the computer closed and took her phone upstairs. In the bedroom, she stared at the line that took her from her place to his, memorizing every turn. Then she fell into bed—fully clothed—make-up and all. She struggled to fall asleep; her mind raced and she could feel the beat of her heart as it pulsed through her body. When she finally fell asleep, her dreams displayed wild, vivid images of red, orange, and yellow. In each one, Roy's face haunted her—the orange glow of his glasses constantly watched her as she waited for the morning light.

***

With Jade and Henry out the door and a quick call to Karen to pick her son up after Kindergarten, Claire left the house—absent of her purse and phone—forgetting even to set the alarm. She walked out the door with only her keys.

With the route committed to memory, she closed in on her destination: Hauser Circle. 1787 would be just up ahead. Her blinker indicated her intent to turn right, but her arms had suddenly gone heavy. Even if she wanted to, she could not turn the wheel. She glanced into the rearview mirror and breathed a sigh of relief when she realized no one was waiting behind her, and so she did not move.

From the intersection, she could not tell which of the older homes was 1787—which one belonged to Roy. Huge maple trees lined the boulevard. Flowers and bushes provided much of the color in front of the light-colored string of homes. No swing sets or forts or swimming pools were visible in the front or back yards from her line of vision. It was obvious to Claire it was a neighborhood filled with elderly people. A gray-haired couple strolled down the sidewalk in the opposite direction of her SUV. She studied the man, wondering if he might be Roy.

A large black pickup sped around her, nearly clipping the front of her silver Lexus as the man jerked it back into the lane. Through her closed windows, she could hear his muffled insults as the younger man turned onto Hauser Circle wagging his middle finger in her direction. With her blinker still indicating a right turn, Claire quickly followed the truck and pulled up next to the curb. Her knuckles were white as she gripped the steering wheel. Laying her head against it, she again wondered what she was doing. It was not the first time she'd asked herself that question in the past twelve hours.

Pulling herself together, Claire checked the house number where she was parked—1776. Instantly, she turned her head to the left and stared at the houses up ahead. She pulled back onto the street, creeping along, her eyes searching every house for signs of the man who had taken her innocence.

*1777, 1779, 1781…*Claire pulled over again, this time in front of one of the larger homes on the block. She wiped her palms on the front of her jeans and adjusted her sunglasses— sliding them higher up on the bridge of her nose. She tugged the brim of her tan baseball cap down just a bit. Dropping the car's visor, she sat up taller to hide her face behind it. As she did, she kept her eyes fixed on a gold-colored house with brown trim. A small ceramic inlay affixed to the brick on the garage front marked the address: *1787 Hauser Circle*. The yard was meticulous. The grass was a lush green and there was an abundance of flowers in multiple gardens. The bushes were perfectly pruned; Claire wondered how a man as evil as Roy could take the time to care for flowers. A red Ford Escape sat under a huge silver maple tree that shaded the front of the house and the driveway.

Her hands shook and she slipped them under her legs to stop them.

The dwelling was a small 1970s style home. The entire neighborhood looked the same: split levels and ranch-style homes. Mature trees and bushes stood erect in both the front and back yards, showing years of growth.

A sudden tap on her passenger window initiated a small scream she stifled between clenched teeth. She felt a rush of blood to her face as she nervously searched for the correct button to lower the passenger's side window.

"Can I help you?" A small, stern-looking, gray-haired woman stood next to her car, her face pressed close to the small opening in the window.

Trying to concoct an instant and believable lie, Claire nodded. "I'm looking for..." But her mind went blank. She searched for something she could say. "Ah...Hauser *Lane*." The words came out almost as a question rather than a statement.

To Claire's surprise, the old woman laughed. She waved her hand in the air as if she were shooing a fly away. "Oh, people make that mistake all the time. This is Hauser *Circle*." She emphasized the word *circle* so Claire would understand her mistake. "Hauser Lane is two blocks that way." She pointed behind Claire and off to her right.

"Oh," Claire said as she looked in that direction. "Tha...thank you for your help."

"You're very welcome. I was drinking my coffee when I saw you sitting out here, and... well, we're a pretty close neighborhood. We look out for each other—neighborhood watch kind of stuff. Been doing it for almost forty years now." The old woman smiled down at Claire. "We're like family. Only good folk in this neighborhood, ya know."

Claire swallowed hard. She wanted to scream *Roy Moses is not good folk!* But instead, she bit the sides of her cheeks. She thanked the woman for her help, but her voice sounded forced; the woman must have picked up on the strain. She tipped her head and gave Claire a curious look.

She started to pull away from the curb when she heard the woman knock again. "The thing is, you'll have to turn around because this here street is a circle. It doesn't go all the way through. Once you turn around, just turn left on Cascade

Street and go two blocks." The old woman patted Claire's window. "If you don't find it, you just come on back and we'll try it again. But it's pretty hard to miss."

Lifting her foot off the brake, Claire cast a wave and forced a smile in the woman's direction as she watched her walk back up her sidewalk and through the black metal gate that was positioned in front of her front steps. She moved the car forward, just out of the woman's view, but still not past the one that *whitepages.com* had deemed to be Roy's house.

What am I doing? she asked herself again. What did she hope to accomplish? Her shoulders slumped forward, and she closed her eyes for a moment, again recalling the events of that night thirty-two years ago.

When she opened them, her breath caught midstream. An old man shuffled down Roy's driveway. With one hand, he pulled a small green oxygen tank. Claire's heart jumped into her throat and she felt panic set in. She covered the lower half of her face with her hand. *So, is that Roy?* She searched for anything that looked like the Roy she had known, but she saw nothing. This man was bald on top and the sides of his head were rimmed in thin tufts of white hair. His glasses were small and dark-framed. Roy had been tall and muscular, but this old man was hunched over at the waist and appeared to lack muscle anywhere. If it was Roy, the hands that had once pressed down so hard against her face and body were now curled and misshapen and looked as if they lacked the strength to hold down a baby, let alone a ten-year-old girl. Back then, Roy had been so sure of everything he did; it showed in the way he carried himself, but this old man watched the ground with every step he took, as if one wrong step could send him tumbling. *It can't be Roy, can it? He's aged too much.*

Still hiding behind her hand, she watched as he turned in her direction, shuffling along the sidewalk. He came to a stop at his mailbox. Letting go of the oxygen cart, he leaned a hand out to balance himself against the silver container. His other hand pressed against his chest. Claire watched as he gasped for breath.

As she became more intrigued with watching the old man, she forgot about hiding her face and her hands dropped into her lap. She tipped her head to the side and scrutinized his every move, still searching for signs of the Roy who had violated her. Suddenly, he turned and his eyes locked with hers. Claire could not breathe; she fought to draw in the cool air that blew through her vents. She wanted to scream. Without a doubt, she knew the man was Roy. Even from where she sat, his steel blue eyes gave him away. He waved, unaware of who she was; then he went back to the task of gathering his mail and shuffling his way back toward his house.

Stepping on the gas, Claire quickly drove past his driveway and into the turnabout at the end of the road. Wiping the sweat from her forehead with the back of her trembling hand, she pulled over to the side of the street, all the while watching Roy make the slow climb back up his driveway. She clamped her jaw tightly shut to keep from screaming. She white-knuckled the steering wheel, holding on securely despite her slick hands. Roy neared the top of his driveway—one hand holding both the mail and his chest, the other pulling the oxygen tank slowly up the slight incline. He was obviously struggling to make it back to the house, but that did not matter to Claire. She felt nothing but anger toward him. That anger churned into rage—and the silence in the car changed to parts of words and phrases she muttered to herself. "Roy, you miserable son-of-a-bitch...you took everything...my poor mother..."

Her hand slid along the inside of her car door, reaching toward the door handle. As she pulled it toward her, the door popped open. Claire stepped out; her legs wobbly and weak, but steady enough to carry her up the incline. Her teeth gritted together so hard that she heard them grind as she tightened her jaw. Memories of the past pushed aside any thoughts of the present or future. She made the quick and easy climb up the driveway, silently approaching Roy from behind. He had stopped moving again as he adjusted the plastic cannula, adjusting it so the oxygen could flow freely.

She sidestepped around him, placing herself between him and the house, noticeably frightening him with her sudden and soundless appearance. Claire angrily stood face to face with the man who had taken everything from her—only this time, she was in control.

Roy's face tightened in a mixture of pain and fear. "Please don't hurt me. I don't have anything. Just don't hurt me." His voice trembled as he begged for mercy.

Claire laughed out loud and inched closer. "You mean the way you hurt me when I was just a little girl? You mean the way you took everything from me, even things I wasn't willing to give? I didn't have a choice, did I, Roy? You took it all from me." Her words hissed through her still gritted teeth. She watched his face for any sign of recognition, but there was none. Roy shook in fear; his mail dropped piece by piece onto the blacktop driveway. "You don't remember me, Roy, do you? Well, let me reintroduce myself. I'm little Mary Claire O'Brien. Edward and Theresa's daughter…the one *you* molested." She watched as his chin went slack with memories.

"Ohhhh." The word came out in a rush of air as Roy squirmed sideways. His hand pressed harder against his chest. Sweat dripped down both sides of his face. "Mary Claire?" His words were a mere whisper. The confidence and swagger of the Roy Moses from her past had clearly disappeared, leaving a shell of who he had once been. "I'm…I…"

"Stop it, Roy! You don't get to talk!" She reached out and poked a shaking finger against the hand that covered his chest. Her actions scared her, but she could not back down. "There is nothing you can say or do that will ever make up for what you did to me—not just back then, but what you have done to me every single day of my life since. I have never forgotten, and I won't let you forget it either. I want you to go to your grave remembering what you did to me, remembering what you did to an innocent little girl."

Roy winced. He pressed both hands against his chest but did not move. Claire sucked in a breath and stepped backward. With her hands clenched at her sides, she ran to her car. She slammed the door shut, all the while never taking her eyes off Roy. He swayed as he turned to watch her go. He grabbed onto the oxygen cart to keep himself from falling. When she turned the key, the engine sprang to life. Holding the top of the steering wheel, Claire picked up an imaginary rifle and positioned it in Roy's direction. *BANG!* she mouthed at him; her lips formed the word a second time—this time with more emphasis as she leaned closer to the windshield.

Suddenly aware of what she had done, Claire shook her head and opened her eyes wide as if to awaken herself from one of her nightmares—only she did not wake up. Roy still stood in his driveway, his mail splayed all around him, and she was still pointing her pretend gun at him. She quickly dropped her hands to the steering wheel. What had she done? What was she thinking? There it was again. That thought. What was wrong with her?

Slamming the car into drive, Claire raced past the gold house with the brown trim and down the street, turning back onto Cascade Street and as far away from Roy as possible.

CHAPTER 16

Claire had not visited her mother in over two weeks. Since her run-in with Roy, she hadn't had the energy to drive the ten miles to the outskirts of town, let alone the strength to keep a one-sided conversation going. It was more than she could handle on one of her good days. Who cared if her mother circled the dates she visited; who cared if there were long strings of unmarked numbers on the calendar? Most of the time, her mother did not even know what was going on around her; she was lost somewhere inside of herself—in a world that had taken place a lifetime ago. Claire did not care about anything except the pain that continued to grow inside of her—sucking her downward with the force of a black hole. Her entire body ached, physically and emotionally. All she wanted was for someone to make it stop.

She slept her days away, only dragging herself out of bed long enough to throw food at her kids and push them out the door in the mornings. The cupboards and refrigerator were nearly barren compared to their usual abundance, and she scrounged to find something to set on the table for Jade and Henry to eat. Once the door closed, she scooped the leftovers into the overflowing garbage can, leaving the crumbs to settle on the unswept floor.

Within minutes after the door closed each morning, she climbed back into bed, pulled the covers over her head, and lay completely still until empty sleep took hold: no nightmares— no thoughts of Roy or her father or the life she had been born into—no thoughts of losing Michael or Jade or Henry. She felt nothing. She *was* nothing—a different kind of invisible.

This had become Claire's life—routine and silent. She no longer knew what day it was—nor did she care.

One morning in mid-May, after she had fallen headlong into one of her empty sleeps, the phone rang, culling her from the depths of nonexistence. The shrill sound swam through the air several times before she remembered where she was—that it was 11:00 on a sunny morning and she was still in bed, smelling of sweat and grime—of unwashed laundry. Claire picked up the receiver and dropped it back into the cradle before rolling over. But the piercing noise started again almost immediately.

"Hul-lo," Claire said as she grabbed the phone and pulled it under the covers. She slurred the word—her sleep resembled drunkenness.

"Mrs. Stanton?" the caller questioned. "A-are you alright? You sound…"

"I'm fine. Who is this?" Claire snapped.

"Mrs. Stanton, this is Linda Marcus from Autumn Woods. I haven't seen you in a while, and I was…" She paused again, uncertain if she even had the right Claire Stanton. "A-are you sure you're okay? You just don't sound…"

Claire's voice grew louder. "Fine. Didn't I just tell you I was fine?" So that was the way this game was played. She was not just going to be chastised by her mother, but now the nursing home administrator was calling to drag her over the coals for not visiting her mother as well. "Is there something you wanted, or did you just call to harass me?" The rudeness of her voice scraped like fingernails on a chalkboard, even to her own ears; rudeness had never reared its ugly head before her life fell apart, but now it was part of who she was. This Claire, the one who just barked into the telephone, was the person she had *never* wanted to become—her father.

"Well, yes, actually; I'm afraid I have some bad news. We transferred your mother to the hospital. It doesn't look good."

Claire threw the covers off and slid to the edge of the bed. A sharp electric current buzzed through every nerve in her body, pushing out the hopeless feeling that had filled her just seconds before. She pressed the phone tighter to her ear, needing to hear every word Linda said—every pause, every sigh that might tell part of the story.

"Oh, my God, Linda! What happened?" The tone of her voice was kinder but filled with panic.

"Like I said, it's not good news. We found her on the

floor of her room this morning. She was unconscious. I think you should get to the hospital as soon as possible. I'll meet you there."

She heard Linda draw a sharp breath. "Mrs. Stanton, I think you should know—I've also called Father Bill."

Claire dropped the receiver. The administrator's last sentence cut clear through her and she doubled over in agonizing pain. It truly was the end.

Pulling herself together, Claire raced through the shower, winding her wet hair into a knot at the nape of her neck. She rifled through her closet in search of something clean to wear amidst the overflowing baskets of laundry. She threw on a pair of faded jeans and a light blue blouse. She pulled a black belt through the loops and tightened it two notches tighter than she ever had. She hit her cheeks with a spot of blush and wiped a slur of lipstick across her lips. She ran her toothbrush around her mouth and shoved in a piece of gum. The clock in the foyer read *11:22*. Less than twenty minutes since the call that brought her back into the world.

She pressed speed dial on her cell phone and waited impatiently.

"Karen!" Her voice trembled as her friend answered the call. "They took my mom to the hospital…"

"Claire, just go. I've got it covered."

"I love you!" Claire's words were nearly lost amidst a sob.

"Love you too, Claire. Call when you can."

***

The sanitized hospital smells nearly overpowered Claire as she raced through the double glass doors; she leaned against one wall to steady herself. Linda met her in the entry. She grabbed Claire's arm and supported her as she led the way to the ICU. Few words were spoken between the women as they took the elevator to the third floor. There was nothing left to say—nothing left to do but pray.

As they approached the room, Claire peeked through the window into Room 313. A small, child-sized shape lay tucked into the bed. Linda held the door open and ushered Claire into the room. Once inside, she was met by a cacophony of noises.

The machines beeped, hummed, and flashed numbers and symbols that were beyond her comprehension. Settling her eyes on her mother, Claire began to cry. Tess looked so frail, so tiny in the narrow hospital bed. *When had this happened? When had she grown so pale?* She seemed lost beneath the covers. Her skin blended in with the white sheets, and she looked like a ghost—living half in this world and half the next.

Claire drew in a shaky breath. The ICU smells were stronger than those in the entry. Here it reeked of death—buried beneath a layer of bleach.

Slowly, she turned toward Linda; the woman pulled her into her arms.

"Mrs. Stanton..."

"Claire. Please call me Claire."

"Claire," Linda said tentatively, "your mother fought a good fight. But..." she paused before stating the obvious, "sometimes the hardest thing to do is say goodbye."

"But I-I don't know if I'm r-ready." A sob shuddered through her as she let Linda hold her the way her mother had always done.

Finally, stepping away from the woman, she leaned over the railing of her mother's bed and placed a tender kiss on her forehead. "Oh, Mom. I'm so sorry," she whispered. She waited as she watched her mother's face, willed her to open her eyes and acknowledge her presence—but for all her wishing, she got nothing. Claire picked up Tess's hand and stroked it with her thumb. Her hands felt so soft, softer than she remembered.

Unnoticed, Father Bill quietly slipped into the room, stopping, first, to speak with Linda. Claire, lost in her own thoughts, jumped as he laid his bear-sized hand on her shoulder. As she turned, he opened his arms and she fell against the softness of his chest.

"Claire," he whispered as he patted her on the back. "It's hard. It's always going to be hard. But, truly, it's for the best. She's not going to have to suffer any longer."

Her words stuck behind the giant lump that had grown in her throat. "I know she'll be so much better off, but I just don't know if *I'm* ready."

Father Bill continued to hold her. "I know, Claire," he

said, tipping his head sideways toward the bed, "but I think *she* is."

As the priest performed her mother's last rites, Claire lost focus. Instead, she read the numbers on each machine, making mental notes of where they were now so she would know if they increased or decreased. The sound of the priest's voice and the whooshing and beeping of the machines mesmerized her, and she floated in and out of memories of the past.

After everyone left, Claire pulled the blue vinyl recliner as close to her mother's bed as possible. Through the side rails on the bed, she continued to stroke her mother's hand and arm. *Please, God, let me be able to tell her I love her just one more time*, she begged silently. *Just once more.* But the afternoon passed without so much as even the tiniest movement from Tess—even as nurses came in and out of the room reading numbers, taking her blood pressure, and listening to her heart.

***

Still sitting at the side of her mother's bed, Claire fell into a fitful sleep. She jumped when Dr. Reinhold finally spoke. "Good evening, Claire," he said as he jotted down information on his clipboard. Finally, he listened to Tess's heart before tucking his stethoscope around his neck.

Claire took the clipboard from his hand and stared at it; the numbers blurred together in an overload of information, but determined to understand, she tried again. She asked her family doctor question after question. *What does it mean if this number drops? What should her oxygen level be? What is being recorded by this machine?* She wanted to understand everything that was happening, keep track so she would know when the end was imminent.

She handed the clipboard back to him as she stared at her mom. "Can she hear me when I talk to her?" Her voice was hushed—almost childlike. She felt helpless watching her mother fade away. Words were all she had to give.

Dr. Reinhold sighed. "Well, personally, I think so. I believe your mother knows you're here, Claire. She may not know exactly what you're saying, but she can feel your presence. I think she knows when you touch her hand or when you sit next to her."

Dr. Reinhold watched as Claire picked up Tess's hand, gently rubbing it the way she had when she first arrived.

"The rest of the medical community would agree. They've run tests on people in comas. In nearly every case, brain activity increased when people in comas were spoken to or touched by someone they loved." That little piece of information gave Claire a surge of hope and she sat a bit taller. "I believe they *want* to respond, but they're trapped in a world halfway between ours and eternity—not so unlike Alzheimer's," he said. He folded his arms as he stared down at the glossy floor. He finally laid a hand on Claire's upper arm, over the long scar that lay beneath her blouse. "Your mom's still here—for now. Focus on that."

Dr. Reinhold turned away, again jotting notes on Tess's chart, recording anecdotal information from his visit. Claire watched the doctor and her mother alternately. Again, she prayed for a sign from her mother. She also prayed Dr. Reinhold was right—that Tess could hear her.

Finally, dropping the clipboard into the slot at the end of the bed, Dr. Reinhold pulled a folding chair toward Claire's. He positioned himself directly in front of her, touching his knees to hers. He bent forward, resting his elbows on his knees as he reached out and took her hands. "Claire, your mother doesn't have a lot of time. It could be hours or days. I don't know. I wish I had all the answers, but I don't. I'd have to be less than honest if I didn't tell you the best medicine you could offer your mother right now is prayer. Keep praying. And keep talking to her." Claire looked at her mother before turning back to Dr. Reinhold. "But, Claire, when you're ready, you have to tell her it's okay to let go."

Dr. Reinhold laid a hand on Claire's cheek before he left the room; she felt the warmth of his touch long after he was gone.

As she listened to the machines, she watched her mother's face. She rocked back and forth. Her mother looked as if she had become smaller in just the handful of hours Claire had been with her, but she also looked at peace. Her skin was pale, almost translucent. It was the color of death—as Claire imagined it to be. But somehow it did not feel sad.

Claire lowered the railing on the side of Tess's bed and crawled in beside her mom. She snuggled against her, nestling as close to her as she could—just as she had done as a child. *Mom, are you here? Are you listening?* she thought.

Claire closed her eyes and collected the words she needed to say, drawing the strength to let her mother go. "Mom, I love you! I've always loved you. You were strong when I couldn't be; you were strong enough for both of us. And after my father died, you taught me how to live, how to love again. You gave me hope—something I never imagined I could ever have."

Tears stung her eyes as they rolled across her cheek and dropped onto Tess's shoulder. She took another breath and waited for the words to completely form. "Oh, Mom, we didn't always have an easy life. We suffered so much, but you never gave up. You never lost faith that there was something better for us."

Claire tenderly laid an arm across Tess's chest. Her mother had never lost faith, but where was Claire's faith? Where was her faith that summer would follow spring—that happiness would follow sadness—that good times would eventually follow the spiral she had been experiencing.

She closed her eyes again and her mother appeared before her, floating between the light and the darkness. The image felt so real that Claire reached out to touch it. But the picture suddenly faded as her mother aged. Tess, tired and old, still floated in front of Claire. The edges became fuzzy; the image darkened until only a stark blackness remained.

Her voice cracked as she opened her eyes and brushed her mom's cheek. "It's okay to let go, Mom. It's okay to go home. I'll always have you in my memories. That way, you won't really be gone."

Her voice wavered. She waited for the lump in her throat to quit aching. "I love you, Mom. I always have. I always will," she repeated. Claire laid her hand over Tess's heart, hoping her mother could feel her love. Even through all the pain and sadness, Claire felt a tiny piece of joy—of peace.

She wiped her tears on the edge of the bedsheet and

snuggled even closer to Tess. As impossible as it had seemed when the doctor and others had told her to let her mom go, she knew she had to; it did not seem fair to pray for her mother to stay any longer.

Claire laid her head on her mom's shoulder, again, feeling the woman's warmth against her skin. She tenderly placed Tess's hand against her cheek, the way her mother had done a million times before. Claire listened and waited. She waited for a sign that the end had come, that her mother had gone home, but the machine's steady beeps continued their rhythmic song. Tess's chest rose and fell amidst the symphony of sounds. The repetition of the machines lulled Claire into a peaceful dream.

"Mary Claire! Mary Claire! I'm here. I always will be. You were always my precious girl. It was you who saved me, not the other way around.

"Please don't suffer because of the past. Your family needs you. Pay attention to their hearts; pay attention to your own. Let people in; let them see the real Mary Claire—imperfections and all.

"And don't be sad for me, be happy. I'm going home. Wanda is here; she is going to take me with her. Goodbye, sweet girl. I'll love you for all of eternity. Someday, we will be together again."

Claire's eyes snapped open as her mother's voice faded into nothingness. The room was dark except for a small light that seeped in through the window that led to the hallway. The shadows were frozen in place, nothing moved.

The machines told her Tess was gone; she had been released from the prison that had held her captive for a lifetime of misery.

She lifted herself onto one elbow, still holding her mother's hand in her own. Sixty-three years of warmth had suddenly gone cold. The softness of Tess's hand was growing waxy and stiff. Her mother was no more.

Claire smiled thinly. Her heart felt as if it had been torn in half, and yet, she was happy.

She wagged a few fingers in the air, one final wave before laying her hand in her lap. She let her mother go.

Claire could barely whisper, but she knew her mom would hear what was in her heart. The words she spoke floated outward, through a sob. "I love you, Mom."

And in the stillness of the room, Claire heard her mother whisper, *"I love you too, Mary Claire. I always will."*

CHAPTER 17

Claire forced herself to keep moving. She could barely remain upright; yet she knew if she stopped, the darkest moments of her life would sneak back in and pull her under in a riptide of emotions. So, she kept them at bay—would not allow herself to feel anything. The funeral arrangements consumed her every waking moment. Meetings with Father Bill, the funeral director, florist, musicians, and caterer had become her final duties as a daughter. She knew she didn't need to do any of it; it could all be done by the people at the funeral home, but she wanted to—needed to—and she had to do it alone.

Checking the car's clock, Claire cut across two lanes of traffic before pulling into the turn lane that headed into the mall. In front of Bloomingdale's, she impatiently waited for a small black convertible to back out of a parking spot close to the door. Forty-five minutes was all she had between appointments—leaving her no more than thirty minutes to find something acceptable for Henry and Jade to wear to the funeral.

Henry was easy. She nabbed a white dress shirt off a carousel rack and a pair of tan slacks from a wooden display table—both in size 6. Next, she pulled a striped tan and navy tie from a small selection of children's ties. It had been less than two months since she bought him new dress shoes, so, unless his feet had exploded in the past few weeks, her son was covered.

Jade, on the other hand, was not as simple. Anything Claire picked out would be *lame*—in her daughter's words. She searched through several racks in the Juniors Department before finding a black sleeveless dress with an asymmetrical white layered ruffle around the waist. She grabbed a short, thin black sweater off a table near the dresses and held the two together. Resigning herself to the fact that time was running short, she decided the outfit would have to do and would not make Jade look like a twelve-year-old hooker like so many of the other outfits.

Claire dug through a mass of dresses before she found a size one. With her arms overloaded, she raced to the shoe department and grabbed a pair of black patent leather slip-on sandals with a two-inch heel from a round table. She dropped the armload of clothes onto a brown and orange patterned chair and waved the shoe toward a lethargic middle-aged clerk, calling out the size from two displays away. When he returned, she did not wait for his help but instead grabbed the box and slipped on one of the shoes. She peeked at the shoe in a low placed mirror and quickly tossed it back into the box. "I'll take these," she called over her shoulder. If they fit her, they would fit Jade.

With her arms again loaded down, Claire rushed toward the checkout but made a quick detour across the aisle when she spotted a small silver butterfly necklace. Her mother had always loved butterflies. Over the years, Jade had given her grandmother an assortment of butterflies that could fill an entire dresser: jewelry, clothing, stuffed toys, and even a large orange and black Monarch that hung from the ceiling of Tess's room. Her mother had always told Jade that if she could come back as anything, it would be a butterfly; they were free to go anywhere they wished. Claire picked up the box between her free thumb and little finger—holding on tightly to keep it balanced amidst the precarious stack she carried as she wove her way to the checkout.

As she plopped into her car, Claire picked up a pen and a small yellow pad of paper and checked *clothing* off the list she had created before dawn. *Five minutes to spare.*

She pressed the speed dial button for Michael's cell as she pulled out of the lot.

"Hi, Hon. How ya doin'?" Michael asked, his voice filled with concern.

"I'm okay—all things considered. How's it going on your end?"

"I'm trying to wrap things up here as quickly as I can, but nothing's moving as fast as I had hoped. I *will* get out of here before three; I promise—come hell or high water."

Claire laughed. "Do what you need to do, Michael," she said as she shifted into park. "Hon, I need to go, though. I just pulled into the florist's, and I—"

"Great! Ditched by a bunch of *pansies*—guess that makes me a true *wallflower*," Michael teased.

"Ohhhh! Boo! Hiss! I have to go before you tell any more of your stupid flower jokes. Later," Claire called into the phone.

"Love you," Michael said, but his wife was already gone.

***

Claire pulled into the Reeves' driveway to drop off the outfits for Jade and Henry. Since Tess's death, Karen had seamlessly stepped into Claire's shoes—caring for the children—even housing them for a few days to make life easier for her best friend. Jade and Henry had both fought the arrangement but had finally conceded. Henry promised Claire they would be on their best behavior, but Jade said nothing at all. She could not deal with Jade's attitude, at least not until after the funeral. Then, she knew, they would have to find a way to create common ground between the two of them. Until then, she did not have the time or energy to commit to anything except her mother's celebration of life.

With two Bloomingdale's shopping bags hanging from one arm, Claire pressed the lever on the Reeves' front door and let herself into the house. True friends did not knock—and friends as close as the Reeves and the Stantons were really more like family.

Claire could hear Karen in the laundry room, moving clothes from the washer to the dryer—likely laundry that belonged to Henry and Jade.

"Hi, Karen. It's me," she called out.

"Hey, Claire. I just made some iced tea. Throw some ice into a couple of glasses and I'll meet you on the screened porch. I'll just be a minute." Karen's voice was muffled by the kitchen and laundry room walls.

Claire did as she was told; she loaded a tray with ice-filled glasses and the pitcher of iced tea.

"You aren't washing Henry's and Jade's clothes, are

you? I can do that," she called from the kitchen. "They shouldn't have that many; it's only been a couple of days,"

"No big deal—I just threw them in with our stuff." Karen repositioned a bobby pin in her hair as she walked into the kitchen. She looked tired and worn, but she still tossed a weak smile at Claire. "But maybe, just maybe, you could teach your children to use a laundry basket." Both women laughed.

"Yeah, well, good luck with that. I've threatened to throw away anything that doesn't make it into the basket—and still—nothing changes."

"Two days. They've been here two days, my friend, and half of Henry's clothes were under the bed—some clean and some dirty."

Claire shrugged. "No surprise there. *Those* genes came from his father." Again, she chuckled.

Carrying the tray out to the porch, Claire set it on a low, round, slate-topped table and filled the glasses nearly to the rim as Karen cut a lemon and brought the slices out in a small red bowl.

"So, how are you? I mean, really?" Karen asked.

"Well, yesterday was hard, but today's better." Claire sipped her iced tea. "I think that's the way it's going to be. Each day will get a little bit better. Today's the first time I've laughed since she died—actually longer, really."

Karen did not have words to make Claire feel better, so she pulled her into a hug and held on tightly before letting go.

Creatures of habit, Claire plopped into the chair on the left and sighed. "I'll always miss her. It's just that, well, growing up, Mom and I, we really only had each other."

Karen tipped her head, somewhat confused by the comment. "I thought your dad was alive when you were young."

The truth, the whole truth was there, on the tip of her tongue, but she wouldn't let it escape—couldn't even tell her best friend. "Well, *he* was why we needed each other." Claire stared up at the ceiling as she rested her head on the back of the overstuffed chair.

Karen knew better than to pry. Friends or not, there were some things that were told in their own time—when the teller was ready; it was not her place to push.

"Anyway, the past is the past. Tell me; how's it going over here with my hormonally adrift daughter and my suddenly independent son?"

Karen's eyes grew large as she arched her eyebrows. "You weren't kidding when you said Jade was up and down and all over the place. That girl bounces from one emotion to the next with the ferocity of a tornado." Karen smiled. "Honestly, the kids are fine. Jade's definitely made the change into adolescence, though."

"I told you, didn't I? Do you remember being like that as a teenager?" Claire asked.

Karen drew a long sip of iced tea. "I'm afraid what I remember and how I really acted may be as different as night and day. In my mind, I was the perfect child, but you'd have had to ask my mom how I really was. But since she's gone, I'll just go with the whole perfect thing. How about you? Were you the emotional rollercoaster your daughter is?"

"Hmmm, honestly? No. I mean, I probably could have been, but my mother had been through so much by that point, I didn't dare cause her any more grief. Jade, though, she doesn't seem to care how much pain she causes any of us."

Karen suddenly stood and walked to the far side of the screen porch; her lips pinched tightly together. She stared into the distance. "Claire, I don't think—well, I have something I think you need to know."

"Okay?" Claire asked rather than responded as she moved toward Karen.

Karen set her iced tea on the table, catching the edge of the tray. She watched it slosh over the top, making miniature puddles on both sides of the glass. "I think there might be more to Jade's emotional rollercoaster than we know about."

"More? What do you mean?"

Karen rubbed her ice-cold hands together, unsure whether it was to warm them or help calm her nerves. She wrapped her arm over Claire's shoulder and steered her back to her chair, then she knelt on the decking in front of her. "Well," she said, searching for the sequence of words she had spent the morning putting together. "Last night, I went to pick Jade up at soccer practice, but there was that huge fire up near the elementary. You heard about that, right?"

Claire nodded; you would have to live in a bubble to not know about the fire. "Go on," Claire urged, her stomach already doing flip-flops.

"The police were redirecting traffic, so I was about twenty minutes late picking up Jade." Karen's story sounded rote—as if she was reading it.

Déjà vu! Claire could feel panic set in as she scooted to the front edge of the chair. She placed her tea on the table and balled her hands into fists before tucking them under her thighs. "G-go on," she said again—unsure as to whether she really wanted to hear the rest of the story.

Like the lines of a play, Karen took her cue from Claire and began again. "Well, there were lots of people around when I got there, but I couldn't find Jade anywhere. I finally went into the office to see if they could page her, but the office staff was already gone." Karen hung her head and blew out a long breath. "I could tell Mr. Ryan was in his office, so I knocked lightly on his door. When he did not respond, I pushed it open." She closed her eyes and tipped her head back before turning toward her friend. "Claire, Jade *was* in Will's office, and she was crying. She was sitting in a chair in the corner of his room." Again, Karen blew out a long breath.

"Just tell me!" Claire blurted. The sweat beaded along her hairline as she relived the same scene from weeks earlier.

"Well, Will was on the ground, kneeling in front of her. His hand was in her lap, and it didn't..."

"That son-of-a-bitch!" Claire cried as she jumped up, bumping the table and knocking her iced tea to the floor. "That no-good son-of-a-bitch! I knew it! I knew he was bad news!" Her right fist repeatedly pounded into her left hand as she blasted off a long list of expletives to describe the man who seemed to be cut from the same cloth as Roy and her father.

Karen wrapped her arms around her inconsolable friend. "Claire, I'm so sorry! I should have left..."

Claire squirmed out of Karen's hold and ran from the room, heading through the kitchen, toward the bathroom not more than fifteen steps from the porch. There she emptied the contents of her stomach into the ceramic bowl while Karen held her hair away from her face—continuing to apologize.

Grabbing the hand towel from the hook, Claire dropped back against the wall of the bathroom, settling herself next to Karen. In silence, the two sat side by side, knees pulled tightly to their chests, for what felt like an eternity. Then, finally, there, in the safety of the deep, red-colored bathroom, Claire shared her story—bits and pieces—not the whole truth—not about Roy or her father or her past, but about her faults as a mother and her suspicion of Will Ryan.

CHAPTER 18

The clock read 2:47 a.m. and Claire had not yet been to sleep. Once again, she pulled the covers, only to toss them off seconds later. She missed Michael's constant presence. He was so consumed with Senator Prescott's case, that even when he was home for short periods of time, he often slept in the den—not wanting to wake her with his early departures.

Her thoughts tumbled in all directions: her mother, Jade, Will—each one clamored for her attention. Her anxiety spun out of control, moving faster and faster until she became nauseous, fighting to keep last night's dinner from reappearing.

Claire finally rolled onto her stomach and lay spread-eagle across the king-sized bed, kicking her foot in time to a beat that played only inside her head, but after less than a minute, she rolled onto her side and pressed her knees toward her chest, locking them tightly in place with her arms. Everything quieted for a few moments as she silenced her mind, saw only the murky color of nothingness. But within seconds, from that tiny spot in the middle of her giant bed, something began to take shape. She could not name it at first, but it felt familiar—like something from long ago. It was just a speck of a thought at first, increasing in size until each of its long single threads wound together into a full-blown plan that played out over and over in her mind—each time changing just enough to add a new layer of—*revenge.*

Just before dawn, Claire walked through her plan one final time. Will would not expect it from her—would not expect the wrath Claire was capable of.

She took a deep breath and held it until her lungs burned, then she released it as slowly as she had drawn it in. With one arm tucked beneath her pillow, she allowed her mind to wander outside of her plan—to her mother's funeral.

Yesterday, her family had taken their place in the front pew of the church, tucked neatly together like pieces of a puzzle, arms locked for support. At some point, Claire took her eyes off the casket and glanced at her perfect family. Not like the O'Briens her father had portrayed back in Manchester. Back then, their lives had been a tangled fabrication. Appearances were deceiving. The family he portrayed had been deceptively dangerous—treacherous to those within.

"Sometimes in our lives, we're so focused on following one path…" Father Bill looked directly at Claire, "that we miss out on all the other roads that might take us someplace better."

Claire carefully wiped her tears with a twisted tissue. Tiny pieces littered her lap and she brushed them to the floor with a sweep of her hand. *Are there better roads? Am I on the wrong one? Am I headed in the wrong direction?*

She glanced over at Jade and her heart skipped a beat. The road she was pushing them down wasn't the perfect path at all. They *weren't* the perfect family they portrayed either. Her husband had spent almost no time at home in the past month, and because of her stupidity, Jade had been fragmented into a million little pieces.

Each moment that passed brought new struggles for the people she loved: Jade's internal self-destruction, Henry's loss of his sister's attention, her own pain of letting go of her mother and her children, Michael's job eating away their family time— and of course, the internal struggle with her plan for Will Ryan.

Vindictiveness had not been a part of Claire's life since before her father died, but since her dark visit to Roy, she struggled to drive out the malevolent thoughts that haunted her on a daily basis. She had wanted to destroy Roy, but she wanted to ruin Will even more. He had chosen the wrong person to tangle with—no one got between a mama bear and her cubs— no one.

Michael had not been apprised of Will's transgressions. As far as Claire was concerned, this was *her* battle to fight— no, *her war to win.* In the past week, she had finally regained some of the control she had let slip through her fingers, and no matter what Father Bill said about taking new roads, Claire refused to turn back. She felt her hands tighten as she gripped an imaginary steering wheel, following the curves of the road she had put Jade on. She needed to protect her daughter—not

Michael's daughter—*her* daughter, from the man who was no better than the men who had destroyed her own childhood.

***

Early the next morning, Claire showered and pulled her hair into a tight ponytail. She slipped on a pair of denim capris and a white lacy tank top. Then she pulled a pale green blouse from the closet and hastily punched her arms through the sleeves.

She set the day in motion by waking Henry and helping him get ready for school. PBS entertained her son as he ate his breakfast. His fork made loopty-loops in the air as he giggled over the antics of whatever show was on.

As an appeal for money burst onto the screen, her son asked, "Whe's Wade?"

"Henry, don't talk with food in your mouth." Claire gave him her mom look and watched his little shoulders sag in disappointment.

"Thorry," he said. A pinkish drizzle of strawberry cereal slid out of one corner of his mouth. He took a swallow of skim milk, then wiped the back of his hand across his mouth and onto his shorts, and asked again, "Where is she? She's s'pposed to eat breakfast with me. She never misses this show."

Claire slipped a small water bottle and several plastic storage bags containing food—a turkey sandwich, celery and carrot sticks, and a juice box—into a brown paper bag and wrote Henry's name in large block letters across the front. She drew two eyes and a thin curved line of a mouth below it. "Well, hon…your sister isn't going to school today."

"How come? Can I stay home too?" He excitedly bounced up and down on the stool.

Claire ruffled his sandy-blonde hair. "Sorry, bud. Jade and I have something we need to take care of."

"No fair!" he whined as he crossed his arms and clapped them down across his chest. "I don't wanna go to school if she gets to stay home."

Claire leaned across the counter, leveling her eyes with her son's. "You're right, Henry; it's not fair." She tipped her head to the side and gave him a little wink. "But it's also not fair that you get to go on an all-day field trip to the zoo and Jade

126

doesn't."

Slowly, the message registered. "Oh, yeah! I f'got!" Henry jumped down from his stool and pumped his arms into the air. He danced and hooted, even hip-butted Claire just above her knee. She grabbed onto the edge of the counter to keep from falling. Suddenly, he stopped. He threw his arms out to the sides. "Well, let's go, Mom. What are we waiting for?"

Claire laughed. "You go brush your teeth. I've got to get some things from the garage." She watched as her son ran up the stairs, sliding a hand along one wall just as she had done when she was younger. *Oh, Henry. Wouldn't it be nice if all our problems could be fixed that easily?* she thought. Then she turned and headed into the garage.

***

Claire stacked three large cardboard boxes in the back of her Lexus. From a wooden workbench drawer, she grabbed a long red and white nylon rope and a pair of leather work gloves. She stood on a stool and snagged a new blue tarp off a high shelf. Finally, she pulled a shovel from the tool barrel, measured the weight in her hand, then exchanged it for a heavier one. She slid the shovel underneath the boxes, hiding the metal scoop beneath the seat. The rope, the gloves, and the tarp, she hid inside the smallest box, tossing two paper grocery bags on top. She interlocked the flaps to close the top. Wiping her hands on the back of her capris, Claire scanned the garage, studying the items on the shelves before pressing the button and watching the tailgate close—hiding her cache. Then she walked back into the house.

"Henry," she called, sticking her head through the kitchen doorway, "are you ready?"

"Roar!" Two claw-shaped hands shot out from one of the wooden cubbies. Claire stumbled backward as Henry jumped toward her. "I'm the King of the Jungle!" Henry yelled as he jerked the door open and raced into the garage. "Come on, Mom. We don't want to miss the trip!"

Her heart was racing when she pulled out of the driveway—but she did not think it had anything to do with the sudden appearance of *the King of the Jungle.*

***

When she returned, Claire parked in the driveway rather than the garage. She pulled several dead flowers off the plants on her way to the front door. *If only getting rid of people was that easy,* she thought. The key turned in the lock without a sound, and she closed the door behind her in the same way.

As she turned the corner at the top of the stairs, Claire noticed the door to Jade's room was still closed. She understood better than anyone the meaning behind a closed door— protection. She did not even try the door handle; she knew it would be locked. She plucked a long, thin piece of metal from above the door frame and poked it into the small, round hole. The lock clicked as she pressed on the lever and tried to push the door open, but it wouldn't budge. Something had been jammed against it, holding it closed. Claire pressed her shoulder against the wood, putting all her weight into the task. The door opened just wide enough for her to squeeze through. As she did, her daughter's desk chair, loaded with a stack of books, tipped into the wall, sending the books tumbling to the floor.

Jade screamed. Even in the dark, Claire could tell she was petrified.

Claire reached for her, but Jade slid to the far side of the queen-sized bed and jerked the covers over her head.

"Hon, it's me." Claire touched her daughter's back through the thick covers.

The room was unusually dark for 8:37 in the morning. The only light in the large space came from a small night light plugged into an outlet under Jade's desk. A heavy quilt Tess had made years before had been thrown over the curtain rod, blocking out the morning light.

"Jade, please talk to me," Claire begged, her voice quivering.

"Go away! Leave me alone!" Jade snarled through gritted teeth. She slapped at her mother's hand from beneath the covers and moved as close to the far edge of the bed as she dared.

The stagnant, sweaty aroma nearly made Claire cough. "Jade, you have to talk to me. Tell me what's going on." She waited for her daughter to say something, but Jade remained silent. "Please, honey." She swallowed hard before adding,

"Did something happen with Mr. Ryan?" Claire leaned closer, hoping Jade would say something, anything, but there was only silence. Even with no words, she knew the truth—her daughter's silence told her everything she needed to know. Anger roiled inside of her, and she was afraid to move; she wanted to save that anger for Will.

From the edge of her daughter's bed, Claire worked her way through the plan again—step by step until it almost became a reality. *I'm doing this for you, Jade,* she thought.

"I said, go away!" Jade bellowed, drawing her mother away from her thoughts. Claire saw just the back of her daughter's head as it popped back under the covers.

She slowly stood; the anger inside her spun itself into a hurricane of rage. "Alright, Jade. But this isn't over. I will fix it."

She pushed her way past the pile of fallen books and the tipped chair, silently moving down the stairs and out the front door.

Will Ryan would pay for turning her daughter into a frightened, angry little girl. He would get what was coming to him.

But there was one stop she had to make first.

CHAPTER 19

Autumn Woods held ghosts of her mother. Everywhere Claire looked, she caught glimpses of Tess: the back of a woman turning a corner in a wheelchair, an old man struggling to turn on his TV, a red and yellow patchwork quilt folded across the end of a bed in a random room. Memories flooded the hallways and poured into Tess's room as Claire moved closer.

She touched the room placard: 210—her mother's room. She traced the numbers with the tip of her index finger, committing to memory the deep cuts in the brown and white fake woodgrain sign.

Finally, she stepped into the room and dropped two empty boxes on the bed. The room had grown cold and lonely in the past few days. Claire flipped on the overhead switch, but the bright light was too harsh and illuminated her mother's absence more than she could bear. She blinked several times before snapping it off and turning on the bedside lamp instead. The softer glow danced across the brightly colored quilt as the loose shade shifted from side to side.

Claire stood in the middle of the tiny space that had been her mother's home for the past three years: a nine-foot by twelve-foot tiled area—three pale blue walls and a thin cream-colored curtain defined her room. That curtain served as the dividing line, separating Tess from a long line of residents who had come and gone during her time there. A twin bed with a bookcase headboard, a tall built-in dresser, and a small matching nightstand were the only pieces of furniture the home provided. Claire and Michael had bought Tess a tan leather recliner when she moved in, but there was little room for anything else.

Claire tucked her legs beneath her as she curled up in the recliner. She tugged her mother's quilt off the bed and pulled it over her lap, taking in the view of the room from Tess's perspective. The view did not make Claire sad, but it didn't bring her joy either. She felt nothing at all. From this vantage point, she finally understood what her mother saw—*the end*. Tess had spent the last three years sitting in this chair waiting for the end to come—and it finally had.

Claire felt the sting of tears grow and she wiped them away with the corner of the quilt. Tess's scent still lingered on the fabric. She pulled it to her face, gently rubbing it against her cheek the way her children had done with their own blankets when they were toddlers.

The perfumed smell bogged down her memories with a stream of *What ifs*. What if her mother had not gotten Alzheimer's? What if Claire had told Tess about Roy from the very beginning? What if her father had not been so controlling and abusive? What if they had stood up to him? What if she had been around to help protect her own daughter? *What if? What if? What if?* Claire knew she could play this game all day long, but it would change nothing.

The boxes waited on the bed. With a drawn-out sigh, Claire checked her watch and began packing her mother's belongings.

The quilt, carefully folded to fit into the bottom of the larger box, was the first thing she packed. Claire smoothed out the wrinkles as she placed it inside. Next, she opened each drawer, neatly folding and stacking items to be donated. She carefully placed pictures and personal items into the smaller of the two boxes. Breakable items, she wrapped in pastel tissue paper. She was careful to hold her memories at bay, to keep them from crashing into the task at hand, making it harder than it already was.

When the dresser was empty, Claire attacked the closet. Claire looked at the clock. She felt a growing sense of urgency to get the packing done—to get back to the task of dealing with Will Ryan.

The closet emptied quickly. Nightgowns, sweaters, and shoes all went into the donation pile. Undergarments were tossed into the trash can. Little was worth keeping except for a few photos and cards that had been tucked into a robe or jacket pocket.

Claire rubbed her lower back as she worked out the kink

that had grown there. She backed out of the closet and into the corner of the nightstand. She winced as she rubbed her hip, but it wasn't the bruise that had already begun to form that bothered Claire; it was what was in those drawers. They would be the hardest to pack. They held all of the things Tess had saved over the years: cards and mementos—things that held special memories for Claire too.

Tears fell as she opened the top drawer, but she forced herself to keep moving. She carefully removed each item. She had not meant to take so much time, but instead of throwing them into the box, she found herself sorting everything into piles: cards, letters, newspaper clippings, photographs. Once she had everything from the top drawer sorted, she placed each pile into the box, gently smoothing it with the palms of her hands, laying a piece of tissue paper between each stack. Then she moved on to the second drawer.

Finally, she knelt and pulled the last drawer open. Because of where the recliner sat, this drawer did not open as far as the others. Methodically, she emptied its contents, just as she had with the other two. As she wiped the inside of the drawer with an old rag, Claire's hand bumped into something she had missed. She pulled a wooden box into the light. The lamp's glare reflected off of the glass top, sending a flood of memories through her. The hairs on the back of her neck stood at attention and goosebumps spread down her arms. She tossed the box onto her mother's bed. Her hands recoiled and she clasped them tightly together as she stared at the old container.

Memories! The box swarmed with them. Not the inside; she didn't even know what it held, but the actual six-sided dark wood structure. It burned through time—dragging her with it. Back in Manchester, the box had been tucked inside one of Tess's dresser drawers—buried beneath heavy sweaters in the second-hand bureau. At eight years old, Claire accidentally discovered it when she retrieved a sweater for her mom. She picked it up and carried it downstairs to ask about it, but her mother grabbed the box and told her to forget she ever saw it— to never mention it to *anyone*. She told her that no matter what, it was off-limits.

The only time she had broken that rule, she had been

beyond sorry. Her mother had been immersed in cleaning. While she was busy, Claire tiptoed into the room and opened it to take a quick peek inside—but her mother knew immediately. Music played; a few haunting bars of a melody escaped. Panicked, she slammed the lid shut, but her mother had heard the tune from downstairs.

"Mary Claire!" she called as she raced up the stairs with a dust rag in her hand, her hair tied up in her usual blue cleaning bandana. "I told you to *never* touch that box. Do you understand me?"

Claire's nod had been so small that her mother had angrily repeated the question.
"I said, do you understand?"

Tears rolled down Claire's cheeks as she stared at the floor; her head moved in a full-fledged nod. It was not that she had broken the rule that made her feel remorseful—it was the way her mother had looked at her, the few words she'd said before she pushed Claire from the room and closed the door behind her. For the first time ever, Claire felt so ashamed, she couldn't even speak.

"I am *so* disappointed in you." Her mother clicked her tongue three times as she stared at her. Claire had never forgotten that sound, and even to this day, she could hear those clicks as if she was still standing outside that bedroom door long ago.

She glanced over her shoulder—toward the door of her mother's room. She waited to hear Tess's voice scold her yet again; she waited for those tongue clicks. But none came.

Cautiously, Claire moved toward the box. She was petrified. Even with the air conditioning on, sweat dripped down her neck. She stripped her blouse off and tossed it onto the chair. She adjusted her tank top as she stared at the box.

What could possibly be in there? What could her mother have kept hidden in the box that was so important she did not even want her own daughter to know? What would she find? Whatever it was—good or bad—Claire knew she owned it now.

She swallowed hard as she felt her heart bang inside her chest, trying to escape. Anxiety was like that for Claire. One minute she was fine; the next she was in a full-blown panic attack that kept her frozen in time. *Stop it, Claire!* she reprimanded herself. *Just breathe!*

For nearly a full minute, Claire counted her breaths, metering them as she drew them in and blew them out again.

The small container bounced ever so slightly as she eased down onto the mattress, fearfully inching her hand closer to the box. Maybe it contained nothing at all—or maybe it contained the answers she had been looking for. She touched it with one finger, and then her thumb. She pulled it toward her, then immediately let go.

A too-small—faded and cracked—black and white photo of her Grandpa and Grandma Hadley, two people she only knew from pictures, had been tucked into the glass frame cover. Their eyes seemed to study Claire as intently as she studied them. Her mother's face floated between her grandparents', making it obvious she was part of each of them.

Claire cautiously lifted the box, but she could not keep from shaking. She twisted the wind-up key on the bottom, but it turned without resistance, and she knew the gears of the music box were stripped. She continued to stare at the dark wood. The intricate carvings on its edges and the curved sides had been burned into her memory, but other than that one time, she had never looked inside; she hadn't dared. Disappointing her mother again would have been devastating.

Her heart raced, sending threads of emotion through her, and she fought the urge to put the box back into the drawer and leave it there, but her curiosity was too strong.

Slowly, she lifted the lid. The golden gears and pins were still, and even though she knew the box was broken, Claire felt disappointment tug at the corners of her mouth.

The room suddenly felt too dark. She needed the light. Leaning off the edge of the bed, Claire flipped on the overhead light. She dropped the cardboard boxes to the floor and smoothed out the sheets around the box.

At the very top of it lay Tess's wedding ring. To anyone else, it was extraordinary—a large, flawless diamond, surrounded by ten smaller ones that had been embedded in the gold band. It was too beautiful for anyone in Manchester, and surely too fancy for a woman who rarely left her house. The ring was just another symbol of prestige; it was a sign her family stood above the other residents of the town. The O'Briens were untouchable. It had been another of her father's ill-fated attempts to make them appear like the perfect family.

The day he died, Tess had removed her ring. It had just disappeared; Claire hadn't asked where it went. She never cared.

Lifting the ring into the light, Claire was tempted to slide it on her finger, but she didn't. The ring had been part of the past—a time in her life when happiness had only been a dream. Nothing on earth meant less to her than this ring, and knowing her mother felt the same, she was surprised she had kept it all these years. Claire knew she would not keep it, and she wouldn't save it for Jade or pawn it off on anyone else she loved. The ring brought only painful memories of her tragic past. No, she planned to lose it—in a parking lot, in a mall, somewhere where it could never be traced back to her. With no past, she was certain it would bring more joy to the finder than it had to her mother.

Claire stared into the box, unsure of what to do next. If it was filled with only memories of her father, she did not want to keep looking. It had taken her years to bury them; she didn't want them thrown back at her all in a single morning.

Snapping the lid shut, Claire bent down and placed it in one of the cardboard boxes. That was it; she was done with the past. But even with her mind made up, she remained on the bed. She was stuck in time somewhere between the past and the present. Sweat beads formed again, and she wiped the back of her neck with her hand.

Time and distance had made her stronger. She had become a better person. Maybe it was because of her father's cruel parenting she had grown into the person she had become—his exact opposite. Maybe the past *did* form the future—you continually went back to it, like a dog-eared page of a book, rereading parts until you understood the author's message as it was written. Maybe the contents of the box would help Claire understand *herself* better. Perhaps it was all a great big puzzle—pieces of her past, snapped together into a picture she could finally understand.

Claire lifted the box back onto her lap and sighed. She was not in control; the memories were.

Gingerly, she opened the lid one more time, but this time, music sang out—just a few single tinny notes. Her heart raced again as she looked around the room. Was her mother sending her a message? Apprehensively, she continued the quest into her mother's past.

A yellowed newspaper clipping had been placed just below the ring—an obituary announcing the deaths of her grandparents—married for an eternity, dying on the same day just hours apart—both from heart failure. Her grandfather's life taken by a heart attack, her grandmother's from a broken heart. When he passed, she had simply lay down and stopped breathing. Claire knew about them from the stories Tess had told her over the years, stories that had become as real as if she had been there.

Other newspaper clippings hinted at family events from her life back in Manchester: a single picture of Claire's first communion, a Brownie Scout photo, and a snapshot of her sitting on the curb during the only Summer Daze parade in town she had ever been allowed to attend. There had never been family photos—at least not until after Edward's death. No one had ever cared enough to snap a lasting memory of her family. The three of them had been kept hidden from the outside world except on rare occasions, and only if the situation necessitated. That had been fine with Claire. Photos marked memories, and the memories of her first ten years weren't meant to be kept.

A faded pink piece of stationery lay directly below the obituary. Claire opened the letter, unfolding it gently into her lap. She carefully pressed the creases flat with the palms of her hands. She recognized her mother's perfect script handwriting immediately, even though it was obvious it had been written decades earlier. When she started reading, the words jumped from the page and Claire choked back a sob.

She held the letter tightly in both hands as she focused on the wavy words that swam across the page. The letter professed love for someone; love so deep, it made Claire feel as if she was eavesdropping on an incredibly private conversation. It started *Dear Cal*. Cal was not her father.

Claire's heart slammed against her chest with an irregular beat. This was beyond her comprehension. Had her mother been having an affair while she was married to her father? Claire scanned the letter, searched for a date that would confirm or dispute that her mother had cheated on Edward. She knew for a fact that Tess had never had a man in her life *after* her father's death; she had sworn off men completely. Because of Edward's abuse, her mother had never trusted another man— she had never been able to love again. Tess had told her as much. But had she been lying? Was that how she had survived—in the arms of another man?

Claire could not blame Tess if she had whittled away her days with someone else; she had been in school and her father was gone each week—hours away from Manchester. Even though she understood it, the thought nearly capsized her. She tried to imagine her mother with someone else, but she could not. Her mom had been devoted to Edward, not out of love, but out of *need* and fear. She had no money, no car, nowhere to go—nothing of her own. Both of Tess's parents had passed, and her sister could barely afford her own life, let alone support Tess and Claire. That was just the way it was back then; it was the way Tess had told her it had to be—no questions asked.

The box was nearly empty. With an unsteady hand, Claire picked up the first of the three items that remained tucked into the bottom of the box. A second yellowed newspaper clipping laid upside down—perfectly cut, not torn as the last one had been. This clipping was worn and wrinkled as if it had been unfolded and refolded repeatedly. It was a second obituary.

Claire read it, then reread it, but it didn't make sense to her. She squeezed her eyes tightly shut, but the small piece of rectangular paper kept floating back into view. Finally, she gave up. She opened her eyes and pulled the newsprint closer, scanning the clipping until she got to the one sentence that took her breath away.

Taylor, Calvin Fredrick
Calvin Fredrick Taylor, 24, Amherst, Colorado, was killed in a

motorcycle accident on October 14, 1975. He is preceded in death by his grandparents, Hans and Dorothy Taylor, William and Mildred McClure, and a sister, Jane. He leaves behind his mother and father, James and Lois Taylor, and his brother, John. He will be forever missed by his beautiful wife Theresa and his precious baby girl, Natalie. Visitation is scheduled for October 17 between 6:30 and 8:00 p.m. at the Larson-Geller Funeral Home. The funeral will be held on October 18 at 11:00 a.m. at St. Francis Catholic Church in Amherst.

He will be forever missed by his beautiful wife Theresa and his precious baby girl, Natalie. Claire stared at that line until it blurred into the rest of the words. Her mother had recently called her Natalie.

Her head felt like it was going to explode; her insides continued to tie themselves into tighter and tighter knots until she could barely breathe. She felt like she had been kicked in the stomach. She could not focus, couldn't understand the message tied to those sixteen simple words. She understood each word separately. It was the meaning of them strung together that got lost.

She repeated it. He would be *missed by his baby girl Natalie.*

Was Cal her father...not Edward? How was that possible? How could that be? She would have been only a year and a half when he died. *Was she Natalie?*

The sky caved in, and the ground dropped from beneath her. Her entire life had been a lie, and Edward was *still* at the helm, orchestrating the whole thing. No, that wasn't fair—not even to the monster that had raised her. Her *mother* had done this; it had been her choice not to tell Claire the truth. For her entire life, she had believed she was the daughter of evil. How could her mother have done this to her? How could she have let her live her life thinking she was genetically connected in any way whatsoever to Edward?

The room spun and it continued to pick up speed. Claire curled into a ball on the bed. She still clung to the tiny news clipping.

She rocked back and forth as this newfound knowledge

gutted her like those poor deer from her childhood. She felt empty—and yet, whole at the same time. The man who had hated her more than anyone could ever imagine was not her father at all. She did not carry the evil gene that had been a part of him. It finally made sense. Edward had hated her for one reason—she did not belong to him. She was not *his* flesh and blood.

She whispered it out loud. "Edward was *not* my father." Then she said it again, this time with conviction. "Edward was *not* my father!" A smile broke free and Claire rolled onto her back, repeating the phrase over and over, releasing herself of nearly four decades of oppression. She tried another thought on for size. "My father's name was Cal. My name is Natalie *Taylor* Stanton." She giggled with the freedom this small piece of knowledge had given her.

No wonder she had felt like nothing more than a stranger to the man she believed was her father. She *was* a stranger. Her entire life had been a lie; an illusion of Edward's. Anger slowly pressed in, pushing out the fleeting moments of joy. She felt like she had been cut in half—Edward's final trick. It made for great entertainment—except to her.

Claire ran her index finger along the front edge of the box. *There was more.* She knew that. *But what?* She pulled the box into the crook of her arm. She lifted her head enough to peek inside, and as she did, she felt her anger burn. Her mother had not told her the truth. Edward had treated them like they were the scum of the earth. Even her real father had died—leaving them to suffer through a life they should never have known. Fury blazed through her as she sat upright. They had all hurt her. How many more lies would she find?

Claire sighed long and loud. With a scoop of her hand, she deposited the box back onto her lap. *Answers or more questions?* she asked herself as she looked inside. She did not know if she could go on, but she did not think she could stop either. She had just lost control over one more part of her life and she felt herself searching for a foothold—but there was none. The memories and the photos that had been locked away inside of her had just been shredded into a million little pieces and thrown to the wind. She was not sure if they could ever be reassembled—and she wasn't sure she even wanted to try.

Two rings lay in the box, tied together with a piece of white ribbon. The first had a tiny diamond chip pressed into a narrow silver band and the other, obviously a man's ring, was just a narrow piece of metal. Claire held the rings in the palm of her hand. The contrast to the ring Edward had given her mother was stark. This set of rings was simple and pure. She untied them and slipped them both on, holding her hand out to admire their simplicity. Compared to the two-carat diamond Michael had given her, the tiny diamond was nearly invisible, but even in her anger, the rings were priceless.

Claire reached back into the box to pull out the last item: a multi-page folded letter. As she lifted it, a photo fell out, landing face down. It was a wallet-size photo, and even without seeing the front, Claire knew whose picture it was. She picked up the photo and held it gingerly between her thumb and finger. Her hand trembled as she tried to read the inscription on the back, but the blue-inked words were faded and smeared and the handwriting was tiny—making it nearly impossible to make out more than a word here or there.

Claire pressed her shoulders back and smoothed the front of her tank top with her free hand. Then she took a quick swipe at the mascara she knew had smeared below her eyes. Even though she knew it wasn't possible, she didn't want her real father to see the mess she had become. She wanted to make a good first impression. No, that wasn't correct. It wasn't a *first* impression; at some point, she had lived with him—he was her father. Knowing it was futile to even attempt, she tried to conjure up a memory of him, but she was left with only memories of Edward and his wickedness.

Gently, Claire turned the picture over, holding it in the palm of her hand. Her breath stopped midstream as her *dad* stared back at her. His eyes were her eyes—large and green. His shaggy sandy blonde hair was the same color as Henry's, and he and Jade shared the same thin lips. She touched his face, traced the outline of his strong jaw.

Staring at the picture of her father, her *real* father, the years fell away, and suddenly, she was a little girl. For the first time she could remember, she was daddy's little girl.

CHAPTER 20

Claire's hands trembled as she turned the paper over. Her name was printed in large block letters on the opposite side. She held the letter to her chest and closed her eyes. *Pandora's box!* she thought. Information had already escaped; more information than she could comprehend, but it was too late to turn back now. She knew what her mother had hidden; what she needed to know was the *why*. There had to be reasons her mother had hidden the truth about her father—both of her fathers—but what?

She set the letter in her lap and stared at her name. The black ink of the letters blurred and turned muddy as her tears fell. She read *Mary Claire*, but in her mind, that was a different person entirely. Since her father's—no, *Edward's* death—she had just been Claire, no longer the little sprite of a girl—always looking over her shoulder—surviving day-to-day. Mary Claire was someone who had disappeared long ago. She read her father's obituary again—*his baby girl, Natalie*. She was not even Claire—she was Natalie.

Staring into her mother's empty chair, she unfolded the letter. The crinkling noise of the crisp pages filled the room. She squeezed the pages tightly together in her trembling hands and focused on her name. The information written below those two words had the potential to destroy her or bring her peace. But she didn't have a choice. She had to know.

After the first sentence, tears started to fall, and she made no attempt to wipe them away.

Mary Claire,

If you're reading this letter, I can only assume I have passed or am in no shape to answer any of your questions. I can also assume you know I have kept things from you. I'm sure you have a million questions. But you need to know that everything I did, I did for you. If I had it to do over, I honestly can't say what I would do. My only goal in life was to make sure you had a roof over your head and food in your stomach.

My mind is failing—even I know that. Everything I worked so hard to protect, I am losing. I wanted so much to protect you, to help you, but I'm afraid I may have hurt you by not telling you the truth sooner. Not that you will understand, or even accept it, but the only thing I have left to give you is the truth.

I wish I could be with you—hold you as you find out what I've kept hidden, but that's impossible. Three months from now, I may not even remember I wrote this letter. I may not even recognize you or Michael or the kids. And that breaks my heart. But…you have a right to know everything.

By now, you know that Edward was not your father. A kind, gentle man named Calvin Taylor was. I loved Cal with everything in me—and he loved me the same way.

We fell in love in high school. It was the kind of love that's supposed to last a lifetime—but it didn't. Your father was killed in a motorcycle accident on his way home from work. A car ran him off the road and sent him down a hill into a river. He died immediately. He never felt any pain, he didn't suffer, and for that, I am grateful.

When I found out, my world collapsed. I lay in bed for days on end, crying for what was—when all the time I was missing what Cal had left me—you, Mary Claire. He left me— you. I saw him in your eyes and in your smile and in the way you tilted your head when you asked a question. He was still there, but it took me weeks to notice.

Honey, your father loved you more than life itself; his little Natalie was the most important person in his life. He would hold you for hours on end. I used to tell him he was spoiling you. He would just laugh and keep right on holding you. The only regret I have is that you weren't old enough to remember him.

We were young when we married—just babies ourselves, really. He was two years older than I was, but he waited for me to finish school. We had almost no money, but it didn't matter. We were so happy, and that was all we needed.

Cal had no life insurance. The bills kept piling up after his death, and I didn't know what to do. I needed a job, but there were no jobs out in the country. The car we owned was literally a heap of junk, so I moved us into town, to a small two-room apartment, above Jake's Bar in Amherst. In exchange for rent, I waited tables, bartended, cleaned the place after it closed—anything to make sure we had a place to live. You spent your days playing in a playpen in the back room of the bar.

We had no one. Families were different back then; they could barely afford to take care of their own. My parents were dirt poor, and Cal's couldn't afford to take us in either. So you and I were on our own—alone, but together.

One day, a man came into the bar: sophisticated, distinguished, and at least ten years older than me. He had money. His suits and his car proved that. But he was a flirt. He bragged about his job and his travels to anyone who would listen. He laughed too loudly and spoke so everyone could hear him. I didn't trust him, so I stayed away.

Almost every week, he would show up at the bar. He talked about his cabin and how he loved to spend his weekends hunting and fishing. He flirted with me the same as he did with all the other women. Then one weekend, he started paying more attention to me. He asked me out—begged me to have dinner with him, to have a drink. He left me huge tips, and because of that, I couldn't afford to alienate him. Finally, I gave in.

When we were alone, I saw a different side of him. He was kind; he opened doors for me; he brought me flowers and gifts; he took me dancing. But I still didn't trust him—so I kept you a secret. I know it was wrong, but I always went out with him after you fell asleep.

Edward proposed to me that July, just nine months after Cal died. You were just two years old at the time. I told him I couldn't give him an answer until I showed him something first. I invited him up to the apartment later that day.

I raced upstairs, cleaned, cooked, and dressed you in a pretty pink outfit I bought at a second-hand store. I couldn't wait for Edward to meet you. You deserved a father, Mary Claire, even if I wasn't ready for a husband.

When he arrived, you were in the back room. He held me, begged me to give him my answer, when you toddled into the room. I watched Edward's face, expecting joy, but instead,

Mary Perrine

I saw anger. He was outraged; he screamed at me. He told me he would never have wasted his time on a whore like me had he known. He called me used goods. Said I didn't deserve him; a man of his means deserved something more than I could ever give.

I pleaded with him to listen. I tried to explain about Cal, but he didn't want to hear any of it. He slammed the door— leaving both of us in tears.

I was a proud person, baby girl. I refused to let Edward's rejection hurt me. I picked up the pieces and went on as if nothing happened. We went back to the life I had built for us. But business slowed, and my hours got cut. I started stealing food from the bar—a hunk of cheese, a ball of hamburger, a bun. Then I started digging through the leftovers customers didn't eat, tucking them into my bag when no one was looking. But Jake found out and put a stop to it. He watched me like a hawk, and I had to find other ways to feed you. Our electricity had been disconnected and the heat was the next to go.

A couple of months later, Edward reappeared. He said he had been hasty in leaving, and he promised to make things work if I married him. I didn't have a choice, Mary Claire. I did it for you. I married Edward for you, my darling.

At the wedding, when I had to say I would love Edward with all my heart— until death do us part, in good times and in bad, in sickness and in health—I froze. I just stood there. I knew I didn't love him, but I believed Edward would take care of us, so I said "I do" before God and the rest of the world. I now realize how big those two small words are.

Edward had no family, at least none he claimed were still alive. He kept his work life and his personal life separate. He sold his cabin and picked a place where he could hunt and fish on the weekend when he was home. That's how we ended up in Manchester.

We settled into a dream life. The house was finer than anything I had ever seen. Our cars were new, our clothing was beautiful, and the jewelry he bought me was overwhelming. We never had to struggle to pay a bill, never had to count pennies at the grocery store. I felt like I was living someone else's life.

And even though I didn't love Edward, I felt I owed him

144

for taking us in. On weekends when he was home, I was the perfect wife. But he came to expect it, more and more all the time, and not just from me—he wanted you to be the perfect daughter too.

You were just a child; he was too hard on you. He expected too much. He disciplined you in ways that were too harsh. I tried to stop him. In the beginning, I think he felt bad about his actions. He tried to be kinder to you, but the older you got, the more he wanted you to be perfect. Soon he became cruel in his punishments.

Edward controlled everything. When he realized how unhappy I was, he took away my car; he was afraid I would take you and run. He isolated us from others. We were only allowed to see or speak with anyone else if he was around. Our only outings were to the grocery store and to church—and even then, he stood so close, I could feel his breath on my neck. I lived in constant fear.

I'm so sorry I picked that life for us, Mary Claire. I would have left, but I couldn't find a way out. Divorce was not an option—he would have taken everything. He had become so hateful that he would have hunted us down like animals. I was afraid. I was afraid he would kill one or both of us. And I couldn't let that happen. So, I stayed.

I don't even know how to tell you what happened next. In some ways, I'm proud of myself, and in other ways, I hate myself for what I did.

The night Roy molested you—I was there. I saw him touch you, hold you down, press his hand across your face so you couldn't scream. I had to cover my own mouth that night to keep from screaming; I turned away. I wanted to save you, but I knew he would turn the story around and make it your fault somehow. Edward would never have listened to me or to you. He would have believed Roy, and he would have beaten you for lying. So, I did nothing—at least not that night. Instead, I waited for the perfect opportunity.

One Saturday afternoon, nearly six months after Roy's last visit, after another of our particularly violent screaming matches. Edward stormed out of the house with a six-pack of beer and headed to the garage. An hour later, he screamed for me to bring him more beer. I set another six-pack on the table and turned to walk out. But I stopped in the doorway. I watched Edward caressing his golf clubs as he cleaned them, paying more attention to them than he did to either of us. I couldn't stand it. I turned back toward the door, and with all my might, I pulled a wooden shelving unit over. A loaded toolbox landed a direct hit on Edward's head. I am not proud to admit this, but it took me all week to unscrew that shelf from the wall. I shoved shims under the back legs, tipping it forward just enough to make it easy to pull over. Then I loaded an old metal toolbox with tools I knew he would not miss.

The police report stated it was an accident, that Edward had pulled it over on himself accidentally, but I knew the truth. The only accident had been marrying him in the first place, making you suffer all those years.

Mary Claire, I'm so sorry I didn't find a way out before that point. Please forgive me. I made peace with God a long time ago, but I need to make peace with you too.

I loved you so much, and Cal loved you even more than that. I can't make up for spending all those years with Edward. I didn't tell you about Cal or Edward before because you had been through enough. With Edward's death, you changed—you were finally happy. The truth would have set you back.

I love you, Mary Claire—my sweet, precious, Natalie; I always will. I beg you to please forgive me for all I've done. Please understand that everything I did, I did for you. There was no other way out. I did it all for you, Mary Claire...all of it.

Mom

"Oh, Mom," Claire whispered through a sob.

Truth! That five-letter word squeezed tightly across her chest. This was all surreal—like it was someone else's life. She could not deal with it—none of it, at least not now.

Claire refolded the letter and tucked it back into the wooden box. She closed the lid and set it in the box on the brightly colored quilt. *Pandora's box* was right—everything had escaped, except hope—but she was not even sure what she hoped for anymore. Her entire life had once again been turned upside down.

***

12:15 p.m. Three hours had passed; it had seemed like just a blip on the clock.

Claire buried the box beneath a stack of unused tissue paper and set the smaller cardboard container inside the larger one. She moved the donation pile to the chair and pulled the sheets off the bed. She carefully folded them and placed them on top of the clothing. It could all go. The box and the few items she had chosen to keep were all that mattered anymore.

With the stacked cardboard boxes in her arms, she took four steps backward toward the door. The room looked surprisingly dark, even with the overhead light now on. It was not the image she wanted to be left with, but it didn't matter. A million pictures swam through her head—this was just another one that would soon disappear.

CHAPTER 21

Claire raced into the driveway at the middle school and abandoned her car in the first open parking spot. Her hands still trembled from the information in her mother's letter. It was too much; things were happening too fast, winding together into a massive ball of barbed wire—stabbing at her senses—her past, Will Ryan, Jade—she had to let something go or she knew she would break. She closed her eyes and let her mind go blank. The only thing she could focus on right now was Jade—saving her daughter; that had to take precedence over everything else—which meant taking Will Ryan down.

She popped the back hatch open and ran her hand along the handle of the shovel to make sure she had not only imagined hiding it there before she left home. She pulled out the last empty box and pressed the button to close the hatch. After pushing the lock button on her keychain until it beeped, she headed up the cracked cement sidewalk toward the front doors of the school—consciously avoiding each one of the cracks as she absently repeated the sing-song chant from her childhood. *Step on a crack, break your mother's back.*

The tiny hairs on the back of her neck tingled as she pulled the heavy glass door open and stepped into the foyer. She glanced over her shoulder, trying to shake the feeling someone was watching her. For the first time ever, she felt like an outsider in the school—like someone was standing behind a one-way mirror, taking in her every move.

After a short discussion with the head custodian, she followed him into the building, through the usually locked doors, and slipped into the commons like she belonged there.

Claire knew the inner workings of Willow Brook Middle School as well as anyone who worked within the system. Until now, the school had chugged along without so much as a hiccup—even with Will Ryan at the helm. Other employees had stepped up and were compensating for his inept leadership. But she knew that even well-oiled machines needed maintenance from time to time. Through her volunteer work, Claire knew every cog of the school and how each one worked together—which ones fit together too snugly, and which ones needed tightening. The single broken piece, about to set the entire school into self-destruction, was Will Ryan.

"Hmmm," Claire snorted quietly. "You are *not* taking this school down with you, Will."

Slinking past the office, she headed directly to Jade's locker. The locker bay was devoid of students except for a few stragglers who had already missed the tardy bell. The heels of her shoes echoed as they clacked against the tile floor, and she rose onto her toes to keep from drawing unwanted attention to herself.

The combination for her daughter's locker had been committed to memory; Claire had stopped in to pick up forgotten work more than once since Jade had started at Willow Brook. Working quickly and quietly, Claire rifled through the contents of her daughter's locker, searching for evidence. Finding none, she gently closed the metal door. The click rang out through the stillness of the locker bay and she glanced toward the office to see if anyone had noticed. Will Ryan leaned against the opened door, standing half-in and half-out of the office, but the noise had not drawn his attention away from his task. He seemed focused on an unemotional, one-sided conversation with the secretary who sat behind the tall counter taking notes. Claire ducked behind the lockers and eavesdropped on his side of the conversation.

"I'll be back on Monday for that meeting. Call Tammy and remind her we're meeting at 7:45 that morning. Didn't realize she'd be gone *again* today," he muttered. He let go of the door and turned to leave but thought better of it and caught it with his foot, blocking it open just enough to shoot off one final order. "And call Claire; tell her I want to meet with her before the next board meeting."

She leaned back against the lockers. Where was Will going? She couldn't let him just walk away. The plans she had already put in motion were quickly falling apart. The pieces didn't fit together the way she'd pictured them in her head. He was supposed to pay for his crime against Jade—not Monday or over the weekend—but later *today*—when the school was empty.

A new, poorly thought-out plan began to take shape and Claire slipped off her shoes and crept between the lockers, hidden from the office staff. She peeked around one set of lockers and saw Will's quick departure had been thwarted by a parent. She ducked back down, not willing to risk getting involved in a lengthy conversation with a teacher or secretary. She raced out the side door to her car, backing out too quickly, gently bumping into a red Kia Sportage in the row behind her. She slammed the car into drive and raced out of the lot and onto the highway, narrowly missing a second car that switched lanes. "Slow down, Claire!" she chastised herself, but the words didn't register. She could feel her anxiety skyrocketing as she turned right and headed up a small hill, pulling into a gas station. She made a U-turn and parked her SUV next to an overgrown dogwood bush.

From her vantage point, she could see the intersection of the school parking lot. She would be able to tell which direction Will headed when he passed through the stoplights.

Will's black Cherokee made a full stop at the red light before it turned toward her. She unbuckled her seatbelt and slid low into her seat as he passed in front of her car. She impatiently waited for a white Honda Pilot to pass before she pulled onto the highway.

"This is crazy!" Claire whispered as she pressed down on the accelerator to stay with the traffic as it picked up speed. Flipping on her blinker, she pulled into the left lane and raced around what appeared to be an older, accident-prone Chevy Trailblazer—again following the Honda Pilot too closely. The voice inside her head would not shut off; it grew louder and louder, nearly screaming for Will to pay for his transgressions against her daughter.

"What are you doing?" she asked herself out loud. "Stop this! Stop it now!" She quickly removed both hands from the steering wheel and wiped their wetness along the front legs of her capris as the car momentarily steered itself. "Don't you see? I can't stop!" the voice answered. "He has to pay." Another voice, that of reason, joined the fray and the two of them battled it out, each one screaming to be heard over the other. As they argued, she continued to drive, ignoring them both. At this point, it took less effort to continue following Will than it did to make the decision to stop.

Suddenly, the car grew quiet; the two voices seemed to have reached some sort of agreement—or they had simply grown tired of her ignoring them. The loud silence made her nervous and she reached over and turned on the radio, pressing the scan button, allowing it to flip through the stations until she settled on one playing eighties hits. A Madonna song pumped through the speakers and she tapped the steering wheel to the beat.

Will drove the speed limit, never traveling faster than the signs warned. Almost ten miles north of the school, his car turned onto an entrance ramp, putting him on the freeway heading west. Claire continued to follow him, thankful the Honda headed in the same direction. Even with the Honda between them, she never lost sight of the black Jeep.

A commercial blared through the speakers before Blondie's "One Way or Another" began to play. She turned up the volume and sang along. *"One way or another, I'm gonna find ya! I'm gonna get ya—get ya—get ya—get ya..."*

Claire took it as a sign.

CHAPTER 22

Keeping her eyes focused on the road, Claire pressed a button on the steering wheel and commanded the woman to *Call Karen at home*. As the phone rang, she reached over and hit the volume button twice. The phone rang a third time before her friend picked up.

"Hi, Claire!" Karen sang. Her upbeat voice grated on Claire's nerves after their conversation just two days earlier. Karen had been as remiss as she had in getting to Jade on time; she was responsible for letting Will take advantage of her daughter a second time. Perhaps there were more. She gritted her teeth and drew in a deep breath before speaking.

"I need a favor, Karen. Michael's out of town. Surprise! Surprise! And I need you to watch the kids today—tonight." She sighed loudly. "I don't know for how long—the weekend, maybe?" Claire bit her lip, unable to decide how long her mission would take. "Yes, definitely the weekend. "I should be back by Sunday night at the latest." She cringed; if she could not tell her best friend about her plan, then she knew what she was doing was wrong—but she no longer had a choice.

"Claire, yes, of course! You know Matt and I will do anything for you. But what's going on?"

Claire let out a second sigh as she pressed down on the accelerator to cut around an oversized truck that had merged onto the freeway in front of her. "I just need some time to myself. I thought I'd leave town for a couple of days and get my head on straight."

"Do you want me to go with you?" Karen asked. "Matt can watch the kids. Girls' weekend, maybe?"

"No, I need to be alone." The sharp and sudden whir of a siren pulled Claire's attention to her rearview mirror; a police car directly behind her impatiently signaled for her to pull over. She jerked the car off the side of the road, kicking up rocks behind her. "Karen, I have to go. Just tell me you'll watch the kids."

"Yes, but, Claire, wa…" The line was already dead.

The police car sped around her, working his way through the long line of cars on both sides of the road that had all pulled onto the shoulder. She felt her shoulders drop in relief; she was certain he had been after her, had somehow figured out her plan.

The cars, one by one, moved along the shoulder, picking up speed before pulling back onto the freeway. The white Honda took the next exit ramp and Claire tapped her brakes to leave more distance between her and Will. On the other side of the overpass, two cars moved down the entrance ramp. Again, she slowed; this time to allow them to jockey into position between her and Will. One of the cars pulled around his Jeep Cherokee, but the other car kept pace with him, and she stayed in the line of cars, distancing herself from Will just enough to still track his every move.

The sunshine beat down through the side window and Claire twisted her visor to alleviate the direct light. That movement sent Claire reeling back through a web of memories.

***

It was her eighth birthday. Her father had stumbled into the house that Friday afternoon with a dark-haired woman in a low-cut, sleeveless dress attached to his arm. She could smell the alcohol as soon as the door opened, and she made a beeline to her bedroom. Something smashed against the wall in the main part of the house as she tugged her blanket off her bed and hurriedly jerked the homemade quilt up over the sheet, smoothing out the wrinkles as quickly as her tiny hands would allow. She kept a watchful eye on her bedroom door in case her father staggered in.

She knew she would spend the afternoon tucked beneath the wide, low shelf in her closet. The tan speckled linoleum floor had felt cool against her bare arms and legs as she slid beneath the shelf, tightly pressing her back against the wall.

Sunshine streamed through the tiny crack in the door; if she shifted her book exactly right, she could see the words or the pictures, but not both. Three *Little Golden Books* were stacked beneath the blanket near her head; a fourth one,

Pinocchio, she held in her hands as she shifted the book in the sun's rays, whispering the story to a tiny rag doll she had tucked into the crook of her neck—a gift her mother had made and given to her that morning.

The fighting came in waves, intensifying as the afternoon and evening dragged on. A third voice joined the argument from time to time, but never as loud as the other two. At one point, the fighting grew so violent, she pulled the blanket tighter around her tiny body and turned toward the wall. As the sunlight slid lower in the sky, the closet grew too dark to read. She held the doll in one hand, stroking her cheek as she repeatedly whispered to her, "It's okay, Betsy. I'm here. Shhhh! Don't cry. I'll take care of you." Her words grew farther and farther apart until they stopped altogether and the only sound she made was a repeated puff of air.

Her bedroom door flew open, and she awoke with a start. She was confused as to where she was, but instinctively knew she needed to remain silent. She pressed herself tighter to the wall and pulled the blanket in so no one could see it beneath the shelf, but as she did, her doll slid out to the middle of the closet floor. Too afraid to scoot out to save her, she lay still—drawing in silent, shallow breaths and holding them for as long as she could—one after another.

She heard her bed slide sideways as someone pulled it away from the wall. Then she heard it hit the wall as it was flipped over in a rage. Her dresser was dumped next and she heard something hit the door. A few sickly notes of her music box played before another crash silenced it.

Suddenly, the closet door flew open and she squeezed her eyes tightly shut. She heard his foot stomp on the floor, then she saw him grind Betsy's face into the floor. Tears burned her eyes as she stifled a sob. The shelf above her shook as he kicked it and she was certain he would find her, but she remained frozen beneath the blanket—beneath the shelf. And then, he was gone. The front door slammed. She heard his car start and the crunch of the gravel as it traveled down the driveway. Then, there was silence.

She removed the blanket from her face and looked across the closet floor. Betsy's tiny cloth body was flattened;

her face had a gaping hole. Grabbing the edge of the shelf, she slid from beneath it. She picked up Betsy and cradled her in her arms, rocking her doll back and forth. Through sobs, she sang the familiar lullaby.

Finally, she lifted the heavy, low shelf from its supports and leaned it against the back wall. She slid her hand along the baseboard near the left corner of the closet. Two small finishing nails protruded from the wood about twelve inches apart. She pulled on the ends of the nails and the piece of the baseboard came off in her hands. She kissed the doll and tucked her into the hole she had cut out between the sheetrock and the floor. "I am so sorry, Betsy!" she sobbed. "I should have known I couldn't protect you from my father; no one could." She pushed the baseboard back into place, pressing the two nails into the tiny holes. Then she lowered the shelf onto its supports. Sliding beneath it, she curled up next to the wall and cried herself to sleep.

***

Jade is just like Betsy, Claire thought as she continued her mission; Will Ryan was her father and his friend Roy all rolled into the most horrible person to ever exist. Claire hadn't been able to save Jade any more than she had been able to save Betsy. Tears trickled down her cheeks as she followed the Jeep off the freeway, up an exit ramp, and into the quaint little town of Durham.

Claire looked at the clock on her dashboard. Nearly three torturous hours had passed since she'd left Willow Brook.

CHAPTER 23

An artsy stone and metal sign stood near the Welcome Center on the edge of town; it simply stated *Durham, Welcome Home!* At the base of the sign, flowers bloomed in a rainbow of rows. The storefronts had been remodeled to resemble a 1950's town—a time when life had been simple and safe.

Nearly seven blocks from the Welcome Center, Will maneuvered his Jeep into a parking spot in front of the Wishy-Washy Laundry. Claire made a sharp right, turning down a side street about twenty yards from where Will parked. She made a tight U-turn at the entrance of a small *no-vacancy* parking lot and eased her car into a spot—too close to the stop sign. Will climbed out of his car and fed a coin into the parking meter before heading down the street, away from Claire.

From this angle, trying to read the storefronts proved to be an impossibility, and she threw her door open and casually strolled down the sidewalk, moving in the shadows of the storefront canopies. She slipped her oversized sunglasses on and feigned window shopping as she watched Will pull open a large wooden door about three doors down from where he had parked. As he entered the store, Claire stepped into the doorway of a store called Home Again and peeked at her watch—*4:56 p.m.*

Within seven minutes, Will reappeared with two bouquets of flowers, both wrapped in green and white floral paper. Claire spun on her heels and raced back to her car. A meter reader pulled up to a car just two vehicles behind her as she slammed her door and pulled back out onto the main drag—again in pursuit of the man she despised.

Flowers? she questioned. Why would Will buy flowers? He rarely spoke to anyone—man or woman...even the children at school didn't really know him. So why flowers? And why two bouquets—one larger and one smaller?

A line of four cars exited the far end of town ahead of

her Lexus. Another large, artistically designed sign touted *Until next time!* Three of the cars made a gentle turn following the road that ran parallel to the edge of a lake. A bright yellow Volkswagen signaled that it would be turning just ahead of Claire. She impatiently waited for the elderly woman to make the turn before she sped up to catch up to the parade of cars led by Will.

Within minutes, his car slowed and pulled into a church parking lot. Claire slowed too but didn't dare stop. She kept her eyes on the Jeep—making sure the church was his actual destination and not a turnaround. Just past the churchyard, she pulled onto a narrow, rutted road that looked as if it hadn't been driven on in years. The thick weeds brushed against the bottom of the car as she made her turn and headed back onto the highway and past the church again.

Claire drove slowly, keeping just enough speed to not draw attention to herself. The tiny stone building was old but seemed to be well cared for. Its tall steeple rose toward the heavens, while the spire hosted a large white cross that looked, according to the scaffolding, as if it were about to get a fresh coat of paint. The grounds were filled with enormous trees and an array of blossoming bushes.

Several cars indicated their intent to turn into the lot as she passed the first driveway. She sped up once the church was out of view and pulled into a lakeside park less than a quarter mile down the road. She killed the engine and laid her head against the steering wheel. Why was Will here? Why would he be at a church, of all places—on a Friday afternoon?

Suddenly, a thought came to her and she restarted her car and headed back toward the church. This time, she sped past the grounds and eased back onto the rutted road. Her hands tightly clutched the steering wheel as the car bounced in and out of the grooves that had been worn into the soil long ago. She drove just far enough to keep from being seen by anyone on the highway, then she slammed the car in park and climbed out. She stretched to relieve the achy tightness that had grown in her body over the past few hours before making her way toward an opening, which may or may not have once been an old trail. Following it proved harder than she expected in her wedged sandals, but she carefully followed the uneven path in the direction of the church, skidding on gravel and slick grass more than once.

As the cross of the church came into view, she heard muffled voices. She stood perfectly still, listening, but could only catch a word or two above the music of the crickets and a few birds. Slowly, she inched her way as close to the group as she dared, remaining hidden in the thicket. She nearly tripped over a rotted tree stump as she took a step backward. Carefully, she planted herself on the edge of it, behind an oversized bush, and spread the branches to create a window into Will's world.

Before long, the group exited the parking lot and began a journey of sorts, not *into* the church, but behind it. Several people carried bouquets similar to Will's, but none were nearly as large. Claire left her spot and worked her way through the undergrowth of the forest, staying parallel to the group. A branch snapped under her foot and she froze in place. The voices continued to move away from her, seemingly unaware she was watching. Just to be certain, she waited a full minute before continuing her trek.

A squirrel scampered ahead of her and she tried to shoo him away, more from fear than from the attention he might gather. The group stopped at the edge of the gated cemetery. The black iron gate creaked as it was swung open by an old man. A shiver ran up Claire's spine, *almost* enough to bring her back to her senses.

Beyond the cemetery was a view unlike anything Claire had ever seen. The graveyard was positioned on a bluff. Just beyond the ridge, monstrous trees poked at the edge of the brilliant blue sky. An unending line of mountains painted the background as far as she could see. It wasn't until the man who had opened the gate started to sing that she remembered where she was and why she was there.

A haunting melody floated through the cemetery, but the words were lost in the breeze. Claire dropped to her knees and remained still as she watched. Laughter and tears tied themselves to the words people spoke—all too quiet for her to hear. Before long, one group after another started to drift away from the cemetery and back to the parking lot—only Will remained.

As the last car turned onto the highway, Claire stepped into the clearing. She brushed debris from her knees and soundlessly strolled toward the open gate. After entering the grounds, she stopped and watched Will. He sat on the ground near the foot of a pair of headstones; one knee was pulled tightly against his chest and his other leg remained out in front of him. His chin was tucked into the crook of one arm as it balanced on his knee. He was speaking out loud and the tenderness of his voice unnerved Claire more than she would have expected. Almost invisibly, she moved through the headstones, making her way toward him. About ten feet away, she knelt down and listened. His string of words flowed like a never-ending river. He talked about his job and the people of Willow Brook. She felt her cheeks burn as she eavesdropped on his private conversation.

After several minutes, she knew she had made a mistake. *Not this way. Not here. It isn't right, no matter what Will has done.* Claire silently rose and turned to leave, but the movement caught Will's attention.

"Hey!" he yelled as he jumped up, taking several steps in her direction. "Claire?" Will seemed shocked to see her—confused. "Why are you here?" he asked angrily. It took only a few steps to close the space between them. He grabbed her by the arm and jerked her toward him like a rag doll. "Answer me! I asked you why you were here."

"Let go of me!" she cried. "You're hurting me." She tried to twist out of his grip, but it only tightened as she tried to get away.

A single bulging vein above his temple pulsed. "Not until you explain yourself. Did you follow me here?"

Claire again tried to free herself—tried to pry Will's fingers from her arm. "I-I..." she stammered.

"The truth, Claire—not some cockamamie story; I want the truth," Will snarled as he squeezed her arm just a bit tighter. His eyes were rimmed with red and his always perfectly pressed suit was wrinkled.

Slowly, the fight in Claire died. Her shoulders sagged and she felt Will ever-so-slightly loosen his grip. She fought back the tears that were building. She stared at the place Will had been sitting, and for the first time in days, she felt the tiniest bit of sympathy for him. It was obvious someone important to him had died recently.

She watched the blades of grass slowly rise back up where they had been standing.

"Now, Claire! Answer me!" Will demanded as he gave her arm a slight tug.

A ripple of anger danced inside of her, again, and it brought back her purpose. He was a monster—he had molested her daughter. She couldn't afford to feel sorry for him.

"Y-you bastard!" she stammered.

Will stepped backward, almost as if he'd been slapped. "What the hell..."

"You!" Claire pounded her free fist into his chest repeatedly. "You!" she cried. "You took everything from me...from Jade! How could you?"

Will grabbed her other arm to protect himself, but Claire continued to fight. She threw her weight into him, sobbing uncontrollably.

"Claire, what are you talking about?"

She tried to kick him in the shin, but he swung her around, facing her away from him, and grabbed both arms in one hand, pinning her tightly against him.

"Seriously, Claire. You're going to lose. Stop fighting and tell me what you mean."

"You bastard!" she growled through gritted teeth. She tilted her chin downward and tried to bite his arm.

"Enough already!" he yelled as he wrapped one hand across her forehead, pulling it against his chest. "Enough," he whispered.

Defeated, Claire's body trembled as sobs rolled through her. Her weight crumbled against him and the two fell to the ground. Will, still too afraid to let go, waited for her crying to quiet.

He heard her sniff as the crying jag slowed. "Claire, talk to me," he demanded in a softer voice.

She took several deep, jagged breaths before she could even utter a sound. "You...you son-of-a-bitch, you stole Jade's innocence." Her words were a whisper, but Will cringed as if she had beaten him with them.

"Claire," he whispered, "I didn't. I couldn't. I would never…" His throat tightened around the words and refused to let him finish. Claire elbowed him and quickly slid away, kicking her feet to put distance between them.

"Right, Will. That day in your office, when I was late picking up Jade—you were all over her when I walked in. Then again when Karen came to get her. She told me what she saw; your hands were in her lap." Claire created even more space between them, sliding backward in the freshly mowed grass. "How could you? Don't even deny it. At least be a man and admit what you did."

With much effort, Will stood. His knees trembled under his weight. His shoulders slumped forward; his eyes shone wet in the evening sunlight as he looked at Claire. Sadly, he walked back toward the place Claire had found him. He stood there, looking from one headstone to another. He wrapped his arms around himself as he rocked from one foot to the other. Slowly, he began to speak. The words were so quiet, at first, Claire had to lean forward to hear them.

CHAPTER 24

"One year ago this week, I woke up with everything a man could ever want." Will closed his eyes and smiled for the first time Claire could remember, but the fleeting smile collapsed into sadness. "And later that day, I lost it all."

Minutes ticked by as Will retold the story, replaying the footage first in his head, and then relaying it to her. "I was working late, trying to get some work done at school before the end of the year. It had just gotten dark; not much later than it is now. I called Kelly to say I'd be home in about thirty minutes. I asked her if we needed anything. *Milk*—she said we needed milk." He sucked in a deep breath. "A gallon of milk may have been the difference between life and death—my life and their death." Tears streamed down his face and he wiped them away with the back of his hand.

"I stopped for less than five minutes to pick up the milk that no one would ever drink. I pulled into the driveway. An old rusty car with no license plate sat in front of the house. I pulled around it and drove into the garage." Will stopped again; his voice shook as sobs swallowed parts of his words.

"I walked into the house through the garage door. Two men were hauling *my* stuff out of *my* house. One hit me in the head with a metal rod while the other stabbed me in the shoulder as they ran out." Will touched his shoulder where she imagined the scar was.

"Oh!" Claire whispered so quietly Will couldn't have heard.

Will dropped to his knees at the base of his wife's grave; his arms hung by his sides. "They escaped, but I didn't care. I had to find my family.

"I raced up the stairs, screaming their names—but I heard nothing. I looked in our bedroom, but they weren't there. I prayed they weren't home—that they'd gone out in the boat or next door—anywhere but there." His entire body trembled as he struggled with his words. "Then I went to my daughter's room. I knew before I even went in."

Will's weight fell backward as he balanced on his heels; his head flopped forward and his chin rested against his chest. "Kelly was on the floor—ten stab wounds, the coroner said; all I saw was blood." A rush of air escaped through his mouth as if he had been punched in the stomach. "She wasn't breathing when I got to her; she didn't have a chance." He sobbed openly, making up for an entire year's lack of emotion. "Aubrey..." His voice strained as he spoke her name. "She was naked. They raped her before they killed her. My baby was eight years old—eight years and one day."

His body convulsed with sobs as he rocked back and forth. All she could do was watch him; there was too much pain in his words—too much hurt. Tears streamed down her face, but she remained frozen, staring at the mounds of flowers that lay on the two graves. Silence filled the air as the night sky began to take shape.

The question needed to be asked; Claire could listen to his voice no longer. "Will?" But he never moved. "Is-is that *why* you hurt Jade?"

"Oh, my god, Claire! How can you even ask me that after what I just told you?" He stepped in her direction but didn't trust himself not to grab her again. "Did you hear anything I said?" His voice grew louder, frightened her. "They *RAPED* my little girl! Do you think I would want that to happen to *anyone* else?" he cried. "They *raped* her, Claire! She was eight! Did you hear me? Do you see my pain? Do you understand that I would give anything in the world to hold her again—to protect her like a father is supposed to?" He wrapped his arms across his chest as his rage lifted. His next words were almost lost amidst the evening breeze that jostled the leaves. "We were happy. We were a family. And now—now I'm—alone."

Claire wrapped her arms around Will, holding him, crying with him until there were no tears left to fall. She knew Will had not hurt anyone, not her daughter, not anyone else. She knew he couldn't; it wasn't in him to do so.

No matter what she had thought of him, no matter what

she had seen or had not seen back in Willow Brook, she knew he was just another victim of a past that held on and refused to let go. Will was trying to move forward, but like her, he was being pulled back by haunting memories of his past.

CHAPTER 25

The gray sky had moved in before Claire left the hotel room carrying nothing but her purse. The early morning humidity was already oppressive; she wished she had more than just perfume to mask the smell of yesterday's clothing. As she waited to check out, she dug through her bag in search of a piece of gum—anything that would take away her morning breath. She smoothed out her top, trying to erase the previous day's wrinkles, but was unsuccessful in her attempt.

She had showered and run a brush through her hair, but she still felt conspicuously grimy with her grass-stained knees and her tear-stained blouse.

The clock over her shoulder read 7:43 a.m., but already the weekend crowd was up and moving. The dining room was full as people picked their way through the continental breakfast. She turned away from them, hoping no one noticed her lack of luggage or filthy clothes.

She was positive she couldn't have parked any farther from the hotel. When they had left the cemetery, she followed Will to his house and the two talked into the wee hours of the morning. By the time she arrived at the hotel, the lot was full; she felt lucky to have found a spot at all.

They had spent the evening talking about Jade, about Will's family, about Willow Brook—becoming friends through their misery. Even though Will offered, she had refused to spend the night—had driven the eight miles back to town to the only hotel in Durham.

Large drops of rain began to fall when she pulled out of the hotel's parking lot to head home. Before she reached the highway, the driving rain came. Not much farther down the road, hail pelted the windshield, rocking the car with such intensity, Claire was certain it would come through the glass. The wipers ferociously swished back and forth, seemingly fighting a losing battle. The tires hummed as the SUV floated over the water, feeling as dangerously out of control as Claire herself.

She knew she should pull over and wait out the storm, but her common sense seemed to have washed away with the falling rain. She fought the storm, catching glimpses of the pavement in the second that followed each swipe of the wipers. Their steady rhythm pulled Claire inward.

Long zigzag strands of light repeatedly lit the sky as if opening curtains into Claire's past—disappearing as quickly as they entered. Each clap of thunder jolted her back to the present.

FLASH! Staring up from the bottom of a bathtub; scratching at Edward's arms and hands, trying to hold her breath just a little bit longer. *BOOM!*

FLASH! Her mother standing between her and Edward, a fence of protection as he waved a tire iron above his head—threatening to kill her. *CRASH!*

FLASH! Her doll's face—torn and filthy—crushed beneath Edward's foot. *CRASH!*

FLASH! Roy's hands pushing down on her face, threatening to kill her mother if she so much as whispered one word of his transgression. *BOOM! CRACK!*

FLASH! Edward's mangled face—his dead eyes—a river of blood pooling on the garage floor. *CRASH! BOOM!*

FLASH! Waving goodbye to her mother for the last time. *BOOM! CRASH! CRACK!*

FLASH! Calvin Fredrick Taylor, her father, her real father. *CRASH!*

FLASH! Losing Jade as she slipped further and further inward. *BOOM!*

The sky had grown almost as dark as night, making it nearly impossible to travel through the storm safely, but Claire hadn't noticed. She was focused solely on her memories.

FLASH! Will Ryan—not the man she thought he was. *BOOM! CRASH!*

FLASH! This time, the lightning stayed bright as if it were lighting the entire world—not flickering, not flashing. The only sound that followed was the resounding blare of a horn and the screeching of tires.

Claire could hear the high-pitched sound of the horn, but

it didn't initially register. At the last second, she jerked the wheel hard to the right, but the car did not respond. It skipped along the top of the water that had pooled on the road, hydroplaning out of control. The steering wheel was useless in her hands, but still, she tightened her grip as she pressed both of her feet against the long brake pedal, trying to stop the car.

Suddenly, everything slowed; even her scream had been swallowed by the surreal slow motion. The truck's lights moved toward her and she braced herself for the impact, pulling one arm across her face for protection—but it did not come. She wondered if she was dead.

The car was still—unusually angled near the shoulder of the road, half in the mud and half still on the pavement. The rain had slowed, leaving tiny water droplets falling against the glass. The rapid swish of the wipers was the only sound she heard. The windows had fogged on the inside and she could barely see through the thick white film.

Her hands still gripped the steering wheel—her knuckles white. With the palm of her hand, she cleared one small spot from the inside of the windshield and cast her eyes upward through the small opening.

The ugly gray clouds had given way to one small blue spot, an opening, large enough for Claire to slip through. *Move toward the light,* she thought, but she didn't move. She took her hands away from the steering wheel in search of blood but found none. She gave her arm a pinch and yelped in pain.

She cleared a larger spot on the windshield. The sun's face slowly slid into the opening of the clouds and a brilliant rainbow began to dance against the dreary sky. Claire took a deep breath and turned the defroster up all the way. Somehow, by the grace of God, she was alive.

As the window cleared, she watched both the rainbow and the sun intensify. She slipped her foot from the brake as she turned to check her blind spot before pulling back onto the highway. When she turned forward again, a small black and orange monarch butterfly landed on the windshield directly in her line of vision. Its wings fluttered in the breeze before it flew from the windshield—in the direction of home. "Mom," Claire whispered.

CHAPTER 26

Henry raced up and down the edge of the field, mimicking his sister's moves. Sweat beaded on his forehead and he wiped it away with the bottom of his red Brookers t-shirt. Claire smiled as she kept her eyes on the game and her son. Pride swelled into a golf-ball-sized lump in her throat; she struggled to swallow it down.

In recent weeks, her children had grown incredibly close. Jade rarely let Henry out of her sight, but the closer she grew to her brother, the more she pushed *her* away. Claire had slowly come to terms with that. As long as Jade remained close to Henry, she could be patient. It didn't stop her, however, from feeling jealous of their relationship. Maybe *jealous* wasn't the right word to describe what she felt; it was more of an emptiness—a sadness—knowing she had never had a sibling.

In recent weeks, her sleep had been plagued with a recurring nightmare that continually stirred those emotions, leaving her grieving for the sibling that never was. Every nightmare felt real, yet this one felt like more than just a bad dream, and she couldn't shake the feeling it may not have been a nightmare at all.

***

Her mother was getting fat. Her stomach looked like a huge basketball balanced on her lap, leaving little room for her to snuggle. Even at five years old, she knew something was different. Her mom had begun to move like the old lunch lady at school—tipping from side to side when she walked. Climbing the steps to the second floor was a chore and her mom stopped to rest at least once each time she went upstairs. Sometimes her mother would lie down with her, pulling her tightly against the bulge of her stomach. She learned to sleep facing her mom, curling around the big bump that separated them.

Her father hated her mother's stomach, though. He called her bad words; he told her she was as big as a truck.

Sometimes he oinked and called her a pig; other times, he would beep and call out, "Wide load backing up!" He called her *ugly* and *stupid*. He said she was always in his way and he would shove her aside like she wasn't important. Finally, he kicked her out of his bed—said he would not sleep with a cow.

One Friday night after dinner, her mother entered her father's office with a beer bottle in one hand and a frosty mug in the other. She followed her to the doorway, holding on to the back of her maroon dress, hiding, but as her mother stepped into the den, she let go. She didn't dare enter; she tucked herself behind the wall and peeked around the corner with just one eye. The boundaries for her had been clearly drawn.

Her mother moved almost invisibly toward her father's desk. Her movements were slow and graceful and seemed out of place for someone so large. She held the mug at an angle and carefully poured the beer into it, not letting the foam overflow the top of the cold glass. Without a sound, she set them both on the desk and turned to leave.

Her father caught her mother's arm and jerked her toward him. He shoved his rolling chair away from his desk and pulled her onto his lap. With one hand, he rubbed her back then lifted her hair and kissed her neck. Her mother quickly wrapped her hands tightly across her stomach and froze. Her expression was one of pure terror. She repeatedly moved her eyes to the right, signaling for her to leave, to go to her room—but she could not.

Her father's hands traveled over her mom's belly, circling the ball that had grown there. At first, the movements were gentle and slow, but within seconds, they grew frenzied—out of control. He began making wider and wider circles around her stomach as his face turned dark.

The same fear she saw on her mother's face began to grow on her own. She knew something was going to happen; she could feel it. Her father's elbows and shoulders took ever-widening paths, no longer traveling in circles, but instead, moving up and down, back and forth. Without warning, his left elbow caught the handle of the mug, dumping it over. Beer spilled onto his papers and dribbled down the drawers and onto the white carpet.

Her father jumped up, nearly knocking her mother to the ground.

Grabbing tissues from his desktop, her mom soaked up the beer, daubing the golden liquid from the tops of his papers first. Her father stood back yelling at her to work faster before his papers were ruined. His hands tightened into balls and she saw him pound the air between the two of them.

Her mother worked more quickly—but obviously not fast enough. He grabbed her by the shoulders and threw her against the wall.

"Y-you worthless cow!" he stammered. "Look what you've done! My work is ruined!" he shrieked as he picked up the papers and threw them at her mother. She wanted to scream, to tell her mom to run, but she was invisible—had to remain that way to protect them both.

Her father leaned closer to her mom; he pressed his face so close to hers that their foreheads almost touched. He screamed words that were not meant to be heard by a five-year-old. Again, her mother hugged her stomach as she silently accepted consequences for actions that were not hers.

When her mom would not look at him, he grabbed her chin and cranked her neck forward and upward. "Look at me, you bitch! Who do you think you are?" he seethed between gritted teeth. He spit in her face—but still, she did not move. Suddenly, he threw her into the wall again; this time, she stumbled and fell to the floor. As she tried to stand, he pulled his leg back and kicked her in the stomach—just once, but hard enough to make her mother scream so loudly and so long, she had to cover her ears.

She turned and ran; she was afraid she would be next. Even being invisible did not always protect her.

From the depths of her closet, she could still hear her mother screaming. She heard the front door open and slam shut, then she heard the garage door open and the car speed away, pelting rocks against the siding of the house as it roared down the gravel driveway.

She pulled the covers away from her face and took a breath of the cool air on the other side of the blanket. She leaned her head farther out, listening for her mother, but the house was silent.

Finally, she dug her way out from beneath the shelf and slowly opened her closet door. The room was dark. She turned the knob of her bedroom door without a sound and pulled it slightly inward. Slowly, she slid along the wall like an animal hiding from its prey—hiding in the shadows of the night. The house was dark; the silence was loud.

She turned on the light in the hallway outside her father's office. She peeked through the doorway into the room, not knowing what she was searching for. Something small and dark marked the place on the floor where her mother had been.

Tucking her chin down, she stepped into the room, all the while scolding herself for breaking the house rule of never entering *his* office. She tiptoed toward the dark spot. Her legs trembled just knowing she had stepped into the forbidden territory. She knelt for a better look. A red spot about the size of a quarter stained the carpet. Blood, her mother's blood.

Her breath caught in her throat and her body trembled. *Was her mother dead? Where had her father taken her? What would happen to her now?*

She lay down and laid her head on her outstretched arm next to the spot, circling it with her index finger, wondering if she would ever see her mother again; tears filled her eyes and they began to fall. Soon an entirely different fear pushed in. *Her father would be so angry when he saw the stain.* She had to protect her mother and if her mother wasn't alive, she had to protect herself.

She raced to the kitchen and pulled the doors under the sink open; she found an old rag and a can she had seen her mother use time and time again on the carpet. The words on the can were too big to read; she was not old enough to read words with more than a few letters. She sprayed the foam on the stain, repeatedly scrubbing and spraying until the spot faded, nearly disappearing. Her tiny arms ached as she opened the front door and ran through the darkness to the garbage can. She lifted the lid and buried the empty spray can and the damp rag deep beneath the stench of sour milk cartons and rotting scraps of food. She washed her hands and checked on the spot one last time before sliding back beneath the low shelf in her closet.

Night turned into morning, and, still, the house was empty. She waited—another night, another day. Her stomach growled as she looked for food to eat, but lettuce leaves and peanut butter were the only finds that didn't need to be cooked. She hoped her mother would return soon, since the jar she found was almost empty.

Suddenly, she heard the familiar groan of the garage door. Panic set in. She didn't know who was home, but she knew enough to stay invisible. She closed her bedroom door and slipped into the closet beneath the blanket, her back pressed against the wall.

Only one set of footsteps entered the house. They were heavy and she recognized them immediately.

Her father didn't look for her; he didn't call her name. He never left for his job in the city, but spent the next couple days in his office, alone, opening and closing drawers, turning lights on and off—sitting in the dark—drinking from glass bottles instead of eating.

She stayed hidden in the shadows, keeping an eye on him. She found food when he was asleep or passed out on the couch in his den, surrounded by empty bottles and glasses. She ate bread that had turned green, breaking off the pieces that didn't look right, and when she couldn't open the second jar of peanut butter, she took a sharp knife from the counter and carefully carried it into her closet, where she stabbed the jar over and over again until a small hole formed. She licked what she could squeeze out the side of the plastic jar. Lying beneath the blanket, she began to wonder if this was her life now. Would she ever see her mother again?

Then one day, she heard the garage door open and close, heard his car drive away—again she was alone. Would it be for days or just minutes? She didn't know, but just in case, she raided the cupboards, taking boxes of food—even though she didn't know what they were. She hid them all in the corner, under the shelf, tucked beneath her quilt.

Then she wandered the house, imagining what it would be like not to have to be invisible, to not have to hide—to be able to be a real person, to celebrate her birthday.

Around two o'clock, the front door opened. She raced

into her closet and dove beneath the shelf, pulling the covers over her head and body, making sure to cover the food as well. Her pulse raced at the closeness of being caught. How had she let her guard down? How had she missed the sound of the car on the gravel?

Her heart ached for her mother; she longed to be touched, to be held. Suddenly, her door opened. Quiet feet moved across the floor; she prayed it was her mother. The closet door opened; she lay perfectly still, not drawing or releasing a breath. She felt the covers being pulled from her and she tightened her grip on them. "Honey," a soft voice called, "it's Mama." She let go of the blanket and scooted toward her mother and threw her arms tightly around her waist.

Her mom dropped to the floor and pulled her onto her lap. She cradled her, rocking her back and forth like a baby. She felt her mother's tears on her own cheek. She breathed in the scent of her mother as she snuggled her face into her mom's worn sweater.

They sat in the darkness of the closet for what felt like hours, never daring to speak, tightly snuggled together. Her father's footsteps moved back and forth in the upstairs bedroom as they heard drawers opening and closing. Finally, they heard the front door slam and the sound of his car tires on the gravel as he drove away.

Her mother stood and shook the blanket. She put it back on the bed, tucking the corners in tight triangles under the mattress. Then her mom held out her hand and waited for her to grab it. In the kitchen, her mother lifted her onto a stool at the counter before she busied herself making macaroni and cheese—her favorite.

That night, she slept in her mom's bed. She woke to the sound of her mother crying in her sleep, and she snuggled tightly against her. It was at that moment she noticed snuggling had become much easier, but she did not understand why.

***

Henry's victory dance had created an uproar in the crowd. People laughed hysterically at his celebratory moves. He strutted, twisted, turned, and shook his backside at the opposing team. Claire's face turned red as she cupped her hands and yelled, "Henry Stanton! Come here!" But the final whistle sounded, and Henry was swallowed up in the crowd. Claire stepped into the walkway and headed down the bleachers. She felt herself being pushed along, carried forward in the crowd. Everyone seemed caught up in the excitement of the team's advancement to the semi-finals. Claire could feel her own excitement as it threatened to expose the tears of pride she felt for Jade, the star of the team. She feigned a few coughs to cover her emotion.

Claire searched for her daughter in the mass of people. A sea of red swarmed across the field like a moving sheet: players, supporters, coaches. It was at that moment she understood the phrase *looking for a needle in a haystack.*

Still unable to locate Jade, Claire headed in the direction of the last place she had seen her—near the opponent's goal. She squeezed between groups of people celebrating, but she could not travel more than a few steps before someone wrapped their arms around her, congratulating her on Jade's outstanding performance, each one reliving an amazing goal or play her daughter had made during the game.

No one needed to tell her how amazing Jade was; she already knew. At twelve years old, there were already rumors of a soccer scholarship. With each person who congratulated Claire or patted her on the back, she felt her pride grow just a bit more until she was sure her chest would burst wide open.

She continued to work her way through the crowd, weaving in and out, searching for her daughter. She knew if she found Jade, Henry would not be far behind. His sister was his hero and he wasn't afraid to tell everyone he saw.

Trying to avoid being trampled, she made a quick turn to her left, colliding with Will Ryan. He grabbed her arms to catch her.

As she stared into his face, she saw the same emotionless look that had been there since she first met him, but his eyes had softened a bit. They did not seem quite so distant.

Claire smiled at him but knew enough not to expect him to reciprocate. She knew Will wanted to be the person he was before his loss, but he needed time. By sharing his pain with her, he had taken the first step of a million-mile journey. She and everyone else just needed to give him that time.

Will let go of Claire's arms and reached out to shake her hand. His administrative persona took over and she saw no sign of the man who had cried in her arms just the week before. His painful past was still locked somewhere deep inside.

"Congratulations, Claire. You must be very proud of Jade. She had an amazing game today." His voice was deep and low as if speaking about official business, not talking to the friend Claire had become.

"Thanks, Will. I'll tell her you thought so. I am proud of her." She paused before frowning, "She has her moments—but overall, she's a pretty good kid."

Will leaned in, close enough for his whisper to be heard. "Aubrey played soccer too. She was good at it; maybe even as good as Jade." Then he turned and disappeared back into the cheering crowd, leaving Claire with a knot in her heart.

Claire thought about the intense pain that surfaced every day for Will. Activities like soccer games and dance recitals must have been so painful for him. The only way he could protect himself was to keep those memories locked away, but she also knew she was now the one person he could share his sorrow with. They had a special bond—one held together by secrets.

The field slowly began to clear. Spectators began to leave—heading out to celebrate another win. But there were still enough people around to make finding her daughter difficult.

Finally, Claire caught sight of Jade as she stood near the goal line—a crowd of people circled her, congratulating her win. Matt and Karen were there holding on to Henry, keeping him from being trampled—keeping him out of his sister's limelight.

Claire stood up on her tiptoes and watched from a distance; she observed the inner workings of her daughter's world. Lately, that was what she had become—a mere observer, nothing more. A window separated them—a pane of glass, keeping them apart. Sometimes, Claire could see through that window, but most of the time, the curtain was drawn.

As Claire watched the scene, a sudden uneasiness began

to bubble inside. She could feel beads of sweat forming. A burst of nausea blasted into her stomach and she was afraid she might be sick right there on the field. Her body started to tremble as she watched her daughter. As each person congratulated her, Claire saw something different. Lights flashed in her brain: red lights, stoplights. Something was wrong.

The soccer coach pulled Jade in for a congratulatory hug; Claire watched as her daughter's expression changed from pure joy to sheer panic as Jeff picked her off the ground and swung her around. It was a look Claire recognized—one she had had years ago. She wiped the sweat from her brow and urgently pushed her way toward her daughter. Was she reading more into Jade's expression than was there? Was she wrong again? Was it Jeff?

When she reached Jade, she pulled her into a hug, immediately letting go of everything except her daughter. She waited for Jade to pull back, close the curtain that separated them much of the time lately, but instead, Jade clung to her like a child, unable to let go.

Over her daughter's shoulder, Claire watched Jeff high-five some of the other girls—joking and laughing with them. The image of Jade with him cut through her—a likeness that linked itself to an old image Claire kept filed away of herself and Roy. The imaginary photos alternately flipped through her mind until they became one; she couldn't separate them.

Forcing herself to focus only on her daughter, Claire hugged her tightly again. "Jade, you were amazing! I'm so proud of you."

Jade hooked her arm through her mother's and the two of them walked off the field as if nothing stood between them. Henry followed several steps behind, replaying his sister's soccer moves all the way to the car.

It was nearly midnight when Claire fell into her empty bed, exhausted from the day. She had been fighting sleep in front of the television, waiting for Michael's promised ten o'clock return. When she closed her eyes, Jeff's face appeared and reappeared. It haunted her dreams. When she awoke, she could not shake the feeling she had been right all along—she had just had the wrong person.

CHAPTER 27

By two o'clock, there was not a spot a cleaning rag hadn't touched. Sunlight scattered across the quartz countertop as it seeped in through the French doors. Claire gathered her cleaning supplies and carried them to the laundry room. She filled the washer with a load of rags and put the supplies back in the cabinet in their perfect rows with the labels facing forward.

Sometime before noon, she made lunch for the kids. Henry ate in the kitchen but, once again, she left Jade's food outside her bedroom door. The tray had disappeared and reappeared—but as always, her daughter had taken no more than a few bites. Claire wasn't sure how Jade survived; maybe it was candy bars and soda from the vending machines at school or in the park. But any discussion of food ignited major fallout. So, as long as her daughter continued to eat *something*, she wasn't going to fight about it. Picking her battles right now seemed the best choice.

Claire wandered through the living room. Tiny dust particles floated in the sunlight that passed into the room. She sighed, wondering how, even with a weekly cleaning service, she could ever stay ahead of the dust that accumulated daily. Lifting the house phone from a small round table, she lightly ran her hand over the glass surface and wiped away an invisible layer of dust.

She set the base back on the table but carried the phone to the couch. She dialed Michael's office number but did not identify herself when his new secretary informed her Mr. Stanton would be in meetings for the rest of the day and, if she was seeking representation, he was not taking clients at the current time. The woman asked if she wanted to leave a message. Claire hung up without responding. This was what their relationship had become—she needed to contact *his* secretary to talk to her own husband. "We're married,

Michael," she whispered.

Absently, she played with the buttons on the phone, randomly pressing numbers that held meaning for her: birthdays, anniversaries, etc. She needed to talk—needed to have an adult conversation. She dialed Karen's house phone, but no one answered. She punched in Barbara and Walter's number but hung up when their machine picked up. She dropped the phone into her lap and let her head fall backward, onto the couch cushion. For the first time since she was a child, she realized how few friends she really had. No, she had friends; she was *friendly* with everyone, but other than Karen, she didn't have close friends. She had spent her entire adult life being friends with Michael, and later taking care of Jade and Henry. Was that the way it was for everyone? Did people become so busy with their own life, they lost contact with the world. Or had she done this to herself? Had she kept everyone at arm's length so she wouldn't have to share her past?

Tears rolled down her cheeks and fell onto her jeans; she lifted her arm and wiped them on the sleeve of her shirt. She had not cried this much ever, but lately, there was a continuous spring of tears. If they were not rolling down her face, they were threatening to. She had always been strong—had not needed anyone—but in the past several weeks, she had become extremely emotional.

She threw her arm across her forehead and tried to pull herself together. Suddenly, she sat up and dialed a number she had not called in almost a year. Back then, she dialed that number almost as often as she did her mother's.

The phone rang twice. "Will Ryan." The voice was firm and emotionless.

"Hi, Will. It's, ah, Claire." Her voice shook; even she could hear it.

"Yes, Claire. Is there something you need?" She knew instantly she shouldn't have called. The Will who answered the phone was the old Will—all business—not the friend she'd discovered in Durham.

"Never mind. I think this was a bad idea," she said. The silence on the other end of the phone frightened her. She slid her thumb across the phone keys, ready to push the *end* button, when Will finally spoke.

"Sorry, I had to close my door. What's a bad idea, Claire?" Will's voice was softer, more compassionate than just seconds before.

"Calling you. I just thought—well, I'm not sure what I thought, but..."

"Claire, what is it? What's going on? You sound...ah, different."

Damn tears! She thought as she looked up to keep more from falling. "I don't know," she admitted. She sucked in a deep jagged breath. "I just needed to talk to somebody, I guess—and every other number I dialed went to an answering machine."

"So, I was your last choice?" Will asked. Claire could hear his smile.

"No—well, yes, I, ah—yeah." She choked out a tiny laugh. "I guess you were."

"It's not the first time," Will said. "Are you okay? What can I do for you?"

Claire shuddered. Why had she called Will? "Maybe I just needed to hear a friendly voice."

"Wow!" Will genuinely seemed surprised. "Wow," he said again softer. "I've been here for almost a year and no one, not one person in Willow Brook, has ever said my voice was *friendly*. I don't think *you* even thought that until a couple of weeks ago. I'm pretty sure my staff has started a pool to see who can get me to smile first. It's either that or quit."

"It's not that bad, Will. They just need to get to know you."

"It is that bad, Claire, but you didn't call me to tell me that. So, what's going on?"

Claire sat silently for a moment before answering. "Can I come see you?"

There was a long silence on the other end. Finally, Claire heard Will draw a deep breath. "Does 4:30 this afternoon work for you? Heather leaves at 4:00 and it sounds like it might be better if you come after she's gone."

Claire sighed. "That'll work." She almost pressed the end button, but she stopped herself. "Will, are you sure this is alright?" But she got no answer in return. Will had already hung up.

Claire took the stairs two at a time. She turned on the water and waited for it to turn warm. For the first time in nearly a month, she hummed as she showered.

***

"Jade, I need you to watch your brother until I get back. I have a meeting at school and then I have some errands to run." Claire felt her face glow pink as the lie crept upward.

"When do I get to be the babysitter?" Henry whined from one side of the Monopoly board. "Jade always gets to be in charge."

"I have soccer practice, Mom. How'm I supposed to go if I have to watch Henry?" Jade's sarcasm was thick. "Did you forget about me again?"

Claire checked her watch. "What time is practice?" she sighed.

"Five o'clock." Jade rolled the dice and moved the car ahead eight spaces.

"Well, you'll have to go with me to school, then. You'll be there early, but you and Henry can play on the playground." She turned toward her son. "When your sister has practice, can you just sit in the bleachers and watch until I'm done?"

Jade flipped the game board over. "Great plan, Mom! But practice is over at Brandon Park. They closed our field to get ready for the semi-finals, remember?" She brushed past Claire—hitting her with her shoulder as she stormed out of Henry's room. "You don't remember anything anymore!" Jade stopped at the doorway and glared at her mother. "You're just like Grandma before she died."

"Oh," Claire said. It couldn't have hurt more had Jade punched her.

Henry had begun picking up the game pieces; she bent down to help him. "What's wrong with Jade, Mom? She's mad at you all the time." His big brown eyes were filled with such sadness, it made Claire want to cry. "What did you do?"

Trying to hide the pain, Claire knelt on the floor, away from her son, as she picked up the colorful play money that had drifted to the floor. "I wish I knew, Henry. I wish I knew."

Claire dialed Karen's cell. It rang four times before she

picked up. "Hi, Claire. What's up?" Her voice was quiet, not the bubbly one Claire was accustomed to.

"Hi, Karen." Her *I need a favor* was met with unprecedented silence. That was not something she was used to getting from Karen; usually, she offered to help before Claire even asked. "Jade has soccer practice at Brandon Park at 5:00." Claire winced, knowing she had overused her *favor* card. "I'm headed to a meeting at school, and according to Michael's secretary, he has appointments all day—and likely into the night. Is there any way you can get Jade to practice?"

Again, there was an uncomfortable moment of silence—it wasn't long, but enough to make Claire wonder what was going on. "Yes, Claire, I can make it work. Don't worry about it. Do you need me to watch Henry while you're gone?"

"If you could, but… Are you sure this is okay?"

"Yes, it's fine. I'll take care of dinner for the kids after soccer practice, but right now, I have to run." Claire felt her guilt rise.

She pressed the intercom buttons for both kids' bedrooms. "Jade, Karen is going to take you to soccer practice and pick you up again. Be ready to go by 4:45. Henry, you'll stay with Karen during practice. I have to go now. Behave, you two."

Henry was the only one to respond. "Okay, Mom. Love you."

"Love you, too, Henry." Then she added, "I love you, Jade." But there was no response.

CHAPTER 28

The main door to the office was still unlocked when Claire pushed it open. She had driven into the parking lot at 4:24 p.m. but waited a full four minutes before exiting her car—arriving precisely at 4:29.

The outer office was empty, but through Will's open door, she could see him sitting behind his desk. He stood as she walked in, his dark blue polo shirt tucked neatly into a pair of tan chinos.

"Hi," she said sheepishly as she set a cardboard Starbucks carrier on his desk. Two coffees balanced diagonally from each other. A flat paper envelope held two chocolate chip cookies and sat opposite the napkins, sugar, and cream that had been tucked into the last hole. She grinned. "I come bearing gifts. I hope you like chocolate and coffee."

Will lifted the carrier by the cardboard handle and moved it to the table in the corner of his office. He pushed his door shut before pulling out a chair for Claire to sit in. "Who doesn't?" He shrugged as he sat in the chair adjacent to her.

Claire's stomach stirred. Once again, she felt this was a bad idea. But she brushed the thought away as she handed Will a coffee. "Sugar?" she asked.

"A bit informal, Claire," he teased. "Maybe you should just call me Will."

His levity caught her off guard and she stared at him—confused.

"Claire? It was a joke," he said with a laugh.

"I know, but I've never seen...never seen you smile. You should do it more often."

His smile faded as he looked away and began unfolding the napkin he had taken from the container. "There hasn't been a lot to smile about lately," he said.

Claire pushed the envelope with the cookies across the table. "I know exactly what you mean."

Will leaned back, balancing his chair on two legs. "So, I take it this isn't a business meeting."

Claire took a bite of her cookie, swallowing before responding. "No, but I don't know why I'm here either. Like I told you on the phone, I just need someone to talk to."

"So, talk," he said as he crossed his arms across his chest. "I think I owe you some listening time."

The carpet was new, tan with a thin thread of white. Claire picked a line and followed it from the beginning to the end. "It's a long story," she said.

"I've got nothing else to do," Will said as he took a bite of his cookie. He grinned. "You maybe should have brought more cookies, though."

Claire ignored his comment. She drew a deep breath and let the first word fall. The words practically exploded out of her once she began. She told him story after story of Edward and Cal—her fathers: the one she did not remember but loved with her whole heart and the one she knew but hated with every fiber of her being. She divulged the story about the Roy of her youth and the old Roy she had gone to see not long before. She told him how her perfect family was falling apart right in front of her, and about her mother's death. She confessed everything; she left nothing out. Will was privy to information she had not shared with her best friend—and not even her husband.

Sometimes tears trickled down her cheeks, and other times, she would become so overcome with emotion, she could not speak. Will had long ago moved his chair closer to her. He held her hands when she needed him to, and he handed her tissues when she cried. When she sobbed, he held her in a tight embrace until she was ready to go on.

He had no profound words to comfort her, but in the end, she walked away feeling better than she had in years. Will had listened to her—had not judged her or tried to fix any of her problems—he had just listened—which was all she needed.

CHAPTER 29

Just before eight, Claire drove into the Reeves' driveway. Karen's car was gone, but Matt's red Acura was parked on his side of the garage. The double doors were open, so she entered into the mudroom. "Hey, guys, it's me," she called, announcing her arrival. Before she could close the door, Henry barreled toward her and jumped into her arms.

"Hey, Mom! Me and Matt were playin' with his old train. Come and see!" He squirmed until she set him down; then he grabbed her hand and pulled her through the mudroom, past the kitchen, and into the living room. "Look! This was Matt's when he was little."

"Wow! That's pretty amazing." Claire tipped her head to the side, genuinely impressed. "From when you were a boy, huh, Matt? I don't think I have *anything* left from my childhood."

"Yeah, I didn't even know my mom kept it. She wrapped it up and gave it to me for Christmas a few years back. I was totally shocked. My dad and I spent hours playing with this thing. For years, it was set up in the basement of their house, but it disappeared after I left for college. I figured she'd gotten rid of it."

"Well, it's nice to have some *antiques* around," Claire teased. She settled onto the floor next to Henry and let him show her how to run the controls.

From where she sat, she could see her daughter sitting in a rocking chair on the screen porch. The chair rocked so fast, Claire was certain it would take off. Jade's hands were tucked beneath her legs and her lips pressed together to form a thin, angry line. Her eyes were stormy as she stared straight ahead into the living room.

Claire turned her attention back to Henry as he gave her a complete explanation of how the train worked. "Where's Karen?" she asked Matt.

"Mom! Pay attention." Henry grabbed her chin between his chubby hands and turned her head back toward the controller.

"Sorry, bud." She pulled him onto her lap.

"She was in a meeting when you called this afternoon. She called me at the office and asked if I could take Jade to practice."

"Mo-oom," Henry whined.

Claire's face fell. That explained the phone incident. She put one hand over the controller and momentarily tucked her other one over Henry's mouth. "Henry, wait," she warned. "Matt, I'm so sorry. When Karen said it was fine, I just assumed she was free. I feel horrible. You shouldn't have had to leave work to take care of *my* kids." She literally felt sick.

"I didn't," he said. "Karen called Margo Hughes and asked her if Jeff could pick Jade up on his way to soccer practice." Claire's stomach somersaulted at the thought of Jade being alone with Jeff Hughes. "Then she called the Hubers to see if Henry could play over there until I got home. I picked Jade up from soccer practice on my way home. We got dinner started and then we went and got Henry from the Hubers'."

"Oh, Matt, I'm so sorry. I didn't mean for this to be such an imposition. I got called into a meeting at the last minute…" The lie wasn't sitting well; it sloshed in her stomach as it mixed with the knowledge of Jeff Hughes giving Jade a ride. "I didn't think Karen would have to amass an army to make it happen." Claire pressed the train lever upward. The brightly colored train began moving slowly down the straightaway. She pressed it harder and watched it pick up speed as it approached the curve. *Who had she become? Lying! Keeping secrets from her best friend…and her husband.*

Matt stuck his hands out as the train careened off the end about halfway through the turn.

"Mom!" Henry yelled. "You gotta be careful. The train is as old as Matt." He scooted on his knees to help Matt right the train and place it back on the track. "Geez, Mom. Didn't you ever drive a train b'fore?" he scolded.

Claire felt her cheeks slide from pink to red. "Sorry, guys. It's obviously a good thing I didn't go to college to become an engineer." She handed the controller to her son and listened as he instructed her in the fine art of running a model train—specifically, an antique train.

She sensed Matt watching her and she worried he could see through her façade. She tossed her hands to her sides and gave a false laugh. "Well, I guess I've been told."

Matt laughed. "You have great kids, Claire. I *like* spending time with them."

"I know, but I can't believe how awful I feel. I'll make it up to you guys. What time will Karen be home?"

Matt peeked at his watch. "Hmmm, 'bout half an hour or so. She needed to stop by the grocery store on her way home."

Claire bit her lip as she watched her daughter continue rocking at the speed of light. Something was wrong—something more than her current normal. And Claire was certain she knew what it was. She lifted her son's elbows off her leg where he had planted himself. "Henry, why don't you help Matt get the train picked up. We need to get out of his hair. I think we have over-imposed enough already today."

"Awww, Mom. Matt was just startin' to have fun with me," he whined.

Matt laughed loudly. "Yes, I was, buddy. But maybe you could come over tomorrow night and we could play some more." Matt rubbed the top of Henry's head before pulling him into a headlock for his famous tickle torture.

Her son's screaming giggles filled the room, and it made Claire miss the moments when Michael had time to play with Henry and Jade.

Claire stood up and tugged on her son's pants legs, dragging him away from Matt. "Now, Henry. Clean up."

"Awww...alright, you party pooper!" Henry pouted. "Come on, Matt." Then he tried to whisper so his mother would not hear. "Mom's such a girl; she don't understand trains." She laughed out loud for the first time all night.

Claire moved to the porch, where she leaned against the white painted frame. She watched her daughter for a moment before dropping into the chair next to her. She studied Jade—surprised by the young woman she had become. She seemed taller—more womanly than she remembered even this morning. Her face looked different—older somehow. But that was impossible. People did not change in twelve hours—did they?

"Sweetie, are you ready to go?"

Jade continued her speed rocking. Her fingers curled tightly over the arms of the chair.

Claire touched her daughter's hand, but Jade jerked her arm away. Her own arm recoiled nearly as quickly as Jade's had and she folded her hands together to keep from making the same mistake twice.

She whispered, intentionally keeping her voice low. "Honey, what's wrong?"

Jade abruptly stopped rocking. She turned her head and angrily looked at her mother before firmly locking her arms across her chest. When she spoke, her stiff words slapped Claire across the face. "Well, Mother, you should know." She leaned closer to Claire. "If you paid any attention at all—if you were any sort of a mother—you'd know."

Claire stiffened; the buzzing in her ears grew so loud, she pressed her fingers into them. Awkwardly, she tipped back in the chair. Through the buzzing, she clearly heard a name— Jeff Hughes—Jade's soccer coach.

CHAPTER 30

After throwing the dry cleaning over her arm, Claire picked up a few plastic shopping bags from the back of her car and hauled them into the house. She could think of nothing except Jeff Hughes. It was the same as when she had suspected Will of molesting Jade—and when she had paid her surprise visit to Roy. Revenge had become the loudest voice she heard. She could not shake it. But then she also experienced another nagging voice— a warning. She *had* been wrong before; she had accused Will of doing something he had not done—and it frightened her that her instincts had been so off base. This time, she had to be sure; she could not jump to conclusions. She needed to stay calm—needed the facts, and that meant getting Jade to open up to her. But how?

As Claire walked into the house, she heard the slam of Jade's bedroom door—shutting out the possibility of getting Jade to tell her the truth, at least for the foreseeable future.

Henry's feet pounded on each step as he raced down the stairs, jumping from the second step, landing with a thud on the hardwood floor. His little face was filled with grief as he entered the kitchen. "Mom. How come every time you come home, Jade quits playing with me? I hate that."

Claire knelt down and hugged him. "I'm so sorry, Henry. I'm trying to make it better. I really am." She glanced toward the stairs. "How about you go to your room and put in a movie? I need to talk to your sister."

"Are you going to ask her why she's so crabby, Mom? Sometimes she's just mean to you and Daddy, but mostly just you, 'cuz Daddy's not home much anymore." His tiny frown broke Claire's heart.

She pulled out a stool and patted the seat. "Before you go, come sit here and talk to me."

Henry crawled onto the stool. He folded his arms on the countertop and rested his chin on one wrist. Claire pulled the pantry doors open and grabbed two Oreos out of a bag. Then she poured a glass of skim milk and pushed it across the island to her son. At this point, she was not above bribery; she needed all the insight she could get.

Henry picked up the first cookie and dunked it into his milk, swirling it around and around. "Has Jade told *you* why she's so unhappy?" Claire asked.

Henry wiggled in his chair, then climbed up onto his knees. He took a bite of his softened cookie and smiled at her. "This is good, Mom. You never give me store-bought cookies."

Claire laughed. "Well, sometimes we just need to *splurge* a little, I guess."

He swirled his second cookie in tiny figure eights before he spoke. "All she said was that you don't pay attention. She said she just wants you to pay attention."

"To what, bud? To her or to something else?" Claire waited for Henry to finish chewing his second cookie.

"I don't know, Mom," he said as he wiped his face on his sleeve. "She just said you don't pay attention." He picked up the glass and drank the rest of the milk. Then he reached his hand all the way to the bottom and scooped out the soft chocolate crumbs with his fingertips and wiped them on his tongue.

"Nice move there, Henry," Claire said as she handed him a napkin. "Didn't your mother teach you any manners?" she teased.

Henry looked confused. "*You're* my mother," he said.

Her son did not know any more than she did. Claire hugged him and lifted him off the stool. "Now go watch a movie. I'll let you know when we're done talking. Okay?"

"Aye-aye, Cap'n," he said as he saluted her. He spun on his heels and raced up the stairs but stopped halfway. "Thanks for the cookies, Mom." He tucked his hands into the front pockets of his jeans and looked at her with the same sad frown he had before. "I wish cookies would make Jade happy."

"Me too, buddy! I wish it were that easy!"

***

Claire knocked on her daughter's door. "Go away!" Jade yelled. No matter how angry her daughter was, she would

189

not be detoured from this discussion.

She pushed the door open but did not enter the room. She leaned against the door frame and waited for more angry words to be flung in her direction.

"I told you to go away!" Jade yelled through clenched teeth. "Just leave me alone!"

Claire entered the darkened room. She stepped over stacks of books, papers, garbage, and other miscellaneous items that had been left where they landed. She dumped a stack of books from Jade's desk chair and positioned it close to the bed. "Honey, we need to talk. Something's obviously bothering you and I won't go away until I know what it is."

Jade lay spread-eagled across her bed. Her face was buried in her wadded-up comforter, hidden from her mother. Claire knew that tactic; it was easier to lie to a person who could not see your face. She had used it a million times as a child.

She pulled the covers away from her daughter. "Jade, what's going on? Something's happened or you wouldn't be acting like this." Claire waited. "Contrary to popular belief, I'm not stupid. A person does not just change overnight without a reason. What happened? I need you to tell me so I can fix it."

Jade glanced at her mother before turning back toward the wall. Claire could see the side of her face, could see her daughter's tears fall. Jade was near the breaking point; she could feel it.

"Honey..." Claire scooted onto the edge of the bed. She ran her fingertips down the back of her daughter's hair and was surprised Jade did not push them away. "Sweetie, I love you so much. I would do anything for you. You know that, right? Whatever's happening, you can tell me. We can fix it." Her voice grew thick; she was afraid she would cry if she uttered one more word. Her heart ached for her daughter; it ached for herself.

She cleared her throat to keep from crying. "Jade, please? I can't help you if I don't know what's happening."

Claire knew better than to put words in her daughter's mouth. Jade needed to tell her in her own words; otherwise, Jade would deny it—just as she would have denied it had her mother asked her.

"Honey, what can I do? What can I say to make you understand this is fixable?" she pleaded.

Jade flew out of bed, landing in the narrow space between the bed and the wall—opposite Claire. Her fists repeatedly clenched and unclenched. Red splotches grew on her neck and worked their way onto her face.

She didn't even stop to take a breath before she let her mother have it—the words were tight with anger. "See, that's just the thing. You're my mother. Do you even remember that? You're supposed to fix everything—everything! Don't you get it? When I was little, you knew everything before it even happened. You stopped me from hurting myself and you stopped everyone else who might hurt me. You knew—you *always* knew everything back then."

Claire remained still; the words hurt. She had expected rage and anger, but that didn't make it any less painful. In essence, her daughter had just told her she was the worst mother in the entire world.

"Back then, you fixed everything, but now you're so busy dealing with your own problems, you can't even see me. You can't see what's wrong. It's like I'm invisible to you."

Claire's chin shot upwards. Her shoulders slammed backward and her back became as straight as a board. She covered her mouth in shock. She could barely breathe. It was like someone had struck her in the chest with a thirty-year-old board. *Invisible!* Jade had become invisible, and she had let it happen. Hell, she had *made* it happen.

Jade pounded her fists against the wall. Each word came out as a single-word sentence. "You. Aren't. Paying. Attention. Pay attention, Mom! See me! And maybe *then* you'll be able to fix this."

Jade ran from the room and locked herself in her bathroom. Claire heard the click as it echoed through the room.

She cradled her head in her arms and cried. *Oh my god, I made you invisible, Jade. I turned you into me. It's my fault— it's always been my fault—I let it happen.*

CHAPTER 31

The house was empty. Henry had gone to the lake with one of the neighbors and Jade was reluctantly spending the day with her friend Meghan. Being alone had never bothered Claire in the past, but now the solitude almost smothered—swallowed her whole.

Senator Prescott's case still consumed Michael. He hadn't physically or emotionally been home for days. When he was there, Claire barely noticed. Dirty water glasses, half-full cups of cold coffee, and the occasional whiskey glass that littered his desk were the only signs he had even stepped foot in the house. On those nights, he locked himself in the den, following leads and making calls. In the early morning hours, he would fall asleep on the couch, rising before dawn to shave and shower in the downstairs bathroom. He would grab fresh suits, shirts, and ties from the cleaner's hangers his secretary dropped off and picked up a couple of times a week.

Who was Claire to complain? She had agreed to this life; she had promised to keep the home fires burning. He had warned her their life would change. Claire knew winning Prescott's case would launch Michael's career toward partnership, so proving the senator's innocence meant more to him than just a tally in the win column.

Because of his intense attention to the case, Michael had not felt the tension that permeated the house; he hadn't noticed that while he was trying to tightly pull the strings together for Senator Prescott and his family, his own was falling apart. Or maybe he had noticed but had simply chosen to ignore it. If that was the case, then today was just another example of his ill-directed focus. At 5:30 a.m., a colleague had picked him up for another trip south, one of a dozen or more he had taken in the past several weeks—far away from the shattered pieces of their once perfect life.

Claire picked up Michael's pillow and pressed it to her

face. She drew in a long breath but could not pick up the slightest scent of her husband—not even his woodsy cologne. Angrily, she stripped the sheets from her bed and balled them together before tossing them into the hallway.

The house did not need cleaning; the cleaning service had been there just days before and she had practically disinfected it the following day, but she *needed* to clean. Cleaning was power—killing germs, ridding the house of unnecessary clutter. She started in her bathroom, scrubbing the soap scum from the shower, scouring toilets, washing countertops and every surface.

Finally, she picked up the sheets and carried them to the laundry room; she started the washing machine and hauled the cleaning supplies into the guest bathroom. She pulled on her yellow rubber gloves and scrubbed every surface in the room that was rarely used. When she finished, the bathroom sparkled, but it did not look any different than it had before she started. She flipped off the light and headed to the storage closet where she stashed the hose and the accessories for the central vac.

She would never admit she was obsessive-compulsive—although others might call her that—but when she vacuumed, she worked her way out of the room, careful not to leave footprints on the freshly vacuumed floor. Claire worked her way down the hallway and through the guest bedroom.

She bit her lip as she opened Jade's door. It had grown worse over the last few days. Without the light on, the room felt like a prison—similar to the closet Claire had spent hours in as a child. It was dark and dank. The blinds were closed, and the heavy curtains were drawn. A quilt Tess had made for Jade when she was younger had been thrown over the curtain rod—adding another layer of bleakness. Claire was certain it had been weeks, if not months since the room had seen the light of day.

She pulled the quilt down and threw back the curtains. She lifted the blinds and opened the window, letting fresh air seep into the room. In the newfound light, the mess was overwhelming—so much worse than Claire had expected. She picked a plastic bag off the floor and began shoving garbage into it: food scraps, candy wrappers, pop cans, paper—anything that didn't belong.

She stripped the bed, tossing the filthy sheets into the hallway. By the time she was done, two huge laundry baskets overflowed with dirty clothes—or what appeared to be dirty— she hadn't been able to tell since everything had been tossed on the floor. She picked a large animal book off the floor and tucked it back on the shelf—in the correct section, following Jade's organizational system. Other books were buried beneath other things and she methodically placed each one in its place on the shelf.

Jade's comforter was balled up and tossed into a corner—in the same place Claire had left it when she pulled it off her daughter the day before. Claire lifted it to her face and almost choked on the smell. She tossed it into the hallway on top of the sheets. The washer would get its workout. Everything would be washed—everything. She took the curtains down, pulled the shams off the pillows, removed the runner from Jade's vanity, and threw them all into the pile. The mattress pad was still on the bed and she gave it a good tug to release the elastic hold from the far side.

She heard the ding of the washer and she switched the loads, throwing Jade's comforter and shams into the machine first. She made three trips between Jade's room and the laundry room before re-entering with the vacuum.

Claire plugged the long hose into the central vac outlet and slowly ran it over the carpet. With the first pass, she heard noises as bobby pins and small items traveled through the hose. She methodically vacuumed the same spot over and over until the noises stopped, allowing her to move to the next section of carpeting.

The sweeper would not fit on the far side of the bed. She gave the frame a shove with her thigh so she could vacuum between the bed and the wall. Frustration set in when she discovered a whole new array of garbage that had grown beneath Jade's bed. She pressed the power switch on the vacuum and dropped to her hands and knees and began pulling things out from the dark space: a hard-crusted, half-eaten peanut butter and jelly sandwich—at least she hoped that was what it was—several books, one blue and white tennis shoe, several smelly soccer socks, and a few stuffed animals.

Claire finished vacuuming and moved the machine and hose into the hallway. Next, she dusted every surface in the room. From her cleaning bin, she pulled the Lysol can and sprayed the carpet, bed, and air. It was amazing how much different it felt. For a single moment, she panicked. *How would Jade feel?* It was too late; it was done.

In the linen closet, she found a clean mattress pad and set of sheets. She also found a Glade Plug-In air freshener and plugged it into an outlet near Jade's dresser.

She checked the number she had written on the top edge of the mattress: *2*. That meant *3* would follow. The mattress needed to be flipped rather than just rotated. Claire grabbed the lightweight mattress by the handles, pulled it toward her, and flipped it over. In the process, the dust ruffle slid to one side. She pushed the mattress off the bed and balanced it against the far wall. As she pulled on the dust ruffle, planning to add it to the pile of wash, her hand bumped against another book. Claire lifted the corner of the fabric and pulled the book out. She turned it over in her hands. *Jade's diary.* The pink sparkly book held her daughter's innermost thoughts.

Her heart raced. Was this the way to find out what was happening to her daughter? Claire struggled with the knowledge that while she might be holding the answers to Jade's erratic behavior, it was also an invasion of her daughter's privacy. As a parent, where was the line?

Claire set the book on the box spring and left the room— weighing her options. She switched loads of laundry, folding the sheets she had taken off her bed, tucked them inside one of the pillowcases, and put them back in the linen closet. When she returned to Jade's room, the book was still there. She had hoped it would have disappeared. What should she do?

Jade had told her, *You aren't paying attention. Pay attention, Mom! Pay attention and maybe you'll be able to fix it.* Those were her daughter's words. Only a mother could understand how much those words had hurt her.

11:45 a.m.—It would be hours before either of her children would return home. She pulled the mattress onto the box spring and sat on the edge. Her heart began racing again. Did she want to know? Of course she did; she was Jade's mother. She had to know. But what price might she have to pay when she found out?

Claire carefully opened the diary. A pink ribbon marked the last time she had written in it—almost two weeks before, but she chose not to read backward; she needed to learn *everything*—from the beginning.

December 24th was the first date entered; the book contained less than six months of Jade's life. Claire tried to remember where Jade had gotten the diary. She was almost certain it had been a Christmas gift from Lacy.

She began skimming. Jade was a prolific writer; she shared everything about her life, more than anyone would care to know. Soon the dates blended together in a blur as Claire flipped through the book, reading the first couple sentences of each entry, trying to get a handle on the emotion tied to each date. The first three months were still written in Jade's curly handwriting; a heart shape marked every i. But on March 14, the handwriting changed.

As she read that entry, it nearly knocked the wind out of her. The date stuck in Claire's mind; there was something familiar about it, but she could not place it. She leaned across the bed and pulled the calendar from Jade's desk. She flipped the pages back to March and scanned for the fourteenth. There, written in the middle of a circle: *the first day of soccer practice.*

Claire felt her heart squeeze its way into her throat.

She lifted the book closer to her face and reread the words, whispering them out loud.

March 14

I'm scared!!! I've never been this scared in my entire life. I don't know what to do. He told me he'd kill me if I told anyone. He said he'd kill the whole family. He'd start with Henry, making me watch each one die so I could see what I'd done. I'm so scared! I want to tell Mom. She'd know what to do, but what if he finds out?

Claire felt her anxiety kick up a notch. It was true—just as she had suspected. The timing, the events, the person—it all fit. She felt like she was on a rollercoaster and all she wanted was to get off. She felt her pulse beat through her entire body, and she rolled into a ball in the middle of Jade's unmade bed and sobbed relentlessly. Her past and Jade's slammed together as she was hit with a tidal wave of emotion, but she knew she had to pull herself together—her daughter needed her.

Claire forced herself upright. She leaned against the headboard, balanced there for support. She turned the page and read more details of what her daughter had gone through.

Page after page, Claire read terrifying entries. Jade kept specific details of what had happened. Claire pictured it all. She fought to keep her past and Jade's present separate.

Each entry told a different tale, similarly haunting. With each one, Claire felt a change in her daughter's emotional state—fear, panic, anger. Jade was so angry with her coach, but, as she wrote, it became more and more obvious she was angry with Claire for not seeing it, for not knowing it was happening.

With each page, Claire began to hate herself more and more. She had known something was wrong; yet, after falsely accusing Will, she was afraid to make another mistake. What kind of mother was she? Certainly not the kind Jade deserved.

Claire continued to read, each entry casting more and more light onto what had happened to her daughter—each one hurling Claire further into despair. She began to feel an uncontrollable rage toward Jeff Hughes. How could this man have been entrusted to coach young girls? How could the community have let this happen? But even worse, how could *she* have let it happen? Why didn't she know? Why hadn't she seen it? She, of all people, should have known what was happening? She was Jade's mother. Mothers are supposed to know.

Claire curled up on the bed and reread each entry, trying to make sense of what had happened to her daughter. Why hadn't she thought of looking for a diary earlier—when Jade would not confide in her? More importantly, how was she going to handle it?

"Mom?" The word was barely loud enough to be heard. Claire sensed her daughter's presence more than heard her and she quickly turned around.

Jade stood in the doorway; her hands clutching the door frame for support. Claire jumped off the bed and pulled her daughter into a hug. "It's okay, baby. I know. I'm paying attention! I wasn't before, but I am now," she cried. "I know what happened, Jade. I know! And I'm so, so sorry."

Claire led Jade to the bed and pulled her onto her lap like she was a little girl. She rocked back and forth as she apologized over and over.

Jade cried long and hard, but Claire knew that no matter how many tears she shed, Jade would never be able to wash away the images of Jeff Hughes. And Claire would never be able to shake the feeling it had been her own fault. She would always believe she had brought this on herself.

Claire cried—for her daughter and for herself. There was no pain greater than watching your child suffer. The whole thing crushed Claire; she was sure they would never be whole again. All she could do was tell Jade how sorry she was.

The clock on the wall ticked the seconds away—they heard every one of them. But as those seconds turned into minutes, wrapped together as mother and daughter, they were momentarily safe—but they were also victims.

***

The time read *4:15 p.m.* Henry would be home in forty-five minutes; she wasn't ready to give up her time with Jade. They still had not talked; they had only existed. They needed to contact the police, and she did not want Henry exposed to any of the mess Jeff had put into play.

Jade slept on and off with her mother snuggled next to her. Claire reached for the phone and dialed Karen's number. She knew she was home; she had talked to her earlier in the day.

"Hi, Claire. Did you get a lot accomplished with the kids gone?"

"More than you know," she said. "Jade's here with me now and the two of us still need to talk. Henry'll be back from the lake around five. I know I've imposed on you more than enough lately, but we've finally made a breakthrough. Can you intercept him, Karen?"

"NO!" Jade screamed as she grabbed the phone from her mother and stabbed at the power button.

"Honey, that was just Karen. *You and I* have a lot to talk about, and I want to do it without Henry being here."

Jade jumped from the bed and began pacing the room—

rubbing her arms uncontrollably.

"Sweetie, he's too young to know what's going on. Karen can..."

"NO, MOM! She can't. Henry needs to be here with us. Not at their house."

Claire intercepted her daughter as she paced past the bed. Jade's whole body trembled as Claire hugged her. Jade had always been protective of Henry, but with all that was happening, it made sense she would be even more protective of her brother.

The phone rang. Caller ID told her what she already knew. "Sorry, Karen. I guess Jade wants Henry here with her."

"Claire, is everything all right? Is Jade okay?" Karen asked. "I heard her yell..."

"She's okay. Can we talk later?"

"Sure, call me if you need anything. You know I'll be here."

Claire turned to her daughter. "Jade, honey, I know you want to protect Henry, but you can't keep him with you twenty-four hours a day. He'd be fine with Karen and Matt."

"No, M-mom." Her voice was barely audible again. Sobs choked out Jade's words. "N-no, M-mom. I-I w-wasn't."

Claire froze. "Oh my god, honey! Are you telling me..." She felt physically ill. She lost her ability to take a breath as her heart slammed inside her chest.

She stood next to her daughter—trapped Jade's face between her hands and stared directly into her eyes. She needed to understand, needed to make sure she had heard correctly. "Jade, what are you saying?"

Jade pulled her mother's hands off her and buried her face into her shoulder. "It was M-Matt. He was the one w-who did this to me."

Claire felt her knees buckle and she fell onto the bed, with Jade on top of her. The room spun out of control and she closed her eyes to keep from throwing up. She felt like an elephant was standing on her chest, and yet, she could not let go of her daughter.

Matt? Matt was the one who molested Jade? Neighbor Matt? Best friend Matt? How could that be? She knew him almost better than anyone in her entire life. She had trusted him with her children.

Claire lay next to Jade, snuggled tightly against her. It didn't take long for Jade to fall into a deep sleep—probably the first one she'd had since March 14.

As she held her daughter, she picked up the diary and scanned the entries. Jade had never written a name, had never indicated a specific place; she had only described *what* had happened.

CHAPTER 32

Claire's emotions ricocheted out of control—each one vying for her attention, but often bleeding together in a gnarled mess.

Frustration! She needed Michael now more than she ever had, but as usual, his new priority had become work. She had agreed to it. It was as much her fault as his.

Loss! Karen was her best friend—the only true friend she had ever had in her entire life. And with her trust issues, their friendship could very likely become a thing of the past.

Anger! She had trusted Matt with her children, and he had broken that trust. He not only molested her daughter, but he had threatened her entire family—just like Roy had done. It was all a ploy, a scare tactic to force her into keeping his dirty secret. And Jade had fallen for it—just as she had all those years ago.

Fear! She was frightened about what was going to happen next—how all this would play out, what it would do to each one of them. She was afraid for her daughter. How would this affect Jade her whole life? She had over thirty years of firsthand knowledge—of knowing how messed up being molested and abused could make you.

Guilt! The guilt was eating her alive. How could she have let this happen? She was Jade's mother, a victim herself, and yet, she had not protected her daughter.

Sadness! There was an emptiness inside of her. When her other feelings subsided for even a second, the sadness crept in. She grieved over the loss of friendship and trust. She also grieved Jade's childhood. Her daughter was only a child. She had lost her innocence at the hands of Matt Reeve.

Claire could not deal with the sadness. If she let it in for even a second, it would suck her so far under, she would not see the light of day again. Instead, she kept the other emotions on the front burner—where she could tend to them, make plans, stir them when sadness tried to escape.

The whole thing was more than she could stand, and she sobbed uncontrollably.

***

Sometime around eight-thirty, Claire tucked Henry into his bed. After being at the lake all day, his head barely hit the pillow before she heard his steady, shallow breathing. She leaned her head against his doorframe and watched his peaceful sleep. She was so thankful his problems could still be fixed with store-bought cookies and a glass of cold milk. As she pulled Henry's door closed, a shiver ran up her spine and goosebumps rose on her arms. She crossed her arms and briskly rubbed them as she walked back toward her bedroom. Claire's scalp began to tingle and the internal buzzing returned. Had Matt molested Henry too? There was only one way to know for sure.

The sun had not yet dipped below the horizon, but in her mother's absence, Jade had turned on every light in Claire's bedroom, including the small night light she had taken from the bathroom. Her daughter was curled up against an oversized teddy bear that was nearly as tall as she was; her head rested on his stomach and her arms circled his hips.

Claire crawled into bed with the bear lying between them. She locked fingers with Jade and watched her daughter close her eyes. Before long, she felt her own lids droop as well; she welcomed the darkness.

"Mom?" Jade whispered.

"Hmmm?"

"Why? Why did Matt do that to me?"

Claire had asked herself that question more than once. *Why had Roy molested her? Why had Matt chosen Jade as his victim? Why had her father—no, why had Edward treated her so horribly. What was it about them that made them victims, an easy mark? What could she have done differently? What could Jade have done differently?*

"I don't know, honey. I think it's about power. And I think some people just don't understand right from wrong." Claire stroked her daughter's hair with two fingers. "Jade, we need to talk about what happened."

"NO! I can't; I can't tell you. I can't say it out loud; that's why I wrote it all down." She yanked the covers up over her shoulder and buried her face in them.

"Sweetie, I know it's hard, but we need to call the police. You're going to have to tell them everything" Jade started crying. "Honey, I'll be by your side the entire time."

"Promise?" she sniffed.

Claire leaned over the bear and threw an arm around her daughter. "Always."

"I'm afraid Matt's going to hurt Henry. He said he would."

"Oh, honey," Claire whispered. "It's an empty threat. It's how abusers keep you quiet."

"What's gonna happen to Matt?" Jade asked. "And what about Karen? She didn't do anything wrong."

"Well—Matt'll have to pay for his crimes. It's important he doesn't hurt anyone else."

"And Karen?"

Claire felt her tears build again. "I know it's not fair, but she'll have to pay for his sins too."

Jade sat straight up—frantically shaking her head. "NO! She didn't do anything! It wasn't her fault. She can't go to jail."

Claire pulled Jade into a tight hug; she felt the wetness of her daughter's tears roll down her neck. "No, honey. Karen won't go to jail. She's another one of Matt's victims, just like you. But this is going to be really hard on her; it's not something she's going to get over quickly."

Jade squirmed out of her mother's arms and snuggled back up against the bear. "I wish this had never happened. I don't want Karen to be sad."

"Me either, honey. But I don't think there's any way around it. You need to understand; this wasn't your fault. It was all Matt. *He* did all of this. *He* hurt you and *he* hurt Karen; he hurt our whole family. It was him, baby, not you."

Jade was quiet for a long time. "Then why do I feel like *I* did something wrong?"

Claire let her tears fall as she rubbed Jade's back. "You didn't sweetheart; it wasn't your fault." But even as she tried to convince her daughter she was guiltfree, she recalled feeling the very same way.

***

Around midnight, Claire began shutting off lights—one by one until only the night light's glow illuminated just a small section of one wall near Jade's side of the bed before heading downstairs. She sat in the window seat, tucked her feet beneath her, leaned back, and closed her eyes. *Oh, Michael, why aren't you here? What's happened to us?*

The neon green clock on the kitchen stove read *1:23 a.m.* In the darkness of the starless night, Claire ran her hand the full length of the island as she walked toward the porch. She reached out and felt for the handle of the French doors that led outside. From one of the corner gazebos, she shifted a rocker until it faced Karen and Matt's house. For the longest time, she stared at the house that had become like a second home to her. Her anger came in waves, each time resurfacing with a vengeance. As the minutes clustered together, the rocker took a beating, pitching back and forth on the white painted deck.

Almost an hour after she sat down, the rocker began to slow; on its last tilt forward, Claire stood. Looking every bit ghostlike in her long white nightgown, she silently moved down the back steps and across the expanse of lawn that separated the two houses. On the neighbor's front porch, she tilted the gold and red ceramic flowerpot to the side and fingered the key that lay beneath it. She looked up toward the arched windows of Matt and Karen's bedroom. *Tomorrow! Tomorrow, you bastard, you'll pay for what you did to my daughter.* She carefully replaced the key and silently set the large pot back onto the decking. Then, as eerily as she arrived, she was gone.

***

At 8:15 a.m., Claire closed the door to her bedroom and left Jade sleeping in the king-sized bed. After her night's excursion, she had slept more peacefully than she had expected—especially with her daughter by her side.

At nine o'clock, she called Barbara and asked if Henry could spend the day with her and Walter. Barbara was thrilled. "Walter'll finally have a reason to get out of this house and away from that TV," she said in her southern drawl. "That man needs more exercise than just liftin' Diet Coke cans. I don't care what he thinks," she chuckled.

Claire checked on Jade after she walked Henry to the

Harris'. She was still asleep. The bear's glass eyes stared emotionlessly at the ceiling as Jade lay snuggled against him and, for some reason, this angered Claire.

Her heart hammered inside her chest as she closed the door to the den and punched in Karen's phone number. Wednesdays were the day Matt worked from home. Karen often used the day to run errands.

"Hi, Claire," Karen said. "Is everything okay? I've thought about Jade all night long." Claire knew the call from the night before would be on Karen's mind.

She could feel the sweat beading on the back of her neck. "Yes, fine." Her cheerfulness sounded forced, and she hoped Karen would not read into it. "I was wondering if you're going anywhere today."

"Did you need me to watch the kids? Because I can come over. Matt's..."

Perspiration trickled down Claire's neck and the room began to fade around her. She slipped into the desk chair in case she passed out. "No. Nothing like that." She swallowed hard to push the bile down that eased up her throat. "Henry went to the zoo with Walter and Jade's still asleep. But I, ah, needed a few things for Jade, and I'm not feeling the best today." *More lies!* "I was wondering if you were going to the drug store."

"I can." Karen, as always, was more than willing to help. "Do you need them right away? I was planning to run some errands this afternoon."

"No, no, that sounds fine. Just let me know when you leave." She gave Karen a fictitious list of three items she needed: Midol, a heating pad, and, of course, chocolate.

Karen laughed knowingly. "Now I know what's been messing with Jade."

Claire forced a laugh. "Yeah, I should have known." She cringed. *I should have known.*

"Just a sec, Claire." She could hear muffled voices and knew Karen had not muted her cell, instead, had just covered the speaker. "I think maybe I'll go *now*," she said. "Matt needs me to pick up a few things for him too. He's not feeling the best either. There must be something going around."

Claire coughed. The something going around wasn't

something you could catch—it was something that grew deep inside of you—anger! "Are you sure? I don't want to put you out…"

"Not a problem. I should be back in an hour or so."

Claire panicked as she hung up the phone. It was all happening way too fast.

CHAPTER 33

Claire watched through the front window as Karen backed her Mustang out of the garage and turned toward town. Her hands felt clammy as she walked to the den; she wiped them on the front of her jeans before scribbling a quick note for Jade. *Back in a bit.* Then she slid the note under the bedroom door.

From a cabinet in the mudroom, she lifted a gold key attached to an oval plastic key ring. The word *Reeves* was written in thick, black letters. She held it in one hand, squeezing the key between her fingers, creating a zigzagged indentation. Then, thinking better of it, she hung the key ring back up on the hook—that key was for friends. Matt no longer qualified as a friend.

With her running shoes double-knotted, she left the house, wandering across her lawn toward the neighbors'. On the way, she reached down and deadheaded a single flower before walking the last several steps. Silently, she crept onto her neighbor's porch. She glanced down the street in both directions before tilting the flowerpot and removing the key. Even in the late May heat, it felt cold in her hand—more so than it had the previous night. Silently, she slipped it into the lock, turning it to the right. She pressed the lever down, opening the door without a sound. Without any hesitation, she stepped into the entry.

Claire bent down and scratched Karen's tiger-striped cat as he stretched in the stream of sunshine that poured in through the glass door. She listened for Matt but heard nothing. She tiptoed through the entry and down the hall, stopping at the doorway to Matt's office. He was not at his desk.

As she turned into the office, she noticed him asleep on his couch—positioned in the middle of the room, facing the jagged stone fireplace. He lay on his side with his head buried in an oversized turquoise pillow. Claire watched his shallow breaths. He slept as if he didn't have a care in the world.

Again, she replayed the conversation that had kept her awake for the better part of the night. Her one-time friend was now a criminal—a sex offender. He had violated, in the worst possible way, every trust she had ever had in him. He was not worth her time, but he *owed* her honesty. Why had he done this? Why had he chosen Jade as his victim? Had he done the same to Henry?

Claire moved farther into the room and came face-to-face with what felt like another nightmare—only this one wasn't a dream. She slowly squeezed her fists into tight balls—shaking with anger as her rage grew. She pictured beating him—striking him over and repeatedly until he could not hurt anyone else. She was aware she was getting dangerously close to losing control—but she could not stop herself.

Stepping backward, she bumped into the fireplace hearth. As she reached behind her to steady herself, her hand brushed the fireplace tools in their metal stand. She pulled her hand forward and a long, black iron poker came with it. She studied it, held it across her hands as she weighed the damage it could inflict.

Claire clung to the handle of the poker with both hands as she lifted it above her head. She tried to steady it, but her arms shook. Her anger pushed her forward and she could not fight it. It taunted her—*Make him pay! He has to pay!*

Voices screamed inside of her as she struggled with the iron rod. She moved near the arm of the couch, close to Matt's head, as the voices from her past and present wove together—calling out to her.

Kill him! Kill him! Kill him!

Are you afraid?

Your father was right about both you and your mother; you're both more trouble than you're worth.

What are you going to do about it?

What kind of a mother lets this happen to her own daughter? You should have known. You weren't paying attention! Pay attention!

Do it now. This has to end.

You little brat! You'll never amount to anything.

I'll kill your whole family…

Claire's hands trembled. The metal rod swayed in ever-widening circles above her head as the words garbled together.

Kill...pay attention...death...don't deserve...more trouble...hate...

Claire's body swayed as she struggled with the jumble of emotions. She wanted revenge—for Jade, for herself, for her mother, for her family.

The voices grew so loud, she couldn't stand it anymore.

"NO!" she screamed as she slammed the fireplace poker against the arm of the couch with newfound strength. The thud resonated in Claire's ears. The silence that followed was deafening.

Claire crashed to the floor at the end of the couch. "No!" she cried more quietly. "How could you? How could you, Matt? How could you do that to Jade?"

"What in the hell is going on in here?" Karen yelled, coming through the door of the office. "Claire? Why are you here? Matt, what's going on?"

Claire's eyes flew open. Matt was standing so close to her she could feel his hot breath on her face. The fingers of his hand curved into a half-circle and closed tightly around her neck. As she struggled to breathe, but Claire did not see Matt; she saw Edward—she saw Roy. Lights flickered and she could feel herself losing consciousness. She could feel fingernails digging into the sides of her neck, thumbs pressing into her throat.

"Matt!" Karen screamed as she tugged on his arm. "Stop! Matt! Stop! What's happening?"

With every ounce of energy in her, Claire kicked at Matt, landing a hard blow to the center of his stomach, knocking the wind out of him. She pried his fingers from around her neck as he struggled to catch his breath. Finally free, she scooted backward—away from the man she was positive she had killed seconds before. She massaged her throat with her hand as she violently coughed. She pulled herself upward, using the bricks of the fireplace as grips. Her legs wobbled as she awkwardly moved toward Karen and away from Matt.

"I asked what happened. Matt? Claire?" Karen looked from one to the other—angry and confused by what she had witnessed.

Claire never let Matt out of her sight. She would never trust him again.

He dropped onto the leather couch and pressed his elbows to his knees, dropping his head into his hands and tugged at his hair. "It's over," he said. "It's all over."

"No, it's not, you son-of-a-bitch!" Claire yelled. "It may be over for you—" Her voice grew quiet. "But it'll *never* be over for Jade." She walked to the opposite end of the couch from where he sat. "Do you get that?" she said softly. "You took everything from her. She's a child—and you even took that away. You stole her childhood, Matt. That's the worst thing you could have ever done to her." Claire wiped her eyes with her sleeve. "She'll never be the same. She'll never forget this, not ever. She'll carry it with her the rest of her life—everything you did to her—everything—she'll always remember."

She could hear Matt sobbing, but she didn't care. He wasn't the victim. Jade was.

Karen moved toward her; her face was as white as snow. Her entire body shook; she looked like she could fall apart at any moment. Claire touched Karen's shoulder, but Karen turned away from her and moved toward her husband. She knelt in front of Matt and placed her hands on his knees; she pressed her forehead against his. Tears ran down her cheeks and dropped onto his jeans.

"Say it isn't true, Matt. Tell me you didn't do what Claire just accused you of. Tell me you wouldn't," she begged. Her voice quivered as she spoke louder. "Please, Matt. Please tell me!"

Matt never said a word—but he never looked away either.

"Matt?" Karen begged again. "Please!" But Karen had her answer. Claire knew his silence told her everything. Slowly, Karen stood and gently, lovingly touched her husband's cheek. Then she pulled her arm back and slapped him across the face with everything in her. The sound resonated through the room. "You bastard!" she said. "How could you?" Matt did not touch his cheek, even as an angry red handprint began to grow; instead, he stared at the floor and said nothing.

Karen moved behind Matt's desk. She picked up the phone and punched in three numbers: *911*. After the call, she pressed the off button and dropped it back into the cradle. Then she fell into his chair, laid her head on his desk, and sobbed.

Claire didn't know what to do. She stood frozen, behind the couch—three feet from Matt and even less than that from Karen.

Within minutes, the wail of a siren permeated the walls. The lights flashed outside, sending shards of red and blue light into the office, through the open curtains.

Claire opened the front door before the police even reached the front step. She spoke to the officers in hushed tones before leading them to the office. She watched as they pushed Matt to the floor, cuffed his hands behind his back, and searched him for weapons. Karen turned away as they read him his rights.

As the police pushed Matt toward the door, Karen blocked their exit. Matt's head hung forward, his chin resting nearly against his chest. She lifted his chin with her index finger and stared into his eyes. "If you ever loved me, you had better tell them the truth—tell them everything. Don't make Jade have to relive this—don't do that to her."

He gave such a tiny nod that Claire almost missed it. Her shoulders sagged, grateful Jade would be spared reliving much of the nightmare before lawyers or in court.

Karen slowly stepped aside and allowed the police to usher her husband toward the front door. Just before he reached the door, he turned around and said, "Karen, I am so, so sorry."

"There are some things *sorry* doesn't fix," she told him.

Two officers took him outside as two others entered the house to take their statements.

***

After the police left, the two women sat in silence. Once friends, Claire could no longer put a label on what they were. She could think of nothing to say as she stood in front of Karen. No words felt right, so she remained silent.

"Claire, go home. Please just go," Karen begged. "Let me deal with this alone. It's *my* mess."

Claire reached out to touch Karen's arm but pulled her hand back when Karen turned away.

"Karen, it's not your mess. It's Matt's."

Karen leaned against the wall and slid onto the floor; she rested her head against her knees. "Then why do *I* feel so guilty?"

Claire watched Karen for several moments before walking out of Matt's office and out the front door. She stifled a sob as she pulled the door shut. At the bottom of the stairs, she turned and looked at the house—knowing for certain this would be the last time she would ever stand on their porch.

As she walked across both yards, avoiding the questioning looks of the neighbors who were still gathered in the street, she recalled the last words the police officer said to her before he left. "You're lucky, Mrs. Stanton, that you didn't kill Mr. Reeve with that fireplace poker, or this story would have had a much different ending. It would have been you in the cruiser. You're also lucky he isn't pressing charges."

Claire didn't feel lucky. She had allowed her daughter to be molested. She had lost her best friend. And her family had fallen apart. Luck was a matter of opinion; at that moment, she felt like the most *unlucky* woman on the planet.

Claire slipped back into her house and went directly to the den. She made two phone calls—calls she should have made long ago.

Before the receptionist was even done with her greeting, Claire spoke, "My name is Claire Stanton. My daughter needs to speak with someone; she's been molested." She paused as the receptionist wrote down the information needed to make the appointment with a therapist. "Actually," Claire continued, "we've both been molested. I need help too," she finally confessed.

The second call was also direct and to the point. "Michael, I can't do this alone anymore. You need to come home—NOW."

CHAPTER 34

Claire slid across the metal bench, moving closer to Michael, who held a fresh bag of popcorn. "Hey," she said. "I'll share my soda if you'll share your popcorn."

"Okay," he mumbled as he watched his daughter gracefully move the ball down the field. "That's quite the little soccer player we made, huh?"

"Must be my genes," Claire teased as she elbowed him in the ribs. "As I recall, *you* can't even walk and chew gum at the same time. How's that ankle, by the way?" she laughed.

"Unfair," Michael playfully complained as the popcorn bag slipped from his grip, fanning white kernels along the metal bleachers. He shrugged. "Alright, I concede. Give me the soda."

"No way, butterfingers! No can do!" They both chuckled.

Michael wrapped an arm around his wife's shoulder and slid solidly against her, pressing his hip into hers. He leaned over and took a long draw from the straw. As he did, Claire jumped up to cheer for her daughter, dropping the soda into what she believed was his outstretched hand. The uncovered cup tipped onto his lap and drenched his tan shorts with an off-brand diet cola.

The whistle blew; a time-out was called by the other team. Claire plopped down on the metal bench. Michael pressed donated napkins to the front of his shorts. "What the heck happened to you?" she giggled.

Michael smirked. "You know that whole 'got your genes thing'? Well, I kind of wonder if maybe Jade was switched at birth. I'm thinking there could be a family out there looking for some graceful twelve-year-old—wanting to return a clumsy one to her rightful family."

Claire shook her head. "Oh, don't you blame me because you're a klutz!" She gave her husband a playful push on the shoulder as the game resumed.

The bleachers were packed. Those who could not find seats had gathered along the sides of the field, hooting and hollering in support of their team. Jade's name was yelled constantly—by fans, coaches, and, of course, Henry, who never let his sister out of his sight.

Claire searched for Karen in the sea of red. Neither she nor Matt had ever missed Jade's games until the semi-finals a week ago. She wasn't surprised she couldn't find her. The local paper had run the story about Matt on the front page and the TV stations played updates a couple times a week. Several neighbors called to ask how they could help. *Support Karen* was always her answer, but she knew better. Even most of the neighbors viewed Karen as guilty by association instead of seeing her as another of Matt's victims. If Karen had gone into hiding, she wouldn't blame her; as a matter of fact, she didn't blame her for anything Matt had done.

The final whistle blew, sending the crowd into a chaos of excitement—the score was 5-4. Jade and her teammates raced across the field while the Willow Brook fans cheered them on. With Jade in the lead, they met the other team—shaking hands with their opponents and coaches. The line came to a sudden halt as Jade leaned in and whispered to the captain of the opposing team; the two girls hugged before the line continued to move again.

Claire and Michael climbed out of the stands and merged into the crowd. With one hand on his wife's shoulder, Michael steered Claire in the direction of their daughter.

By the time they broke through the crowd, Jade was standing with a local newspaper reporter, a woman Claire had worked with on a handful of school events. The crowd stepped back as the *Willow Brook Gazette* photographer snapped a few shots of the team holding the trophy.

The reporter wrapped her fingers around Jade's forearm and pulled her to the side. She pulled a skinny blue pen from behind her ear with her other hand. "So, Jade, how does it feel to be the state champions?"

Jade stared at the huge trophy she held in her hands, then she passed it over to a confused Jeff Hughes, who stood to her left. "It's amazing! We've worked so hard for this. It just feels awesome!"

The reporter looked toward the other team, who was sitting in a half circle on the ground listening to their coaches. "You said something to the Wildcat's captain. Do you mind sharing what that was?"

Jade kicked at the ground with the tip of her soccer cleats. She shrugged her shoulders. "I just told her that her team didn't really lose. They played hard—and that's what mattered." Jade looked at the reporter. "*That's* what makes you a winner."

The woman scribbled down Jade's words on a small pad of paper before flipping the page. "I know this hasn't been officially announced yet, but there's a rumor you've been chosen MVP. How does that make you feel?"

Jade didn't smile. Claire could see her wheels turning as she weighed her words carefully. "Honestly, I don't think there should be an MVP—everyone's equally important. Soccer teams are like families. You can't be successful if not everyone does their job." She turned toward the reporter and raised her palms upwards. "And the thing is, you either win as a team or you lose as a team."

Claire turned toward Michael and pressed her damp eyes onto his shoulder. She and Jade had only begun meeting with the therapist, but Claire could see the clouds beginning to lift—from Jade, from herself, from their relationship—and it truly felt amazing.

"Excuse me," Jade said as she stepped away from the reporter. She jogged toward her mom and dad with Henry on her heels. Jade fell into their arms as the photographer snapped a couple more pictures.

Over Jade's shoulder, Claire noticed Karen's familiar gait as she walked toward the parking lot. She wore oversized sunglasses and one of Matt's red baseball caps with a bill that had been pressed inward—rounded until the edges just barely reached the frames of her sunglasses. A ponytail of dark brown hair hung through the back of the cap—where her blonde hair should have been. Karen had been taken away—like her husband—only in a completely different way.

CHAPTER 35

Claire had just unplugged the vacuum when she heard a knock on the door. A knock—not a stranger—strangers rang the doorbell; not a friend—they walked in. Neighbors knocked.

She stepped on the rewind button and waited as the cord slithered into the vacuum before heading to the door. Claire could see no one on the porch as she peeked through the sheer curtains. She shrugged and headed back toward the living room. But she heard it again—softer this time—a quick double knock. When she opened the door, a smile slowly spread across her face.

Karen's clothes hung on her gaunt frame. Pale blue circles had grown under her eyes and her skin stretched tautly across the hollowness of her cheeks. Her lips curved slightly downward at the corners; her early summer tan had all but disappeared. But the biggest change Claire noticed was the missing spark of joy that had always been the sunshine of Karen's personality. Her words were flat and metered.

It had been just shy of two months since the day Claire set the wheels of justice in motion—two months since Karen lost the life she knew. Claire had seen her no more than a handful of times—each one in passing, and usually from a distance. There may have been a quick wave or a nod, but, more often than not, Karen looked away.

Claire wanted to hug her, to hold her tightly and never let go. She wanted to turn the calendar pages back six months—to stop everything before it happened—back to a time when they could talk about anything. But that was impossible.

"Hi, Claire." Karen's eyes were cast toward the ground—on some imaginary spot that kept her focused on anything but her friend's face. "Am I intruding? I can come ba..."

"Now's perfect." Claire gently touched Karen's upper arm. "I've missed you."

Karen tucked her hands deep inside her front pockets and raised her shoulders like a child as she finally met Claire's eyes. "It's been two months—I think we should talk."

"I agree. There's so much we need to say." Claire stepped to the side and signaled for her friend to enter. "Come on in. I'll make some coffee."

Karen shook her head. "I don't think that's a good idea. Can we talk out here?"

"Sure," Claire said as she stepped onto the porch and pulled the door shut. "Do you want anything to drink—or eat?" she asked as she again eyed Karen's stick-thin figure.

Karen shook her head. "No. I'm okay."

The two women planted themselves side by side in large whitewashed wooden rockers on the front porch.

"Are the kids home?" Karen asked nervously as she rocked herself with one foot, the other tucked beneath her.

"No." Claire shook her head. "They're both spending the day with friends—sleepovers, actually. I have the day to myself."

Karen's eyes grew wide with concern. "People you trust?" she asked hesitantly.

Claire bit her lip. "You know, during the past few months, I've learned I can't control everything. I can spend the rest of my life worrying about all the bad things that *might* happen or I can trust the world is filled with more good than evil. I'm choosing to worry less. I have to."

Karen pulled a tissue from her front pocket. "I'm sorry. That was a stupid question," she said as she shook her head. "You trusted Matt and me."

"Karen, I still trust *you*. I've always trusted you. You're my best friend. This was never about you. It was Matt who did this."

Karen stopped rocking; her shoulders drooped as she sighed loudly. "Claire, I'm so sorry. I'm sorry it's taken me this long to be able to face you. I can't even look at myself yet. You can probably tell that by the way I look," she said as she tugged on her ponytail. Her voice grew thick and her lashes glistened. "If I can't see myself, then I don't exist—and if I don't exist, then none of this was my fault—none of it happened."

A sudden, single, sharp-edged sob escaped from Claire as she scooted to the front of her rocker. "Oh, Karen, you *do* exist; don't ever think that way. No one should ever feel invisible. You're better than that. What Matt did shouldn't make *you* want to disappear."

"But don't you see, Claire? It was as much my fault as Matt's. I should have seen it. I should have known something was going on." She slammed her fist down on the arm of the chair. "I've gone over it a million times trying to figure out how I missed it—what clues I should have seen but didn't." Her voice dropped to a whisper. "What's wrong with me that I didn't see it? I can't even begin to tell you how sorry I am..." Her voice broke, then faded away; her last few words were buried in silence.

"Karen, I know how hard it was for you—to even knock on my door—but there's something you need to know." She reached over and locked their fingers together. "How this played out—it's on *all* of us. Don't get me wrong—what Matt did was unconscionable and unforgivable—but we *all* handled it wrong." She stared at the late summer bursts of color in her gardens. "Jade needed to tell us what was happening—even though Matt threatened her—she needed to let us know. There were signs before he molested her—things that made her uncomfortable, but she said nothing. And me—I never talked to Jade about sexual abuse or what to do if someone makes you feel uncomfortable—because I didn't believe it could ever happen to one of my children. I was so busy trying to be the *perfect* mom that I didn't see the reality through my rose-colored glasses." Claire wiped her tears away with the back of her hand. "Michael, well, he missed it all. When things got tough, he pulled away. He knew we were struggling, but the case pulled him away from us. He chose work over his family. I told him I would take care of things at home—but I never expected... Well, you know." Claire slid her chair closer to Karen's. "And you, Matt had to hide it from you, more than anyone else, because he loved you—and he didn't want to hurt you."

"But, Claire..."

Claire held up her hand. "When you love someone,

you'll do anything to keep them from finding out what you're really like—who you really are deep down inside. Do you know why? Because you're afraid they won't love you if they know.

"*I* should have known, Karen. I've never told you this, but, as a child—I was molested and physically and emotionally abused. I never told you because I was afraid I'd lose you as a friend if you knew how screwed up I was because of it."

Karen shook as she sobbed out loud. "*I* should have known too."

Claire's eyes widened. "What?"

Karen's chin dropped to her chest and she squeezed her eyes shut. "I was eight. I was so ashamed and so afraid, I didn't tell anyone." She looked at Claire. "I kept asking myself what I did to deserve it. Why did he choose me as his victim?"

Claire tightened her grip on Karen's hand. "I've spent my entire life asking that same question. *What did I do to deserve this?* The thing is, *I* didn't do anything wrong and *you* didn't either—and neither did Jade. It's *not* our shame. It's Roy's shame, and my father's, and Matt's…"

"And Stan's," Karen added.

"Yes—and Stan's. They're responsible. We have no guilt in any of it." Claire cast a weak smile in Karen's direction. "We just have to find a way to let it go. I know that's easier said than done because I've been struggling with it for over thirty years." She squeezed Karen's hand before letting go. "Have you spoken to Matt?"

"I told him I wanted a divorce," Karen said as she continued to shred the damp tissue.

"How'd that go?" Claire asked warily.

"It wasn't easy, but he said he loved me enough to let me move on. I guess that's all I can ask for."

"Have you made any other decisions?"

Karen looked toward her house. "That's why I came over here today," she said. She balled the tissue up, shoved it back into her front pocket, and wiped her tears away with the fingertips of both hands. She sat upright and drew in a deep breath before blowing it out in a rush of air. "I've spent the last couple of months, and a chunk of our savings, trying to decide how to move forward." This time, Karen took Claire's hand.

"I'm going back to Minnesota—back to my family. I'm also going back to school to get my teaching license." Claire felt her heart sink, but at the same time, she saw the first real sign of hope in her friend.

"I want to make a difference. Since I can't have kids of my own, this is how I'm going to do it."

Claire wrapped her in a tight hug. "Oh, Karen. I don't want you to move," she whispered, "but I understand. There are so many bad memories here."

Karen held Claire at arm's length. "Yes, but there are a lot of good memories here too," she said. Then she brushed her palms against one another—symbolically wiping away the mess Matt had put into motion. "And who knows, maybe I'll come back and work for that emotionless Will Ryan." She laughed.

"Well, yeah, about that..." Claire smiled as she shrugged. "There's so much you don't know."

Over the course of the next several hours, Claire shared Will's story, told her about her mother's letter, and shared the news of Edward and Cal. Before the afternoon was over, the two were sitting on the *back* porch laughing about old times, better times—as only two best friends could.

As the evening sky began its slide into darkness, Karen stretched. She carried the wine bottle and two empty glasses into the house with Claire following—holding a pizza box and a couple of paper plates and wadded-up napkins. Claire shoved the leftover pizza into the refrigerator, box and all. Karen rested her hands on the edge of the kitchen sink and stared into the dusk of the backyard. "You know, Claire, I've missed you so much." She turned and leaned a hip against the cupboard, wagging a finger back and forth between the two of them. "I've missed *this*—our friendship." Her eyes sparkled with dampness. "I made a decision this afternoon. After I get my degree, I'm coming back—*back home.* I'm coming back *here.*" Karen hugged Claire and walked out the front door without looking back. "I'll see you later, my friend," she called as she closed the door.

CHAPTER 36

NINE MONTHS LATER

"Are you sure, Claire? You're positive you don't want me to go with you?" Michael leaned over his wife's shoulder and picked up one of the papers she had laid on the desk. "I'm not a big fan of you doing this alone." He couldn't bear the thought of her being away from him any more than she could stand the idea of him ever going on another business trip, but this particular excursion frightened him more than he could say.

After last summer's crisis, he'd given up the idea of becoming a partner at Grayson and Delaney. Instead, he opened a small law firm in Willow Brook. In light of everything that had happened, he had no intention of distancing himself from his family ever again.

Claire had resigned as PTA president. Will no longer needed her as a buffer between himself and the other members; he was coming around. The change in him during his second year had shocked the town, but Claire knew better. She had seen the real Will Ryan long ago—and he hadn't changed at all; he had just started knocking down the walls he'd built around himself.

Jade and Henry were happy and adjusting to life in a flawed family. They delighted in the store-bought cookies, delivery pizza, and a mom who wasn't perfect.

Yet, with everything moving toward the positive, there was still one thing Claire had to do before she could completely move forward—and she had to do it alone. Her therapist had told her she needed to confront her past, not hide from it any longer. As hard as it was, she knew that meant going back to Manchester, to the house she had grown up in.

"No, Michael. This is something I need to do alone," she said as she pulled the paper from his hand and tucked it into a folder with the rest of her notes. "The only thing I need you to do is look after the kids while I'm gone—and I'm *not* going to call you. I know you'll all be fine. I should be back in a couple of days."

Claire picked up her gray and purple duffle bag and pulled the strap over her shoulder. At the door, she pressed her husband's cheeks between her hands. "I love you—always and forever," she said, letting her lips linger on his.

"I love you more!" Michael called as she walked toward her car.

"Impossible," she whispered. "Impossible."

***

At first, the open road felt freeing as Claire settled in for the three-hour drive. Once out on the highway, she set the cruise at sixty-five and let the car take the lead. She had not traveled along this stretch of highway in nearly twenty years; she was surprised by the vast growth. About twenty miles north of Willow Brook, the road narrowed to two lanes with a meager shoulder on each side. She dropped her speed down to fifty-five and guided the car down her lane.

Memories bombarded her the entire trip, begging for her attention. More than once, she fought the urge to turn the car around and return home.

As she approached the small town of Manchester, she felt her anxiety build. Was she ready? She didn't know if she ever would be. She was here and, as much as she wanted to, she would not let herself run back to the safety of her family. She needed to face her past head on.

The main drag looked exactly as it had when she was a child. A couple of churches—including the one she attended every Sunday, the drug store, Eccentrics Clothing, Joel's Hardware, the bowling alley, Northern Lights Floral, and of course, the Elkhorn Bar—all labeled with hand-painted signs— no neon signs, no bright lights of the city. She wondered if they were owned by the same families of her youth and if Manchester had always been a happy place for them.

Between the church and the drug store, she turned right—toward the school. She was sure there were names for the streets, but she had never noticed them before; she wasn't even sure if the corners were labeled with the familiar green signs. It was a small town; directions were given by landmarks and buildings—not by street names.

She parked in front of the school. It hadn't changed at all. It was an unusual array of reddish brick and white stucco. The building was oddly shaped due to multiple additions. She stepped out of her car and closed the door but did not press the lock button. There was not another person as far as she could see.

She followed the cracked and uneven sidewalk to the back of the school—to the playground where she hid, every noon hour, in plain sight. The old swing set with the wooden seats had been replaced. The bright blue rubber seats matched the other updated pieces of equipment. Claire sat down on one of the swings and gently swung back and forth, pushing herself with the tips of her toes. Her lips curled into a devious smile as she dropped her purse on the ground near the swing. She pushed herself backward and began to pump her legs, just as she had as a child. Before long, she was soaring, nearly even with the top of the swing set. This was where she had spent her recesses as a child; this is where she hid. From her vantage point, she saw the same things she had seen back then—small houses to the right and in front of her, and the football field to the left. Virtually nothing had changed—except her.

After the dizziness from swinging subsided, Claire peeked through the classroom windows on her way back to her car. The inside of the school had not changed either. Save for bulletin boards and posters, Mr. Manson's, Miss Groob's, and even Mrs. Handler's rooms looked the same as they had when she was a child. The chalkboards had been replaced with whiteboards, but the tiny ceramic drinking fountains in each room looked the same. Even the black and white checked linoleum even looked familiar.

As she drove away from the school, the Dairy Queen fell into view. She pulled into the lot and went inside; she ordered a small cone—just as she had when she and her mother drove out of Manchester for the last time all those years ago. The Amoco station next door was still open, but the A & W appeared to have long since closed. So little had changed; she doubted it ever would.

Claire followed the highway north. The curvy road

wound around numerous small lakes, cutting through swamps and bogs. As she got closer to the gravel road that led to her house, her heart started to race again. The gray cloth seat belt jumped in time to her beating heart. Her hands grew slick; she held one at a time in front of the cool air blowing out of the vents.

Almost twelve miles from town, Claire slowed to a crawl before turning right and onto the dirt road that led to the house of her past. The soft sand and ruts of the country road pulled the car sideways, reminding her of the Sunday trips to town.

On the desolate road, she never drove faster than thirty miles an hour. Miller's Pond, the gravel pit, and Frank's pasture all linked memories together. Sweat beaded along her hairline and she tilted the blower toward her face. The car began to slow before coming to a stop at the edge of the soft gravel. The house sat around the next cluster of trees. Claire wasn't sure she was ready, but she'd come this far; she wasn't about to stop now.

Wiping her hands on the front of her jeans, she took several deep breaths and eased back onto the road—the car slowly crept around the bend and past the cluster of trees that separated her present from the past.

CHAPTER 37

A floodgate of emotions hit Claire as the house came into view. She struggled to hold them at bay but knew her attempts were futile. She pulled to the side of the road and let the tears fall as the memories exploded.

The old house was still white, but the black shutters had been replaced with dark green ones. Several Adirondack chairs were lined up across the front deck. Flowering plants filled large green planters in each corner of the deck. Other than the color and the décor on the deck, the house looked virtually the same.

The seedlings her mother had planted along the gravel driveway had grown into towering pines. The rock gardens overflowed with color—obviously loved and cared for as much as they had been under her mother's care. She wondered if any of the perennials were the ones Tess had painstakingly chosen years ago, or if too many years had passed for their survival.

She wasn't sure how many times the house had been sold over the years. She had not looked up the name of the owners; she didn't really want to know. All she needed was to see the place—to see it as a home filled with love—then, she could move forward.

Claire put the car in gear and drove up the gravel driveway. She stopped in front of the open garage door where Edward had died. A shiver ran up her spine as a faded image of his blank eyes stared at her. She had heard the noise of metal toolbox hitting the concrete floor all the way in the house and had come running to check on her mother. As she rounded the corner of the building, her mother stood with her hands balled at her sides. She was seething with anger, but as soon as she saw Claire, Tess had whisked her out of the garage and back into the house.

Claire shook the image away and focused her attention on the garage itself. The outrageously large building was nearly as big as the house. It had served no purpose other than to house Edward's prized possessions—his car, guns, golf clubs, and a limited number of tools.

She pulled the door handle open and slipped out of the car, gently closing it with only a small click. The last thing she wanted to do was awaken more sleeping ghosts.

She stepped onto the pitted sidewalk, instantly rising on her toes—tiptoeing toward the house. Edward's presence was thick. It coerced her into those same old habits—forced her back into her childhood invisibility as she climbed the eight steps to the back door.

Softly, she knocked on the wooden screen door. When no one answered, she knocked again. An old woman suddenly appeared behind the screen door, startling Claire with her sudden appearance. The elderly woman could not have been more than five feet tall, and Claire doubted she weighed more than eighty-five pounds soaking wet. "Can I help you?" she asked in a worn-out voice. Truthfully, *could anyone help her*? Looking into the entry, she wasn't certain this was a good idea anymore.

"I, um. I'm Claire Stanton—Claire *O'Brien* Stanton," she corrected—emphasizing the O'Brien in case it might spark a memory for the woman. "I used to live in this house when I was small."

For a split second, the woman's eyes grew large before she repeated the name. "O'Brien, you say? My husband and I got this house years ago from a woman whose last name was O'Brien. Let me think…" She tapped her cheek as if in deep thought.

"Tess O'Brien?" Claire offered. "Theresa, really."

"Yes, yes, that was it—Theresa." The woman never looked away, and Claire grew even more uncomfortable. "She had a little girl about nine or ten—a pretty little blonde thing as I recall."

"That was me." Claire smiled.

"So, you're the little girl who lived in this house, and you say your name is Claire."

"Yes, Mary Claire, actually."

"Hmmm." The woman tipped her head. "You must have

been so sad to have had to leave. Charles and I moved here when the tail end of our brood was still at home." From behind the screen, Claire could tell the woman's smile held sadness.

Claire felt a pressure build in the back of her eyes. "Were you happy here?" she asked.

"Not in the beginning," the old woman admitted, "but as time went on, we grew to love it."

"My fa...—my father built this house about forty years ago. He built it for my mother." She faltered with the word *father*. Edward was not her father, but that no longer mattered.

The old woman pushed the door open and held it for Claire. "Come on in, dear. I have a feeling you'd like to look around."

"Really?" Claire pressed a hand to her chest in surprise. "I don't need to come in. I can just walk the yard."

The old woman pushed the door open a bit farther, waiting for Claire to enter. Her eyes held a knowing look— something that told Claire she knew more than she was letting on. "Somehow I think you need to see more than just the outside of this big old house." As Claire stepped into the entry, the woman patted her on the arm. "You look like you could use some tea. How 'bout if I go make us some?"

"Oh please, don't go to any trouble for me. I'll just take a quick peek and get out of your hair."

"No, dear, it's no trouble at all. You've actually done me quite a favor. I get so lonesome out here all by myself. I just love having company."

She led Claire into the kitchen. The memories instantly began to build. Claire clung to the corner of the doorway to keep her legs from buckling. Everywhere she looked, she saw ghosts: her mother, Edward, the men who infested it on hunting weekends, and Roy—especially Roy.

The old woman took her hand and guided her to the middle of the kitchen. Her hand felt the way Claire imagined, soft and worn—like a pair of old familiar work gloves. "I'm sure the memories are strong, but you'll be all right, dear," she said as she patted Claire's hand. "It's the memories that make us who we are."

The old woman took a small glass from the dish drainer

and drew some cold water for her guest. Claire grabbed onto it with both hands to keep it from spilling but, still, the water sloshed over the top of the glass. "Oh, don't worry about that, just drink. This floor needs a good washing anyway." Claire tipped the glass up and downed the entire thing before handing it back to the woman.

She grabbed a napkin off the table to wipe up the spilled water, but the old woman pulled it from her hands. "I have all day with nothing to do," she said. "You go ahead and take a look around. I'll make us that tea. Feel free to go anywhere you'd like." The old woman's kindness touched Claire. She reminded her so much of her own mother. "And take your time; there's no rush. When you're done, come on back and we'll have a nice chat."

"I think I'd like that," she said.

Claire ran her hands along the woodwork that separated the kitchen from the dining room. Then she pushed the café door open and stood between the two rooms. How many times had she waited for her mother in this exact same spot? How many times had her father—no, how many times had *Edward* thrown her into the doors as he passed by, knocking her out of his way? It was more than she could count.

Claire slowly moved about the house, taking tentative steps as she entered each room. Memories layered one over another—a heavy burden to carry. Again, she wondered if she should leave.

As she stepped into the living room, the ghosts of her past grew stronger and appeared faster than she could push them away. Her feet felt heavy as she moved to the center of the room; yet, everywhere she went, she tiptoed.

The old woman's couch sat in front of the long picture window just as her mother's couch had when Claire lived there—but this couch was pushed tighter to the wall, leaving no place for *little* Claire to hide behind. Slowly, she pulled it forward, crouched down. and touched the floor where she had spent many evenings. What if she had stayed behind the couch on those November nights? What would have happened? Would Roy have found her? Would she have been safe?

Claire chided herself for asking *what if*. She knew

better. Her therapist told her she had to live in the present. He'd told her, *You need to confront the past and then let it go.* That was why she was here.

Gingerly, she sat down in the middle of the couch. After a few moments, she lay down and rested her head on a small navy pillow. With her eyes wide open, she let her memories guide her back to that night of long ago. Roy stood over her. He held both of her hands in one of his large ones—pressing the mass over her face. He pinned her legs down beneath the weight of his knee—and with his free hand, he reached under her pajama bottoms. She froze the vision, separated herself from it, and carefully analyzed it, coming to the realization there was nothing she could have done. She finally believed it had not been her fault. She had done nothing wrong.

She trembled as she sat up, but she felt differently than she had when she walked into the room. Peace had found her. She now accepted she had been too young to fight back—too small to defend herself against Roy.

Claire stood up and slowly walked down the hallway. Before she even entered the narrow space, she had already eased onto her tiptoes again. The door to Edward's office was open; glimmers of the man she had once called *father* were all around her. She held her breath tightly, afraid to release it for fear he would hear. She peeked around the corner, half expecting to see him sitting at his desk; she expected him to reach out and grab her.

The room looked nearly the same as it had years ago. The massive desk was built into one wall and had not been removed. The walls were still the same off-white color they had been when it was Edward's office, but the room no longer had a sterile feel. It was filled with plants and candles and knickknacks that held importance to *this* family. The tall built-in shelves were filled with more photos than books: photos of children and adults—both old and new. She picked up a heavy wooden frame that housed a black and white picture of a man holding a small girl who appeared to be about two years old; the girl's arms were hooked around his neck. Their heads were pressed together. Claire could not see the faces clearly, but the photographer had captured pure joy. The picture had been taken in the living room, just steps away. When she had lived in the house, the only photos these shelves held were ones of Edward's mother—none of Tess or Claire.

She ran her hand along the edge of the desk, but that light touch elicited no emotion. She pulled out the antique desk chair and sat in it. She told herself it was just a room; it didn't control her, yet there was something she couldn't place—something that still made her feel uneasy.

She pushed the chair back against the desk and stood in the center of the large space. Slowly, she turned around in a circle, facing the desk, the window, the built-in shelving, the end wall. Suddenly, her knees buckled and she dropped to the floor and crawled to the place her mother had lay bleeding all those years ago. It had not been a dream; she knew that now. It had really happened. Nothing but the memory marked the carpet, which had most likely been replaced a few times in the last thirty years, but she knew the exact spot her baby brother or sister had ceased to exist. She touched it with her fingertips and drew a small heart on the carpet's surface. Then she stood up and left the room, closing the door behind her—leaving all the memories on the other side.

Claire continued down the hall and into the room that had been her bedroom, the room she'd spent weekends in— hidden away from the fighting. It looked nearly the same. The built-in dresser and desk clung to one wall; although it appeared to have been repainted, the color was still the palest shade of pink—just as it had been years ago. A handmade quilt of rose and white squares lay across the double bed. Strangely, she felt she had never left.

The closet door was closed; Claire gently pulled it open. The familiar musty smell lurched at her with a wave of memories so strong, it nearly knocked her down. Tears blurred her vision as she crawled to the back of the large closet and leaned against the wall.

Light streamed into the small space, making her realize she had never been in the closet with the door fully open before—she had always used it to hide, to become invisible— to stay safe. The door had always been closed. As the sunlight filtered through the door, it seemed to wash away the bad memories, blocking out the darkness she had once felt there. It was no longer a place of refuge—it was just a closet. Without Edward, the house felt like a *home*.

The low, wide shelf had been removed. Claire was certain that in all the time the woman had lived here, no one had ever needed to hide beneath the shelf. She slid toward the side wall and ran her hand along the baseboard. She found the loose nails and removed the narrow piece of trim.

She slipped her hand into the small cutout in the base of the wall and pulled out the doll with the torn face. She was covered in dust from being hidden all those years. Claire held the tiny doll to her chest. "Betsy," she whispered, "I came back for you."

A corner of a birthday card slid out with the doll; Claire pulled it out the rest of the way. She blew on the surface and watched the small dust bunnies float into the beam of light. She traced the large, silvery seven with the tip of one finger. It had been the only card she ever remembered getting in this house. Edward told her cards were a waste of money, but her mother had tucked it in with the groceries and had slipped it under her pillow after she had fallen asleep on the night before her birthday. She knew what it said on the inside without even opening it. She had read it over and over, committing it to memory. *Mary Claire, you are more beautiful than the sunshine. Happy Birthday! I love you! Mom.* It didn't hurt to read it; it was part of her past—and the longer she spent in this house, the farther away her past moved.

Claire reached back into the space and felt around. Her hand touched a small piece of cool metal. With the tips of her fingers, she slid it out of the narrow space. It was a tarnished silver cross on a chain. She had never seen it before and wondered if someone from the new family had used her hiding place.

She fingered the chain and let it fall across her hand until the wide, flat cross lay in the center of her palm. Though tarnished from years of being hidden away, Claire could tell there was an inscription on the back. She rubbed the cross on the bottom of her shirt but still could not read the words. She moved to the window. As the sunshine reflected against the grayed metal, the words jumped out at her. *Calvin Fredrick Taylor-1942.* Claire was shocked. She held the cross to her heart, her *father's* cross—her real father. But how had it gotten into her hiding space? Where had it come from? He had never even lived in this house. Was it her mother's doing? Had she known about Claire's hiding place all along? Did she know that Claire would one day find it?

Claire slipped the small doll into her sweater pocket. The cross she hung around her neck, tucking it inside her shirt; the cold metal warmed quickly against her skin.

She replaced the baseboard, pushing the nails back into place. For over thirty years, her treasures had been locked away in her special hiding place, and one extraordinary gift had somehow made it to Claire when she needed it most.

***

Claire wandered through the rest of the house. It looked similar to the way it had when she was a child; no significant changes had been made. There were new paint colors, wallpaper, and carpeting in all the rooms, but none of those other rooms held the memories the first four had—none of them needed to be exorcised from her past in the same way.

CHAPTER 38

When Claire returned to the kitchen, the old woman sat at the table sipping tea from a china teacup. She poured hot water into a second cup and pushed a bowl of flavored teas toward Claire. Then she slid a plate of sliced lemon, a sugar bowl, and a small pitcher of milk in her direction. She took a small sip of her tea before setting the cup back into the saucer.

"Did you find what you were looking for, dear?" she asked.

Claire sighed. "I don't know—maybe." She absently touched her chest; her hand rested on the cross that lay beneath her shirt. "I'm not sure what I was even looking for. Closure?"

"Well, that's important to all of us," the old woman said as she patted Claire's hand. "You know, this house is the happiest place I've ever lived. I spent hours out in the gardens and sitting on the front porch drinking tea with my friends and my children, and I watched my grandkids climb the trees out back." She smiled. "Oh, don't get me wrong; I caught them all doing a lot of things they shouldn't have too. Things like climbing up the trellis and sneaking back into the house after a night of carousing. Oh, the stories I could tell you." She paused. "But this isn't about me. It's about you."

Claire nodded solemnly but could think of nothing to say.

"You know," the old woman continued, "maybe you could help me with something. I've always wondered what this house looked like before the fire."

Claire felt her knees tremble, and she grabbed the side of the table. Her stomach lurched upward, stirring old memories. Images of dangling from the deck's edge slammed through her.

The old woman's head tilted sideways, and her eyes sparkled. "Do you remember the fire, dear? Were you old enough to remember? No, I don't suppose you were. You probably would have been too young."

Claire reached across her chest and touched her shoulder—ran her finger along the wide white scar that had been there for as long as she could remember. She believed it had been just a nightmare—but according to the old woman, it hadn't been. Her father—Edward had reached out through the smoke to save her, only to dangle her over the edge of the deck—peeling her fingers off his hand—watching her fall to the ground below. No, she wasn't too young to remember, but for years, she had chosen to forget.

"Y-yes, I remember the fire," Claire whispered, "but— I'm sorry, I don't remember the house before that."

"Oh, nothing to be sorry about, dear. I'm sorry you *remember* it. It must have been terribly traumatic for you. I hope everyone got out safely."

Claire nodded.

The old woman absently stirred her tea with her spoon. "My Charles, God rest his soul," she said as she looked upward, "and I moved into this house after your father was killed. I should have sold this house when Charles died. My children begged me to move to the city, but I didn't want to." She looked around the kitchen. "The house is much too big for an eighty-nine-year-old woman to take care of alone. I've thought about selling it over the years, but I just couldn't part with it. I always felt there was something keeping me here." She laid her spoon back on the saucer. She wiped a dribble of tea off the table with her paper napkin, then she reached out and cupped her hand over Claire's again. "I somehow don't feel like I need to stay anymore. I think I've been waiting for *you*."

Claire felt a tear roll down her cheek. She pushed her chair back and wrapped her arms around the old woman's tiny shoulders. "I'm sorry, I haven't even asked your name," she said.

"It's Mary, honey—Mary Claire. It looks like we have one more thing in common than just the house."

Claire cried openly—the two shared time and memories of a house they hadn't even lived in together. After all these years, the memories of the house no longer held her hostage.

As the old woman stood, she wobbled slightly. "Oh my!

Suddenly, I feel so tired. It must be time for these old bones to take a nap. I think I'll go lie down for a while." The woman carried her cup to the sink. "Claire, honey, you stay as long as you need. Feel free to look around all you want. You won't bother me a bit."

Claire hugged the old woman. "Thank you," she whispered. "You're an angel."

The woman laughed. "I wouldn't go that far. You didn't know me in my heyday. I had a pretty wild streak back then." Claire joined the laughter.

The old woman touched Claire's cheek before she walked down the hall and into the room that had once been her own. "Good luck, dear. I'm glad you found closure." Then she waved a few fingers in Claire's direction and gently closed the door behind her.

CHAPTER 39

The house was silent. The trees outside were as still as could be. *The calm before the storm,* her mother used to say, but the sky was blue—clear and blue—a perfect, warm April evening. Claire knew there would be no storms—not anymore. Her storms had finally passed.

She leaned against the screen door and stared toward the top of the hill. Her head pressed against the mesh screen hard enough to leave an indent. Finally, she pushed the door open, shutting it quietly behind her so as not to wake the old woman.

She moved toward the hill, no longer tiptoeing. The ghosts were gone.

Claire slid down the hillside, searching for the exact location she used to lie. She tried to find the small divot that had been created from her weekly visits as a child, but after thirty-some years, the hole had disappeared. It had been filled in with the love of a family that had changed the house into a home. Finally, she settled on a spot and leaned back.

She rested her head in the crook of her arm. So many things had changed. The trees were taller—more majestic now—and the lower garden was overrun with weeds—flowering weeds that looked beautiful to Claire. A female deer nibbled on the spring buds at the edge of the woods.

"I'm going to be okay," she said out loud. "Not perfect, but okay. And that's all I need."

Lying on the hillside in the warm April sun, she thought of her mother and her father. She thought of Edward and even Roy. She thought of Michael and Jade and Henry. She thought of Karen and Matt and Will and Ellen and Aubrey—and she said a prayer for all of them.

***

Claire watched the sun drop below the horizon. As the gray of dusk settled in, she stood and brushed the dirt from her jeans, watching it fall onto the hillside she had once been a part of. She let it go—just like the bad memories. Then she snuck back into the house, just as she had done as a child.

She eased past Edward's office, not even glancing at the closed door. She didn't need to; what she needed was gone. Claire walked down the hallway to her bedroom, the room she shared with the old woman in two different lifetimes.

The door was closed—the old woman still inside.

She had an overwhelming need to thank her, to tell her goodbye. She wanted to let her know she had found peace. Everything had been filed away in places where it no longer hurt.

Claire pushed the door open and quietly moved toward the bed. The early moonlight shone in ribbons across the handmade quilt, across the tiny body lying beneath it. She gently touched the old woman's shoulder, but even before she did, she knew. The eighty-nine-year-old woman was no longer a part of this world; she had passed into the next. Like Claire, the old woman had finally found closure.

CHAPTER 40

Claire turned on the bedside lamp. Tears filled her eyes as she glanced at the old woman. They were both going home.

Leaning against the base of the lamp was a yellowed envelope. She blinked a few times as she brought the words written on the front into focus. She ran her fingers over the writing on the front. It wasn't the first part that caused her angst—it was the second. She read the words out loud. *Mary Claire O'Brien Stanton.* Then below that, in smaller print, surrounded by parentheses, she read, *Natalie Taylor.* Below that, written in block letters, was her address in Willow Brook. What was going on? How could this old woman have possibly known she had once been Natalie Taylor?

Claire touched the old woman's cool cheek. "You truly are an angel," she whispered. "I knew you knew more than you let on." Then she turned off the light and carried the letter to what had been Edward's office.

She drew the curtains and turned on the small desk lamp before pulling the letter from the envelope. She sat in the antique chair—the one Edward had used every weekend. She smoothed out the letter and mentally prepared herself for more truths.

Dear Mary Claire,

Or perhaps I should call you Natalie. I have kept track of you for your entire life. As I write this, I know you are married to a man named Michael, and you are expecting your first child. I am certain there will be more, just as I am certain you will make an amazing mother. We have that in common.

I was a good mother to all my children—including Eddie—your father. Growing up, Eddie was the sweetest boy. He was my oldest child; he made me a mother. We had an incredibly special bond. There was no son who loved his mother more.

Eddie was a smart, kind boy who lived for reading, music, and art. He was the most amazing artist I have ever seen. But all that changed when he turned 15. One day, on the school bus, he was drawing in his art book, the book he reserved for only his most amazing drawings. One of the older students grabbed his book and threw it out the window of the bus. Eddie watched as the binding broke and his drawings scattered along the highway. Something inside him snapped, and he changed from my sweet little boy to an angry young man. He no longer wanted to be Eddie; he insisted on being called Edward. He grew his hair long, picked fights, and got tossed out of school more times than I can count.

On the day he graduated from high school, he left home. No matter how many times we tried to find him, he was one step ahead of us. Then one day, a few years later, a fancy car pulled into our yard in the small town of Carver Springs. The man who stepped out of the car wore an expensive suit and held himself as if he came from money. When he stepped onto the porch, we realized it was our Eddie. We were so grateful to see him. I had missed him so much.

However, Eddie didn't come for a visit; he came for money. The lavish lifestyle he was leading cost him dearly and, even with a good job, he couldn't pay his bills. Charles gave him the money he wanted. After that, from time to time, Eddie would visit, but it was always the same—he needed money.

Then he met your mother. One day, he stopped by the house. But all he wanted was to tell us about this woman he was going to marry. We couldn't wait to meet her, but almost as soon as he told us about her, they had broken things off. Eddie again began coming around—for money.

Charles and I wanted to meet his Tess; she seemed to be the only person who could soften his hardness. Eddie had told us she worked at Jake's Bar in Amherst. We made the 40-mile trip, but we never spoke to her. The entire time, she ran herself ragged taking care of customers—taking care of you. We ate and left her a big tip.

Before long, Eddie told us he had married Tess and planned to raise Natalie as his own. We offered to host a dinner or a wedding reception, but that was not to be. He had told Tess he had no family—and that was the way he planned to keep it. It's hard to keep lies straight when you have so much to hide.

Eddie continued to come for money, and he and his father fought over his extravagant lifestyle. One day, shortly after they married, he showed up at the house. He begged us for cash. He told me they had decided to change the name of their little girl. She would be named after me—Mary Claire. Tess believed I had passed, so she agreed to change your name because it made Eddie happy. How could we say no to giving him money after learning you were going to be named after me? Charles wrote him a check, but when he handed it to him, he told him there would be no more—this was the end. Eddie grew angry and began grabbing everything of value. He took an expensive vase I had gotten from my mother, and several pictures of the two of us together, but he took none of Charles or his siblings. We only spoke to Eddie one time after that.

In those early days, we would see your family from a distance. Eddie looked so happy. He loved being your father. The picture in the den—the man with the little girl—is a picture of you and Eddie. It's the only one I have of the two of you.

But then Eddie began to change again. Money was tight and the lifestyle he promised your mother was threatened. The only way to keep her from spending money was to take away her ability to leave the house. He became cruel and controlling.

Eddie never let on there was a problem. He hid everything from your mother. He hid from the bill collectors; he hid from friends he owed money to. He made extra money by collecting fees from hunters who wanted to come north for a weekend in the woods. We found that out through a friend whose son paid Eddie for one of those hunting weekends.

Around the time you were 9, Charles and I took a short trip to the cities to spend time with one of our children. When we returned, the house had been ransacked. All of our valuables were gone. We knew it was Eddie. We didn't call the police, but we drove to Manchester to confront him.

It was a Friday afternoon in early April—the month Eddie died. Your mother was home alone. We told her everything—everything about Eddie and the money. She said nothing. Instead, she begged us to leave before he came home from work or you returned from school. We left, not knowing what would happen next.

We met Eddie as we were pulling out of the driveway. Charles tried to talk to him, but he was far too angry to talk. He punched Charles in the face and kicked him as he lay in the driveway; I tried to stop them, but even I couldn't get Eddie to listen. Suddenly, a door opened in the house and a gunshot rang through the air. Your mother stood on the step with a shotgun. Eddie raced toward her. I helped Charles into the car and locked the doors. We didn't leave right away. I was afraid of what he would do to your mother or to you. Before long, she came down to the car and told us to go. She said everything was fine; Edward just needed time to deal with the fallout. So, we left. It was the last time we ever saw Eddie alive. The next weekend, he died in the accident.

When you and your mother moved away, she signed the house over to Charles and me. She said it was to repay all the money Eddie had taken from us. She kept the life insurance policy, left Manchester, and made a new life for the two of you.

Your mother sent letters a few times a year. She didn't have to, but she knew how much we loved Eddie—not Edward, the man he had become—but the boy who had been so kind and loving. We sent you birthday and Christmas gifts but asked your mother to put her name on the tags. You have always been one of our grandchildren.

Claire, Eddie never hated you. He loved you, but as things spiraled out of control, he hated himself, and that hatred permeated everything he did and said. I wish you could have known Eddie as a child. He was a lot like you.

Take care of yourself and your family. Don't ever let the pain someone else inflicts on you ruin your life the way Eddie did.

Mary Claire

Claire felt numb. Her shoulders dropped; she had not realized she had been holding so much tension inside. She refolded the letter and tucked it back in the envelope. She pushed in the desk chair and walked to the shelf and picked up the picture of her and Edward. This man, the one holding her, *loved* her? He had a funny way of showing it.

The pins on the back of the frame turned with ease as Claire slid them to the side. She opened the back and removed the picture, replacing it with the one tucked behind it—a photo of five young children and their parents. She looked at the oldest child—smiling, happy. Then she put the frame back on the shelf.

She picked up the phone and dialed *911*. Darkness filled the room as she clicked off the lamp and made her way out of the house.

CHAPTER 41

Claire could hear the sirens in the distance. She knew it would be a good fifteen minutes before the police arrived. The sound echoed through the countryside—over the treetops and across the lakes, winding its way toward the house.

She wandered across the yard, feeling the familiar ground beneath her feet. At the top of the hill, she took one last look. The hillside lay dark, brightened only by the moonlight. She breathed in the fresh evening air—lilac-scented—and smiled as a shooting star crossed the sky. Claire didn't need to make a wish. She had everything she ever wanted.

The sirens grew louder and Claire knew she was running out of time to close the book on her past. She walked toward her car, opened the door, and cast one final look toward the house before climbing in. Then she pulled onto the gravel road. Less than a hundred feet from the driveway, she backed onto a side road and cut her lights—keeping a watch over her angel.

She could see the flashing lights, could hear the siren and the crunching gravel as the police car sped past—not toward *her* house, not toward the *old woman's*—just to a place where the past had been buried.

Once the ambulance drove by, she pulled out of the road and headed south. As she hit the highway, she felt an immense sense of peace. The car's tires dropped into a small hole and bounced back out, jerking the Lexus momentarily to the right. Claire felt the car stumble again and again as she drove along the roughly, paved road. Those potholes were a metaphor for her life. It had taken her forty-three years to understand—forty-three years of stumbling along through potholes to discover who she really was.

Even though she should have been exhausted, she wasn't. She rolled down her window. The cool night air kissed her face, lifting her hair toward the open moonroof. Claire reached over and turned on the radio. A song from her past oozed out of the speakers—a constant beat, too repetitive—*too safe*. A quick press of the button gave her a song with a beat as unpredictable as her future. Claire turned up the volume.

As she drove, she slipped the photo of her and Edward out from her purse. Under the dashboard lights, she took one last look. He was not her father; he was just a man who had been part of her past. Slowly, she raised her hand through the moonroof and let the picture go. She didn't see it fly away in the cover of the night, but she knew it was gone. She didn't need to hold on to her past so tightly. She had just set hers free.

Claire pushed herself deeper into the leather seat— settling into her new life. Amidst the blowing wind and the unfamiliar tune, she was happy.

On that dark stretch of highway that led both to and away from her past, she *finally* realized she was no longer invisible. She had moved out of the darkness and into the light.

More from author Mary Perrine:

THE LIES THEY TOLD
By Mary Perrine

No one noticed me until the day I went missing. Then, they couldn't *stop* seeing me. My face was plastered everywhere: in the news, on social media, and on flyers tacked up around the small Minnesota town of Cedar Point.

I have been invisible my entire life. You see, I wasn't an *oops* baby, a child my parents would eventually grow to love; I was a *dammit*! A baby no one would love. Lily and Laurel, my identical twin sisters, were my parents' dream. I was their mistake. I was Jane. *Plain Jane* is what they called me.

I had to leave, disappear, but my past would not let go. While in hiding, lie after lie followed me—ones so huge, my life read like a psychological thriller. Someone wanted me dead; I just didn't know who.

The truth is, I just *thought* no one saw me, but as the lies fell, I realized *everyone* had seen me from the beginning. I had been a puppet with many masters; each just waiting for the perfect moment to destroy me.

Death, they say, is a terrible thing. But I'm not sure it could hurt worse than the lies they told.

Hidden

For more books by 10,000 Lakes Publishing, visit
www.10kLP.com

Titles include:
Adventure North: 2200 miles by canoe, 49 days in the wild
Her Island: The story Questico's longest serving interior ranger
Justin Cody's Race to Survival
Waters Beneath my Feet
The Eddy

Mary Perrine

From the time I picked up a chubby Crayola crayon, I have been writing stories. I always wanted to be an author, but my mom told me I had to get a job that made actual money. So, after four years of college and $2,500 in student loans (hey, it was a long time ago), I spent thirty-six years honing my writing skills. (Obviously, I am a slow learner.) During most of that time, I taught middle school (because I fall in about the same place on the quirkiness scale as they do) and trained teachers to help students personalize their own learning.

I was an award-winning Minnesota teacher. Some of my awards include the 2006 Fox 9 Top Teacher, 2010 Eastern Carver County Teacher of the Year, and 2011 Minnesota Teacher of the Year—Top 10 finalist. I also present at educational conferences across the United States as well as freelance for companies.

I hold a master's degree, but, while I loved teaching, I jumped ship three years ago, when I retired to a small Minneapolis suburb. I now have time to spend with my husband, Mitch, a retired school principal, my son, Brandon, and daughter, Taylor, (who still come home to see what's cooking), my Parti Yorkie, Harper, and my two grand pets: Baxter, a Wheaten Terrier and Guinevere, a tabby cat.

We spend a great deal of time at our cabin in Northern Minnesota, where I lose at waterskiing, but win at Cornhole and floating in the lake. We enjoy boating, ATVing, and entertaining our massive families. And, of course, there is never a lack of food.

My husband has a gold personality (planner) and I have an orange personality (spontaneous). That makes us a perfect pair. We love to travel. He likes to plan, and I don't ask where we are going until we get on the plane.

Between all the family shenanigans and laughter, I spend time spinning tales—stories that entertain, inform, and teach. So, stay tuned. There will be many more to come.